SCOTLAND
FOREVER HOME

SCOTLAND FOREVER HOME

An Introduction to the Homeland for American and Other Scots

GEDDES MACGREGOR

DODD, MEAD & COMPANY · NEW YORK

Copyright © 1980 by Geddes MacGregor
All rights reserved
No part of this book may be reproduced in any form
without permission in writing from the publisher
Printed in the United States of America

1   2   3   4   5   6   7   8   9   10

Library of Congress Cataloging in Publication Data

MacGregor, Geddes.
Scotland forever home.

Includes index.
1. Scotland. I. Title.
DA757.5.M28   941.1   79—24066
ISBN 0—396—07804—4

Acknowledgments

I WISH to express my thanks to the following: Lady Malcolm Douglas-Hamilton, CBE, President of the American-Scottish Foundation, Inc., New York, for encouraging me to write the book; Mr. Louis M. Clark, CPA, Past President of St. Andrew's Society of Los Angeles, and the Reverend Dr. D. H. C. Read, Minister of Madison Avenue Presbyterian Church, New York, each of whom read a chapter and made suggestions; Mrs. Jean Gowans of the National Trust for Scotland, for providing the photographs; the office of the Lord Lyon for some information about dress; and the Hon. David Harris, Justice of the Supreme Court of Iowa, whose love for all things Scottish and zest for the project cheered me along the way. To Mr. Allan W. Campbell, Edinburgh, I owe a special debt of gratitude for reading two chapters and an appendix and offering valuable criticism of them, and also for most generously placing at my disposal the storehouse of his learning and scholarly judgment.

None of these is to be held responsible for errors that may remain or generalizations that must inevitably offend readers whose perceptions may differ from my own. I know of no way of writing creatively on Scotland without disturbing a few thistles.

Geddes MacGregor

Preface

THERE are three Scotlands: (1) the never-never land of Brigadoon, where kilted Rockettes dance in the moonlight on heather hills, and men, having greeted the dawn with a quaich of Scotch, sally forth to shoot a deer or two for breakfast; (2) the Scottish Homeland, an area of just over thirty thousand square miles inhabited by five or six million people on the northern part of the island we call Britain; and (3) the Scottish Diaspora, consisting of the vast millions of people of Scottish birth or ancestry dispersed throughout the world (in the United States alone an estimated five times as many as in the Homeland) who look to the Homeland with that deep affection and occasional exasperation that people never bestow on anyone but their mother.

This book about the Scottish Homeland is designed for members of the Scottish Diaspora, although I know of no law forbidding Homeland Scots from reading it too. Books about Scotland abound, many of them excellent and exhaustive (sometimes also exhausting) on almost every conceivable aspect of the Scottish Homeland. In the Edinburgh Public Library, for example, is a large room containing books on Edinburgh. There are technical works that tell everything about one castle down to the thickness of the walls and the thread of the carpet, and on a single bridge down to the last nut and bolt. There are also decorative books, redolent of nostalgic memories, with gorgeous photographs to be oohed-and-ahed over during the cocktail hour, celebrating the variety and distinctive beauty of the Scottish countryside.

This book is not like any of these. It is an elementary book all about the Scottish Homeland, introducing it to Scots of the Diaspora. It is on the whole kindly, for how else does one treat the mother one loves, even when she infuriates you? Yet it is meant primarily to be informative, and every Diaspora Scot who reads it carefully will know more about the Homeland than most Homeland Scots ever trouble to learn. My hope is that it will encourage many to visit their mother, having learned what she looks like, how noble her heart, and how great their heritage. She is certainly many things to her diverse sons and daughters all over the world, whose independence of their mother makes them capable of the best kind of love.

Geddes MacGregor

Contents

Illustrations

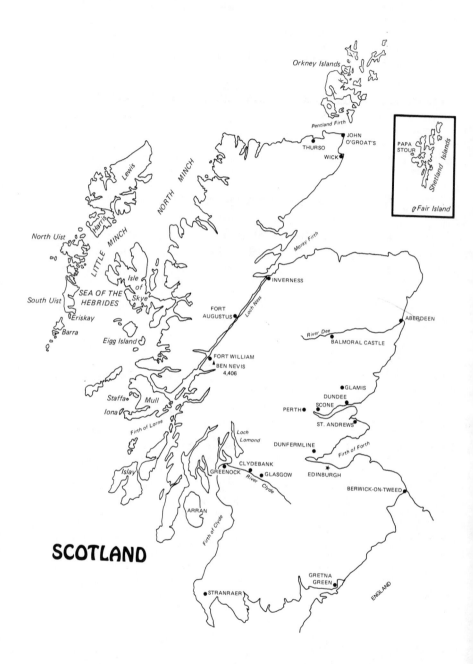

SCOTLAND

1

Atmosphere and Character

There is not a word
Spoke of in Scotland as this term of fear.
— Shakespeare, *Henry IV*

S COTLAND has, in an eminent degree, a haunting character. Every country, of course, has its special flavor, sometimes describable, never strictly definable. Not even the most casual visitor to Egypt or Japan could fail to note something distinctive about each. If, however, you have deep ancestral roots in a country, she will grab you, not to say trap you forever, now enfolding you in her arms like a tender mother, now sulking at you like a malcontent daughter, now berating you like a jealous wife. The ghosts leap out at you, claiming you as their kin. You are the victim of what the Jungian psychologists call the collective or race unconscious. What's more, you revel in it. Rightly so, for it is good for you.

Of Scotland all this is strikingly true. Moreover, she has a strangely eternal quality that makes even Rome seem by comparison almost fleeting. The Scots rarely make such comparisons, and never without provocation. They assume all around them to be fleeting, so that to make such a point would dub you right away as a foreigner, a crime so odious that no statutory punishment for

1

it has ever been devised except, of course, a social ostracism that is absolute.

Sharply contradictory are Scotland's present and past. So also is the character of her people, sometimes charming, sometimes dour. Like her climate, it can be fuzzy today, sunlit tomorrow. Even the limitations of the Scots are as lovable to their friends as they are exasperating to others. Their image abroad is no less full of paradox: a nation of stolid shepherds, skillful surgeons, dependable bankers and engineers that fell for the Young Chevalier, Bonnie Prince Charlie. Scotland is known for its Puritan outlook, yet no less for its drinking and wenching. Its symbols encompass obstinate John Knox and romantic Brigadoon, Scott in his Abbotsford grandeur and Burns at the plow, magnificent victories in war and almost genocidal defeats. In economics, the Darien disaster, Adam Smith, and the nineteenth-century jute boom, Clyde-built ships and fairy-tale islands, belching smokestacks and purple heather-clad glens. Today there is a nationalist movement, yet also apathy toward it; radical socialism alongside deep loyalty to the Queen. How are we to put all this together?

The reasons for the peculiar ambience of Scotland, its haunting fascination and its infuriating prejudices, are not unexpectedly complex. They will unfold as we go on. For the present let us be content with facts that will prepare us for a better understanding of this extraordinary northern land.

It is indeed a very northern land, not on the way to anywhere —unless you happen to be going to Iceland. Its most northerly islands (the Shetlands) are at about the latitude of Juneau, Alaska. Even northern Canadian cities such as Edmonton and Saskatoon are farther south than Scotland's most southerly tip. In northwest Scotland, nevertheless, in bleak surroundings on a West Highland sea loch and north of the latitude of Tomsk, Siberia, are the Inverewe Gardens, containing eucalyptus, rhododendron, many Chilean and African plants, Himalayan lilies, and giant forget-me-nots from the South Pacific. Two-thirds of the inhabitants of modern Scotland live in its central belt, about the latitude of

Inverewe Gardens, Wester Ross: palm trees and South Pacific flora growing outdoors at latitude north of Moscow.

Tomsk. The Gulf Stream saves Scotland from what would be otherwise a virtually uninhabitable climate. Even modern communications systems cannot entirely save her from a certain cultural isolation, with consequences both good and bad.

One of the most delightful consequences of her latitude is that summer brings incredibly long and beautiful twilights. They are, unlike the weather, completely dependable. In the extreme north the sun hardly sets at all but seems, rather, merely to stretch out for a brief nap: not quite the Midnight Sun, but getting close. These long, long, softly lighted evenings are to be found all over the land. The elongated shadows introduce you to a world that you can never see at all anywhere in the United States, and not nearly so well even in London or Copenhagen. It is a strange, romantic world, full of seductive charm, a paradise for lovers, a profound bliss for the mature who seek to hold open memory's door. The sun does not beat down upon you; it distills its warmth and its beauty gently for hours before bestowing on you its last, lingering goodnight kiss. Then, before you can possibly be awake, it is there, greeting you with an already well-developed dawn.

The situation in winter is obviously better left to the darker side of your imagination. I have seen a feeble, blood-red afternoon sun just succeed in penetrating the clouds, punctuating the daytime quasi-night as if making a momentary pastoral sick call to reassure us that our planet is still in orbit, appearances notwithstanding. Unless you visit Scotland in winter you will not see these things. Since I came to America many years ago, I have generally confined my visits to Scotland to the summer months, and I confess that the memory of these dark winters makes me feel a twinge of guilt about getting these indescribably glorious twilights so cheap. To a native Scot it's almost like stealing.

If you will look at a map of Europe you will see what you probably already know: Scotland is part of the island it shares with England and Wales. Compared with them it is not small in area. To our American eyes all European countries seem small. You could tuck all these three countries into Wyoming with room left for about eight Yosemite National Parks. Scotland, very roughly, is 31,000 square miles—to England's 50,000 and Wales's 7,500. Scotland is close to double the size of Denmark and nearly three times that of Belgium. So the Scots do not feel their land to be notably Lilliputian. Also bear in mind that because of the inlets and other geographical peculiarities, Scotland's coastline is about 2,300 miles, more than the highway distance from San Francisco to either Chicago or New Orleans.

Scotland, like other European countries, is packed with a long past. If that past were merely antiquarian it might make little difference; but it saturates the present and lives on in it, enriching the present while also deeply saddening it. This is not a question of age; Uncle Sam is older than most Europeans like to think. Yet almost everywhere in the United States you can get away from the past if you choose. Enjoy a trip to Jamestown or Independence Hall, then set it aside as you enjoy a book about Julius Caesar while riding to work. The past is fun—like science fiction but in the other direction of time. Not so in Europe. A storekeeper in Edinburgh's High Street or a fishmonger in Perth can no more get away from the past than can an inhabitant of Hawaii get away from the Pacific Ocean. In Scotland the past haunts you like a ghost. Even if you know very little about the history, it accosts you everywhere. Many Americans know far more about Scottish history than does the average inhabitant of Scotland, but it has not clung to them. To the inhabitant, some effluence of the past clings like sand to wet feet. Worse than that, he carries it about with him as Sinbad carried his burden. Americans of Scottish descent long to find the Scottish past. Inhabitants of Scotland are trying to get away from it and cannot. Ghosts keep greeting them, friendly or hostile, always a part of them, inescapable. The past enriches yet also limits your life, giving it a peculiar flavor that stays with you forever, once you taste it. It is no mere cultural enhancement like a knowledge of art history or Latin; it is a dimension of your being, whether you know much about it or little.

In all this, Scotland is not different from France or Portugal, but it is distinctive. No doubt about that. Many flowers have perfumes, but roses and wallflowers are strikingly different from each other and from other flora. If you have any scent for atmosphere at all, you will feel it all around you. Drive north from England on eastern motorway A68. If the difference does not hit you hard as soon as you cross the Scottish border, then either you are incurably insensitive to atmosphere or you have fallen asleep at the wheel. Whatever Scotland is, it is different, different from everything else. There is nothing like it on this planet.

The atmosphere, for all its distinctiveness, is also varied. So too—and very strikingly—is the Scottish character. Attitudes can vary not only topographically as do those of New Mexico and Vermont but for an infinite variety of other reasons. We must explore, for instance, the enormous difference between Highlander and Lowlander. You can hardly expect to meet either of them pure and undefiled any more than, in Italy, you could find a pure Florentine or a pure Neapolitan; but you do find predominances. In the United States, as in England, the traditionally strongest differences run between north and south; in Scotland they run east and west. The similarity between Edinburgh on the east coast and Glasgow on the west is like that between iced tea and a chocolate sundae. A fifty-mile trip can take you spiritually at least as far as from Georgia to Maine. There is no Iron Curtain. They don't need one. In my boyhood people in villages two miles apart treated each other as foreigners.

The BBC and other intruders have done their best to ruin these internal insularities, but they have not always been successful. The more one knows of rural life in Scotland in even the recent past, the more one appreciates why they had to have such severe laws against incest. Even today, if you scratch just a little below the surface you may detect regrets that such rivalries have been substantially destroyed by London bureaucrats. The Scots do not very often allude to London, because mention of it demands a very special kind of politely averted gaze and dignified stare into space. In the larger cities such as Edinburgh or Glasgow, where there is naturally daily traffic with London, you may without impropriety refer to it, especially in business contexts; but you would be well advised to make your allusions with the impersonal air of an astrophysicist referring to Jupiter or Pluto.

The distinctiveness of Scotland strikes you everywhere you go. It is written all over her face. (We shall discuss this in more detail later on.) Perhaps first you will notice the architecture: the crow-stepped gable, a cousin of the building style of the Netherlands with which Scotland has traded extensively since the Middle Ages. If anything is not made of stone you may be quite sure it is merely twentieth century. The Scots have a deep reverence for cut stone. If a building is made otherwise, an excuse is usually felt to be required—generally either poverty, cultural decadence, or influence from abroad, usually (here good breeding generally prescribes a sigh) England. Much of the architecture is fortress-like.

The speech is also distinctive. For all its immense variety, it has a common sturdiness to match. Gaelic is nowadays spoken only in remote parts of the country and, to the distress of many, appears to be dying, as Welsh is certainly not in Wales. The Scots like to tell the story of the visiting Englishman who had heard that Gaelic is a very difficult Celtic language, as indeed it is. He returned home reporting that he had been to both Glasgow and Edinburgh and had found that, on the contrary, he had been able to follow quite a lot of the conversation! Unless you go to some remote areas in the northwest, your chance of hearing Gaelic is about as good as your hope of hearing Finnish in Philadelphia or Sanskrit at Princeton.

Even dress is somewhat distinctive from that which you will generally see in the south of England. It seems to match the speech and the streets. I do not refer to the kilt, which the average Scotsman is no more likely to wear to the office than would a Greek secretary go to hers in Athens wearing her national costume. (Nevertheless, if you go to Edinburgh in summer you will see a good number of kilts.) For general street clothes, tweediness is admired in Scotland both summer and winter. Even women, when they aim at looking their best, tend to be definitely tweedier than in London. A London-style dress in Edinburgh might look just a little fussy, if not *légèrement maniérée*. A tweed suit, jacket and skirt, or a heavy tartan skirt with a jacket of one of the lighter Border tweeds, always looks "good"—and in Scotland solid quality never fails to command respect. So although men and women will follow international fashion trends, subtle modification of them gives the streets a very different feel from those of London or Paris or New York.

The Scots have in all things an immense reverence for the enduring and the permanent, the solid and the stable. The old fortress ideal still lurks in the background. All Scots admire England's Durham Cathedral, not very far from the Scottish border. Sir Walter Scott called it "half kirk of God, half fortress 'gainst the Scot." He was not wide of the mark. Edinburgh Castle, poised high on a huge rock, which even the most fleeting visitor sees towering above him in the heart of the Scottish capital, is but a symbol of the national ideal in all its grandeur. You can buy a traditional candy called Edinburgh Rock. It is very sweet and of a consistency that leaves you in no doubt why it is so-called and why it must be recommended only by the most unethical dentists. Aberdeen, built of solid granite, typifies the way the Scots would like to see all cities built. One should try to see it in the sunshine after a shower of rain, when it shimmers beautifully.

In this deep love of lasting quality, the Scots might be said to be to England as Canada is to the United States. Nor does the analogy stop there. The area of Scotland, as we have seen, is not much less than England's, as habitable Canada is not so very much less than that of the United States. Yet the population of Scotland is to England almost exactly as is Canada's to her southern neighbor. Moreover, the Scotland-England population ratio has been much the same since the Middle Ages.

In Scotland it is generally considered bad form to say anything specifically in praise of the English, although as a tactical maneu-

ver faint praise is permissible. The attitude to Americans is somewhat like that of Catholics to Protestants: if the latter have been
born Protestant they may be treated with charity since they cannot be expected to know better, but an apostate is another matter. So if you are anything from a second-generation American
up, you will generally be accounted kosher. For various historical
and other reasons, Americans often feel more at home in Scotland than in England.

The English and the Scots complement each other rather well.
It is a pity they do not get along better at a deeper level, as their
more intelligent representatives recognize. Each envies the qualities of the other. The English envy the rugged and robust qualities of the Scots, which they affect to downgrade for that very
psychological reason. The Scots dare not openly admit to seeing
any qualities in anyone that are not mere shadows of those found
in plenitude in themselves.

By the way, we had better clear up here a simple matter of
terminology. "British" is nowadays a term applied to both English and Scots. It is a term that for obvious historical reasons
does not evoke much sympathy in the American ear, but in Scotland it is a completely neutral term with none of the emotional
overtones it tends to evoke on our side of the Atlantic. Americans
sometimes expect to please the Scots by a little downgrading of
the British. You might as well try to win approval in Boston by
downgrading Massachusetts. Downgrade England if you will, although it is usually better not to deign to mention its existence.

This brings us to the question of pride. National pride is probably found almost everywhere in the world. When it is not developed into belligerency that leads to war it can be a good thing.
Scottish pride, however, is unique. According to a widespread
legend, what is most characteristic of the Scot is his stinginess
with money—or, if you wish to be more polite, his thrift. The
contents of a Scotsman's purse are supposed to be exceedingly
inseparable from its owner. That legend betrays gross misunder-
standing. True, the Lowland Scots are typically thrifty and pru-

dential, which is why they often make good managers and accountants. But nowhere in the world will you find more lavish hospitality, be you a guest in a cottage or in a palace. Not even American generosity, which even our detractors acknowledge, can outdo that of the Scots. Traditionally, however, they do not like ostentation. I can remember an older generation of middle-class Scotsmen who, when they bought a new suit (always the best possible quality, of course), would wear it at home for a while before appearing in public so that their friends would not get the impression that they were showing off. To be too conspicuously well dressed was as bad as being shabby. The idea was never to attract undue notice by being either too shabby or too smart: the former was accounted slovenly, the latter at best undignified and at worst perhaps just a trifle vulgar. Much nearer the mark would be an interior pride as impregnable as Edinburgh Castle.

A London lady advertised for a maid. The one whom she hired turned out to be a very capable Scots lass. After a few weeks she told her new employee how pleased the household was with her.

"But, Mary," she went on, "there *is* one thing that puzzles me. You didn't mention in your application that you are a Scotch girl. You should always do that because most employers like Scotch girls. Why didn't you put it in your application?"

"Weel, mum," replied the girl quietly, "I was always taught that it's very bad manners to boast."

This is as good a place as any, since we have been using the terms "Scotch," "Scottish," and "Scots," to treat them as they occur in Scottish usage. The usage is largely mere convention, but it is accounted important. The form "Scotch," which comes most naturally to English and most American lips, was at one time quite general in Scotland. For somewhat complex reasons it came to be disliked by the Scots and is nowadays used *in Scotland* only in referring to whisky, tomatoes, and such commodities. The basic equivalent of "Irish" and "American" and "French" is "Scottish." So we would talk of the Scottish climate, Scottish history, Scottish scenery, and the like. One does not talk, however, of a Scottish man or woman, but of a Scotsman or Scotswoman or Scot. Furthermore, "Scots" is used instead of "Scottish" in certain connections; for example, one invariably talks of "Scots Law," a technical term.

The distinction between Highlands and Lowlands is well known, although not everyone appreciates the implications of the distinction. Geographically its significance would seem negligible; Ben Nevis, the highest peak in Scotland (also in the whole of Britain) is only 4,400 feet, much less than the higher peaks of even the Adirondacks and less than one-third of California's Mount Whitney. Moreover, the areas called Highlands and Lowlands respectively are not very clearly definable, although if you draw a line from Dumbarton on the west to Stonehaven on the east, everything to the northwest may be included in the Highlands ruling out the Orkney and Shetland islands, Caithness, and the flat coastal land of Nairn, Elgin, Banff, and Aberdeenshire. Even then you will run into disputes.

Yet between Highlanders and Lowlanders is a difference of temper and outlook as striking as that between Germans and French. Traditionally the Highlander is fiery, imaginative, poetic, fiercely loyal, proud, procrastinating, touchy, with a profound natural insight into religion, a vigorous appreciation of whisky, and a tendency to feel jaded when not in the midst of a really good fight. These qualities he shares, of course, with other Celtic peoples, not least the Irish with whom he has common roots, be they much more than a thousand years back. All of us, as the French proverb notes, have the virtues of our vices and the vices of our virtues, and nowhere is this more obvious than in the two main divisions of the Scottish people. Lowlanders are prudent, dependable, hardheaded, industrious; they can also be singularly unimaginative, negative, tedious, and dull. The Highlander will love you and stand by you come what may as the most loyal friend you will ever have on earth. The Lowlander, however, is likely to be more satisfactory as an employer, employee, or business associate.

Till only about two and a half centuries ago, the Highlanders really did live a separate life. Their language, customs, and arts had not changed much since before the Roman invasion of Britain about half a century after the death of Christ. Prior to the Union of the English and Scottish Parliaments in 1707, few people south of Perth knew much about the Highlanders. Among those who gave them any thought, suspicion and fear were the most typical attitudes. Roads and other communications were poor. The Highlanders differed so much from both the Lowlanders and the rest of the inhabitants of Britain that there was almost complete lack of understanding. Their practice of wearing the kilt and of carrying arms wherever they went, together with the fact that they usually knew either no English or very little, made them seem to others to be as ignorant and dangerous as savages are generally supposed to be.

Nothing could have been further from the truth, for the Highlander had great traditions of his own and an ancient and noble culture. The communications gap, however, made them not only objects of distrust; it caused them to look on the outside world with puzzlement and disdain. The brutal persecutions they suffered, notably in the rebellion of 1745, were tantamount to attempted genocide such as is only too familiar in the history of Jews, Greeks, and Armenians. The Highland way of life was virtually destroyed. The Diaspora had begun: an irreparable loss to Scotland, an incalculable gain to the rest of the world, not least the United States. Yet in their kilts and their tartans, their clan spirit, their military courage, their romantic history, and not least the magnificent record of their service in the Highland regiments, they gave Scotland a legacy beyond compare. Nevertheless, Scotland, as we shall see, is much more than the Highlands.

Modern Scotland reflects the racial mix that has taken place both from the earliest times and more recently as the result of vastly improved communications. Into the ancient mix have gone Picts, Scots, Britons (in the older sense), and Angles—four early tribal kingdoms. About the end of the eighth century the Norse began attacking the Pictish regions, and to this day the influence of these Norse invasions may be clearly seen in the outlook of the inhabitants of certain parts of Scotland in the northeast and heard in the typically Scandinavian inflections of the dialect. The net result today is that while you cannot expect to find any ethnically pure representative, you may certainly see some people in whom the characteristics of one ethnic type are strikingly present.

You might even be fortunate enough to receive, at the conclusion of a visit to a Highland cottage, the incomparable farewell: "Now wouldn't it be the fine thing if you were coming instead of going?" If you were to visit one of the remoter western isles they might even sing for you, but that might take more weeks than your stay would allow; first they would have to trust you, and there is no way in which trust can be hurried. Generally speaking, any true courtesy you show a Highlander will be returned a hundredfold. You may sometimes meet undeserved sullen rudeness, mainly in the larger towns; but almost all visitors to Scotland remark on the kindliness of the people. The beauty of the variegated countryside and of many of the cities and small towns is extraordinary, and I shall duly describe it after we have inspected more facts that are necessary background to an appreciation of these delights. In the next chapter, for instance, we shall survey the history of Scotland in a very encapsulated form.

2

Scotland's Story in Outline

Scots wha hae wi' Wallace bled;
Scots wham Bruce has aften led,
Welcome to your gory bed,
Or to victorie!

—Robert Burns, *Scots Wha Hae*

SCOTLAND, after a nomadic period, was settled by a people who actually cleared the land for farming and formed settled communities about six thousand years ago—almost as long before Moses as is Moses before our own time. From then till about the Christian era the inhabitants were cross-fertilized by immigrants from Ireland, England, and the continent of Europe.

When the Romans first invaded Scotland, which they called Caledonia, about A.D. 80, the people they found included a race we call Picts, and the language they heard was akin to Gaelic. The origin of the Picts is mysterious and controversial, although their importance in the making of Scotland is beyond question, and copious evidence of their influence survives today, for example, in artifacts. The Romans, despite their invasions and considerable local occupations, left no appreciable mark on Scotland. They eventually departed after some punitive expeditions in the third and fourth centuries. The notion that Christianity might have been introduced by some of the Roman soldiers is fanciful. Many

Christians were in the Roman legions in southern Europe, but their presence among the troops sent to Scotland is very unlikely. Moreover, while the names of pagan gods have been found on tombs, no Christian inscription attributable to these early Roman occupations has ever been discovered. Nevertheless, before the final departure of the Romans, Christianity had been introduced into what is now southern Scotland. Saint Ninian (c. 360–c. 432), son of a converted chieftain of the Cumbrian Britons, traveled to Scotland from Rome, meeting on the way the celebrated Martin of Tours, one of the patron saints of France, and founding a church at Whithorn, Wigtownshire, called Candida Casa (the White House).

What eventually became the Kingdom of Scotland was the result of an amalgamation of four peoples: Picts, Gaels, Britons, and Angles. South Britain had been conquered by Angles and Saxons. The Britons, driven out by them, settled farther north in the region between the Mersey and Clyde rivers on the west. Meanwhile, the Angles, in about the middle of the sixth century, founded the Kingdom of Bernicia on the east, between the rivers Tees and Forth. Half a century earlier, numbers of Gaelic-speaking people from Ireland had come to what is now Argyll, where they founded the Kingdom of Dalriada, or Scotland. The Picts became supreme in the north, gaining control over both the Scots of Dalriada and the Britons of Strathclyde. In the eighth century the Norse began attacks on Pictland, weakening Pictish control. In 844 Kenneth MacAlpin, King of Dalriada, was able to establish a claim to the Pictish throne, uniting Picts and Scots.

Scotland's future identity as a nation was indubitably promoted by the advent of Saint Columba from Ireland in 563. His mission, and the founding of his monastic establishment on the island of Iona, prepared the way for the union of Picts and Scots. This, in turn, made possible the eventual emergence of Scotland as a nation. Before Scotland could attain anything like its present identity, however, it had to face two major threats: from England and from Scandinavia.

The menace of an English conquest was substantially removed in 685 when a great Northumbrian army invaded Pictland and was decisively defeated at Nectansmere (Dunnichen), Angus. Finally, in 1018, Malcolm II, King of Picts and Scots, defeated the Northumbrians in the battle of Carham-on-Tweed and annexed the Lothians to Scotland. Malcolm's grandson, the Duncan of Shakespeare's *Macbeth*, was the first King of the Scots in the full historical sense, ruling Dalriada, Pictland, Lothian, and Strathclyde. Duncan's reign was brief (1034–1040). Macbeth, Duncan's general, killed him and succeeded to the Scottish throne, reigning until 1057. He was killed, with some English help, at Lumphanan, Aberdeenshire, by Duncan's son, who succeeded to the throne as Malcolm III (Malcolm Canmore or "Big Head"). During his long reign he introduced a new era in Scottish history.

Of paramount importance in understanding the development of Scotland about this time is the fact that between Malcolm Canmore's reign and that of Alexander III two centuries later, the Lowlands became basically English-speaking. With English speech went the organization of social and political life on the lines of the Anglo-Norman Kingdom of England; in the rest of Scotland Gaelic speech and Celtic organization of society prevailed.

The Scandinavian menace was fierce and prolonged. From about the middle of the ninth century the Norse began to make settlements, notably in the Hebrides, in the Orkney and Shetland islands, and in parts of Caithness. The Hebrides were not recovered until the middle of the thirteenth century, the Orkneys and Shetlands not until two hundred years later still, when they passed from Denmark to Scotland through the marriage of a Danish princess to James III of Scotland (1460–1488). Even in modern times these islanders have had a tendency to think of themselves as apart from Scotland. I have heard Orcadians (inhabitants of the Orkneys) talk of "going over to Scotland" (meaning the mainland) as though making a journey abroad.

While the emerging Scottish nation was faced with this double threat from England and Scandinavia, its rulers played one off against the other. Sometimes they would enlist England's help against the Norsemen as against a common enemy; at other times they would join the Norse against the English. In the course of the twelfth and thirteenth centuries, however, Scotland underwent a development that might even be called a revolution bringing in its train, in Church and State, a de-Celticization in manners, customs, organization, and administrative procedure.

That development was initiated by Margaret, the Hungarian-born English princess whom Malcolm Canmore had taken as his queen. Margaret, who is one of Scotland's patron saints, had been nurtured at the court of Stephen I, the saintly King of Hungary, in an atmosphere of deep Roman Catholic piety. Then she had gone to England where, at the court of Edward the Confessor, a similarly devout Catholic outlook prevailed. Margaret had thought of becoming a nun, but was married to Malcolm about the year 1070 at Dunfermline, amid great rejoicing. She is reported to have been an unusually charming and gracious lady, intensely devoted to her faith and most energetic both in good works for her people and in governing the royal household. She insisted on magnificence both in her own dress and in furnishings, not least the table, where the dishes, we are told, were always of gold and silver. The changes she was able to bring about were mainly in the Church; her romanization of it began a more general process that was continued after her death. Malcolm's subjects, except for those in the Lothians, were still very Celtic and naturally resented anglicization of Church and State and destruction of their ancient customs, which they foresaw as the inevitable consequence. Their efforts to stem the tide were not successful, however. The old Celtic method of land tenure, in which the chief of a tribe and his near kindred held the land for the whole tribe, gave way to a new system that was a powerful instrument in establishing greater anglicization.

By and large in the Highlands the old tribal system developed into the clan, while in the Lowlands it grew into a system of families that became units in some ways similar to the clans of the Highlands. The clan, a natural development of the characteristic institutions of the ancient Celtic civilization, cannot be traced back earlier than the end of the fourteenth century. The family, in the Lowland Scottish sense, dates from the twelfth century, resulting from the feudal system of land tenure introduced by King David I (1124–1153) with the other political organization associated with feudal monarchies. Commerce with England was developed. To the new Scottish burghs, organized according to English models and closely copying in many cases the style of English charters, came English and Flemish merchants. The growing influence of English ways in Lowland Scotland, however, made relations between the two countries often uneasy. Nevertheless, compared with later times they were peaceful. But for ferocious attacks by the English King Edward I, they might have remained so.

Edward personally led an army into Scotland and took the town of Berwick, where he brutally massacred the citizens. The Scots offered little resistance. In the summer of 1296 Edward conducted a triumphal march through Scotland, which he left under English military occupation. Inevitably the Scots revolted. Within a year Sir William Wallace, one of the great national heroes of Scottish history, led a popular uprising. On September 10, 1297, at the Battle of Stirling Bridge, with an army that included Highlanders from Moray and other Scots from distant parts of the country, Wallace regained Scotland's independence. Although he was eventually captured and cruelly put to death in August 1305, his leadership had aroused in the Scottish people that love of freedom and that resolve to maintain their national independence that has never since died. The Battle of Stirling Bridge was a great turning point in Scottish history.

When Edward sought to control and also to humiliate Scotland through an administrative system devised to turn the nation into an English province, the Scots predictably found another leader, the second of the two great heroes of this era in their history.

Around the standard of Robert the Bruce they gathered, crowning him King of the Scots at Scone (pronounced *skoon*) in March 1306. He experienced many defeats, the first at Methven, near Perth, three months after his coronation. He was hunted as an excommunicated fugitive and a traitor. Some of his brothers and other supporters who were captured were hanged and quartered, and his wife and daughters were taken prisoners.

Edward died in July 1307, but still the Bruce's troubles were far from over. For long everything seemed to go wrong, and even the loyalty of his people wavered. According to an old legend, the Bruce was sitting one day at the mouth of a cave, so disconsolate that he felt about to give up the struggle, when he noticed a spider. Time after time the spider tried to spin his web across the mouth of the cave; time after time it failed. At last, after many seemingly futile attempts, it succeeded. Bruce, in contemplating this scene, felt his courage return. He heard a voice saying to him: "If at first you don't succeed, try, try, try again." Be that as it may, Bruce did indeed try again. His only hope now was a military engagement with England, in which the English forces would obviously be far greater in number. The risk was tremendous. He was staking his own life and the future of Scotland on the result of one battle; a successful outcome must have seemed unlikely, to say the least.

A combination of great military skill, immense courage on the part of the soldiers, cunning tactics, and miraculously good fortune led to the most spectacular victory in Scotland's struggle for independence. At the Battle of Bannockburn, on June 24, 1314, the little Scottish army routed the English. Scottish independence was assured. The Pope acknowledged the Bruce as King of Scotland in 1323, the year in which the English Edward II was forced to seek a truce. Today the site of the battle, now the property of the National Trust, is adorned with a splendid modern equestrian statue of Robert the Bruce, by C.D'O. Pilkington Jackson, which no visitor to Scotland should miss.

The glory of Bannockburn notwithstanding, Scotland's trou-

Bannockburn: Robert the Bruce

bles with England were by no means over. During the later Middle Ages she looked to France as an ally. After Scotland's War of Independence, which lasted all of the fourteenth century and half of the fifteenth, English influence waned and French took over. All of Scotland's three pre-Reformation universities were founded in the fifteenth century: St. Andrews, Glasgow, and Aberdeen. Trade prospered. The towns revived. National confidence increased. Food was plentiful.

Traditionally, the nobles in Scotland had been strong and the monarchy weak compared with England. But under James IV (1488–1513) the authority and prestige of the Scottish Crown was much enhanced. His reign was Scotland's Golden Age before the tumultuous events of the Reformation half a century after his death. James played a considerable role in European politics while at the same time welding Scotland together by centralizing power and bringing even the remoter regions of the Highlands and Islands under his control. He created a strong Scottish navy. He sought alliances with then powerful Spain, proposing marriage with a daughter of Ferdinand and Isabella but eventually marrying Margaret, the elder daughter of Henry VII of England. This event was of great political importance, for the marriage treaty involved England's first official recognition of Scotland's independence since 1328. In the long run it made possible the Union of the Crowns of England and Scotland under the son of the ill-starred Mary Queen of Scots, James VI of Scotland, who became James I of Great Britain in 1603.

As has happened so often in Scotland's tragic history, progress ended in disaster. To understand what happened we must recall that by this time Scotland depended on France for military power. From the French standpoint, Scotland was useful since it could provide a means of creating a pincer movement for squeezing England in time of war. Naturally, the English were well aware of this, and James's marriage to an English princess had not fundamentally changed the hard fact.

England's fear of the consequences of a hostile Scotland at her back door for long persisted and has never been entirely allayed. Shakespeare well expresses the old enmity in the words of England's Henry V on the eve of the Battle of Agincourt. Henry tells of his fear of

> the main intendment of the Scot,
> Who hath been still a giddy neighbor to us;
> For you shall read that my great-grandfather
> Never went with his forces into France,
> But that the Scot on his unfurnish'd kingdom
> Came pouring, like the tide into a breach,
> With ample and brim fulness of his force.

The Scottish people in the reign of James IV had become accustomed to thinking of France as their ally and of England as their enemy, although no doubt relishing their enmity for England more than their alliance with France. When Henry VIII of England (1509–1547) prepared to go to war with France, he naturally hoped for an assurance of Scottish neutrality. France was then facing pressure on all sides in Europe. What if France collapsed? Would not Scotland be at the mercy of her traditional enemy, England? James's advisers were divided. Some of the older and most distinguished among them questioned whether the traditional outlook was now in Scotland's best interests; they counseled against war with England. The younger advisers, however, were for war, and, alas, James listened to them.

On August 22, 1513, James led a great Scottish army to the greatest military defeat in the history of the nation. Ten thousand men, the cream of Scotland's manhood, lay dead on cruel Flodden Field. Distraught women haunted the streets of the towns, inquiring for news of their men. The desolate sobs and heart-rending shrieks of one woman after another as she learned the fate of her brave Sandy or her handsome Tam must have lingered in the ears of thousands for the rest of their lives, leaving a bitterness from which Scotland has never entirely recovered. Its memories tore the toughest heartstrings. Jane Elliot, who died

nearly three hundred years after Flodden, wrote in her poignant
poem, *A Lament for Flodden:*

> At e'en in the gloaming, nae swankies are roaming
>   'Bout stacks wi' the lasses at bogle to play;
> But ilk ane sits eerie, lamenting her dearie—
>   The Flowers o' the Forest are a' wede away.
>
> Dool and wae for the order sent our lads to the Border!
>   The English, for ance, by guile wan the day;
> The Flowers o' the Forest, that fought aye the foremost,
>   The prime of our land, lie cauld in the clay.
>
> We'll hear nae mair lilting at our ewe-milking;
>   Women and bairns are heartless and wae;
> Sighing and moaning on ilka green loaning—
>   The Flowers o' the Forest are a' wede away.

James himself fell with so many of the rest. On his dead hand
was the turquoise ring the King of France had sent him four
months before the battle. He was forty years old. His son, James
V, succeeded to the throne. He died in Falkland on December 14,
1542, at the age of thirty; his daughter Mary (the future Mary,
Queen of Scots) had been born at Linlithgow six days before his
death. Sadly the dying king thought of how the Crown had come
to the House of Stewart through Marjorie, daughter of Robert
the Bruce, who had married Walter the Steward and whose son,
Robert II (Stewart) had succeeded to the throne. "It cam' wi' a
lass and it will gang wi' a lass," he murmured. The prediction was
not strictly accurate, since Mary's son became James VI of Scotland before the Union of the Crowns in 1603, but it was at least
poetically true. The end of an era was in sight.

We are now on the eve of the Scottish Reformation. The Reformation movement, by the time of James V, was spreading like
wildfire throughout Europe. The form it took varied considerably
from country to country, depending on circumstances. In England, for example, it was mild. In Spain, where reforms had

already been instituted to some extent even before Luther's challenge in 1517, it made no headway at all. Scotland's religious situation was singular. So powerful was the late medieval Church that half the wealth of the little nation was in its hands. Although the nation was politically independent, the bishops and others of the higher clergy had become absolutely and abjectly dependent on Rome. Nowhere in all Europe was the Church more corrupt. The sexual morality of the average cleric was notorious and the butt of much ridicule. Clerical hypocrisy was pilloried in the popular tavern songs of the day, more or less bawdy, such as were collected later by the Wedderburns of Dundee. This is a typical example:

> The bishop would not wed a wife,
> The abbot not pursue one,
> Thinking it was a lusty life
> Each day to have a new one.

The people expected no better. The real corruption lay in the high places of the Church: the trade in pluralities, in many cases highly lucrative sinecures. Such ecclesiastical loot was often held by a man who then did his best to secure more of it for his own bastard sons.

The notorious Cardinal Beaton, for instance, was not only Chancellor of Scotland, a high office of State, as well as, on the ecclesiastical side, Primate of Scotland, but also Archbishop of St. Andrews, Bishop of Mirepoix, France, and Abbot of Arbroath, with some other papal appointments to boot. So hated was he that as he traveled from one castle fortress to another he was usually accompanied by a hundred horse. He was instrumental in burning at the stake Patrick Hamilton, Scotland's first native martyr, in circumstances of unspeakable cruelty even for those days; he watched the proceedings with much satisfaction from a nearby safe eminence. The ruins of his castle in St. Andrews, containing the famous "bottle dungeon," are open to the public.

Of that terrible dungeon more will be said in a later chapter. Why did people endure such turpitude in those who purported to be their shepherds and spiritual guides? The answer is simple, and in it lay the root of the dilemma that faced Scotland at the Reformation. We have seen how important France was, or at any rate seemed, as Scotland's military ally. With France, however, went the papacy: you could not have one without the other. France was and long remained *la fille ainée de l'Eglise et son épée:* the Church's eldest daughter and her sword. No one denies that the late medieval papacy was corrupt. Scotland had become, on the eve of the Reformation, virtually a papal colony. The Scots had to decide whether to keep the French alliance at this price or to choose the Reformation way, which entailed closer ties with England, the traditional enemy. The country was divided, as were the nobles who ruled it. Much could be said for both sides.

One man above all others stood for the second option. Born about the time James V acceded to the throne, he was destined to become the Moses and the Lincoln of the Scots, rolled into one. An oft-repeated story illustrates to what extent he has become the hero par excellence. An American visitor, driven around Edinburgh by a cabdriver, was told that he was passing the house of John Knox. This prompted him to ask who Knox was. The cabbie screeched to a halt and asked, in horror and contempt: "Man, do you never read your Bible?"

The changes Knox wrought were by no means confined to the practice of religion. He was a shrewd politician and a brilliant organizer. He accounted himself no more than a harsh trumpet for the Lord, and indeed his plainness of speech led to the apposite words the Regent Morton uttered at Knox's graveside on his death in 1572: "Here lies one who neither flattered nor feared any flesh." Scottish patriot if ever there was one, and in the minds of many the quintessence of Scottishness, he was more of an anglophile than is popularly supposed. He spent five years of his life as a royal chaplain in England, refused the bishopric of Rochester because of the political enslavement he thought it entailed, and anglicized both his spelling and his speech. Perhaps he did not understand the English very well: Scots and English have seldom understood each other, much to their mutual disadvantage. Be that as it may, he deeply loved and fiercely fought for the land of his birth.

An estimate of Scotland's debt to Knox depends by no means wholly on one's religious views, for the reforms he made possible were as much political and social as they were ecclesiastical. Not all his ideals were fully realized, but he did make possible the transition of Scotland from a very backward to a progressive nation. And he led the Scottish people toward moral independence as well as industry and enterprise. Through his preaching on the Old Testament prophets, the Scots saw not only how much he seemed like one of them, but how Scotland's story resembled the history of Israel. Scottish education, as a result of his insistence on a basic schooling for all, with opportunities for the gifted to go on to one of the universities, came to be highly regarded throughout the civilized world at a time when higher education in England was too largely confined to the privileged classes. The Kirk Knox established underwent many vicissitudes through the centuries, and Scotland's internecine warfare in religious (to say nothing of other) matters has been notorious. However, since the bitter struggle between Presbyterianism and Episcopacy in the seventeenth century (when all Europe was caught in an era of religious wars), which left only a small Episcopalian remnant, almost all of Scotland's religious controversy has been within the Presbyterian framework. After the Reformation, Roman Catholicism persisted in a few of the most inaccessible corners of the Highlands and Islands. Today the considerable Roman Catholic population consists very largely of descendants of the Irish immigrants who came in great numbers, especially during the nineteenth century, in search of work.

The drama of the encounters between Knox and Mary, Queen of Scots, is well known. Mary was nineteen when she arrived in Edinburgh to assume the Scottish throne she had inherited in the first week of her infancy. During the Regency she had been educated at the French court. At fifteen and a half she had been married to the French dauphin, a bilious fourteen-year-old boy as unhandsome as she was beautiful. The wedding in Notre Dame de Paris and the ball that followed in the old palace of the Tournelles had been unusually spectacular even for Paris, for the French monarchy thought to show the world that Scotland had finally come within the hegemony of France.

Widowed at eighteen, Mary came to a Scotland she must have found very bleak: an inhospitable climate; a drafty palace at the foot of Arthur's Seat, the 823-foot lion-shaped hill that is nowadays a central landmark of the city; and (to her Catholic soul perhaps worst of all) a country in which the Reformation had just triumphed under the resolute leadership of Knox.

Mary and Knox were both intelligent. She was also highly educated for a woman of her day. There is no evidence that Knox was, for his time, notably chauvinistic in his attitude to women; but he did abhor political rule by women, not for itself so much as for the peculiar forms of corruption and intrigue he believed existed wherever power was focused in a woman, as, for instance, in Elizabeth of England and in Mary of Guise, the Queen Regent of Scotland during the new Queen's minority. Now had come this young queen, not only a woman but a Roman Catholic, standing for all that he abhorred. Of the many sallies between them, none is more famous than his retort when she chided him for interfering in a marriage she was contemplating. In it lay the essence of the political revolution of which he was the chief spokesman. Let us not forget that in the sixteenth century, politics and religion were as inseparable as the inside and the outside of a bottle.

"What have ye to do with my marriage?" she demanded. Then, remembering what she thought was her past clemency to this pesky preacher and his presumptuous obstinacy in opposing her at every point, she waspishly added: "Or what are ye within this realm?"

"A subject, born within the same, Madam," he flashed back at her. Knox was not of low birth (his father was a respectable small farmer), but he was certainly no grandee, and in royal courts he would look a man of the people. His answer to Mary was by way of saying that a ruler is placed in a position of trust by God and derives authority accordingly; yet the humblest subject has for that very reason the duty as well as the right to see that the ruler's rule accords with God's law. Knox was speaking for every man under God. Moreover, he was enunciating an old medieval principle that a grossly wicked ruler could be deposed by the people and such an act would not be rebellion. It would be a righteous act. This is in fact essentially the principle John Locke was to expound a century later, which was to be invoked a century later still by the Fathers of the American Revolution. Knox relentlessly went on:

"And albeit I neither be earl, lord, nor baron within it, yet has God made me (how abject that ever I be in your eyes), a profitable member within the same: Yea, Madam, to me it appertains no less to warn of such things as may hurt it, if I foresee them, than it does to any of the nobility; for both my vocation and conscience crave plainness of me. . . ."

Mary burst into tears. Knox was, as she often said, "ower sair" (too hard) for her.

In 1565 Mary, with the Pope's approval, married her cousin, Henry Stewart, Lord Darnley. Meanwhile, David Riccio, an Italian *valet de chambre* at the Scottish court, had been advanced with noticeable speed to the position of secretary and personal adviser to the Queen. One evening in March 1566, Mary, six months pregnant, was at supper in Holyrood with Riccio when a band of armed men burst in upon them and demanded that Riccio accompany them to an adjoining bedroom. Riccio, screaming hysterically and clutching at Mary's skirt like a child, was dragged off and slain. Fifty dagger wounds are said to have been inflicted on his body. The following February the Earl of Bothwell murdered Mary's husband, Darnley; a few weeks later Mary married Bothwell. When she was seized a few weeks later still and taken prisoner by some of her nobles, the crowds roared angrily after her in the streets of Edinburgh: "Burn the whore!"

The child that Mary carried in her womb was the future James VI of Scotland and James I of Great Britain and Ireland. As King of Scotland he was unpopular. In England he was at first acclaimed with great rejoicing. Such were the circumstances of the day that the English were disposed to welcome him. But they soon found him completely beyond their comprehension. He was ridiculously vain, pedantic, with scholarly pretensions, unmanly, ungainly, openly proud of his cunning, and altogether both odious and absurd. People murmured that King Elizabeth had been succeeded by Queen James. He obstinately neglected the navy and, after the narrow escape of the country from the Gunpowder Plot by agents of Spain, caused England's seafaring hero, Sir Walter Raleigh, to be beheaded to appease the pride of the Spanish ambassador. James seemed to do everything wrong. Yet paradoxically, it was for him that the most famous version of the English Bible was named: the King James Version.

The Union of the Crowns, far from bringing peace to Scotland, embroiled her in England's troubles as well as her own. The whole seventeenth century was filled with strife. When Archbishop Laud sent up to Scotland what was, or at any rate seemed, substantially the Book of Common Prayer and a symbol of English aggression on the ecclesiastical side, a riot took place on Sunday, July 23, 1637, in St. Giles' Cathedral. The attempt to use it was the occasion of a famous episode. An applewife from the High Street, Jenny Geddes, is said to have thrown her stool at the Dean's head. The riot was followed by the Solemn League and Covenant of 1638 and a General Assembly that defied the King (Charles I) and deposed the bishops. Those who defended its policy were called "Covenanters." The seemingly endless strife that ensued was intensified by the execution of Charles I and by the Civil War. In defiance of Cromwell's Commonwealth, Charles II was proclaimed King of Great Britain, France, and Ireland. He was brought from Holland to Scotland and, forced to accept the

Solemn League and Covenant, was taken prisoner. Cromwell's victories left Scotland seemingly helpless in face of the English army.

Scotland never became a conquered country, however, under Cromwell, as might well have happened. Terms of a union were arranged that had at least the appearance of being voluntary. Administratively, Scotland gained something from the rule of Cromwell's Protectorate. It fared less well in religious matters, for it was during this period that English Puritan influence made its impact on the Scottish outlook, an influence that was temperamentally alien to the Scots and, whatever good it may have brought to England and America, probably hindered Scotland more than it helped. Theoretically, trade between the two countries during Cromwell's time was free and open; in fact, however, Scotland was too poor to benefit fully from it. Both Cromwell's rule and the Restoration of the monarchy that followed England's comparatively brief experience of a military dictatorship were thoroughly English movements. The former was unpopular in Scotland; the latter was welcomed.

After the Restoration, the struggles between Episcopacy and Presbyterianism continued until the English Revolution of 1688, which led to the English Bill of Rights, 1689. The Scottish Parliament had been ready for some time, against popular feeling, to acquiesce in England's wishes for Church and State. England's Revolution was the signal for the Scottish people to find a remedy for their grievances, especially for the rule of the Church by bishops, in whom many Scots saw (often with reason) the source of many of their woes. With the coming of William and Mary to the throne, the Scots secured the settlement they felt they needed: the assurance of an independent national Church governed not by bishops but by a hierarchy of ecclesiastical courts and according to democratic principles. At the Union of the Parliaments of the two countries in 1707, the preservation for all time of the Presbyterian Church of Scotland was made an essential term of the Act of Union. Only in this sense, however, and in the legal recognition of the Scottish ecclesiastical courts, is the Church of Scotland an "established Church." The British Sovereign takes an oath on his or her accession to uphold the independence and maintain the security of this Church. The Sovereign is also required, when he or she crosses the Scottish border, to behave as would a member of the Presbyterian Church of Scotland. Not all Sovereigns have personally liked that expectation. Queen Victoria, however, happened to have notable personal sympathies with the Kirk.

From the time of the Revolution till the Union of Parliaments (less than twenty years), the perceptive must have seen that a choice was inevitable: war with England or union such as in fact came about. King William made himself unpopular in several ways, notably by acquiescing, at least in principle, in a plot of his Scottish advisers that led to the order leading to the massacre of Glencoe in 1692, which had the result of fostering Lowland sympathy for the Highlanders. More will be said later of this episode. Glencoe looks to this day a gloomy, eerie place, a valley of sorrow hewn out of mountains of guilt.

The grim choice between war and union eroded into no choice at all. In 1695 the Scottish Parliament received royal assent to an act establishing a company to trade with Africa and elsewhere. Scottish hopes ran high. English merchants, however, feared what Scottish success in such an enterprise might do to English adventures of a similar kind. The English subscriptions were withdrawn. The Scots, who had raised by themselves nearly a quarter of a million pounds (an enormous sum in those days), had to restrict their enterprise to a settlement on the isthmus of Darien, or Panama. In 1698 the expedition sailed. Scottish hopes grew for a new colony of Scotland's own. Alas, the enterprise ended disastrously. Everything went wrong. Nobody in those days could have known how dangerous Panama was to the health of European settlers. Moreover, Spain claimed sovereignty over the region, and for various political reasons anything like a war with Spain was at the time out of the question. King William withdrew all help to his Scottish subjects in their colonizing scheme. The Scottish Parliament made the appropriate declarations about the rightfulness of the settlement in Darien, but by 1698 the settlers had been virtually exterminated by disease and famine. A second expedition the following year ended in similar disaster. A third eventually had to accept a truce, and most of its members died before returning to Scotland. Darien was a final blow to Scotland's hopes for political independence.

William, in 1700, urged his English Parliament to confer with Scotland about union, but Parliament did not go along with his proposal. At last, however, under Queen Anne, a treaty was made and ratified by the Scottish Estates on January 16, 1707. The voting was 110 for and 68 against, with more than 40 abstentions. Popular disapproval was strong and widespread. Charges of bribery abounded. The Jacobites, who had hoped for a restoration of the Stewarts to the throne, naturally opposed the Union that was concluded on May 1, 1707. On October 23 of the same year the first Parliament of Great Britain met at Westminster.

The Union was an organic one, not a mere federation that would have left open the possibility of secession. Federation had been considered, but the Scots must have known—whether or not they cared to admit it—that in such an arrangement the larger partner would have swamped the smaller, while the smaller could have exercised little or no influence on the whole. Through the Union, however, Scotland could hope to participate in the affairs of Britain. Scotland eventually did just that, and to an astonishing extent. Mutual jealousy has never been overcome, although the climate of understanding between English and Scottish leaders of the United Kingdom has incalculably improved since the Act of Union. Most remarkable of all, Scotland has been able to preserve, as we saw in the first chapter, a notable distinctiveness of atmosphere and character in law, custom, culture, and looks, although not so much as her more emphatically nationalistic sons and daughters would have liked to see. It is important to recognize the distinctiveness of the Union itself. No strict parallel exists. England, a great nation, and Scotland, a comparatively poor and backward one, engaged in a voluntary union that turned out to be in many ways advantageous to both.

In Edinburgh the original North Bridge had been made passable by the year 1772, rendering feasible at last the founding of the "New Town" now called Georgian Edinburgh. The Scottish capital city had already entered into a period of remarkable literary fame. Adam Smith was in his prime. David Hume, the most influential figure behind the development of philosophy today in the English-speaking world, had settled in Edinburgh in 1751. By the 1780s men such as Benjamin Constant were pouring in from the continent. That period of cultural splendor waned, but Scotland's extraordinary contribution in the fields of science and medicine persisted. In the final chapter of this book we shall look at the incredible list of Scottish inventions and discoveries in medicine and science. We shall see also what has more recently brought the spate to a trickle.

The progress Scotland made in the eighteenth century in all fields of human knowledge could not have been achieved without a change in outlook such as came through contact with London. The new Scottish members of Parliament were bringing back something of the tolerant spirit of Addison and Steele. Scotland needed that spirit of the Age of Enlightenment, without which the economic and other progress she was to make in the nineteenth century would have been impossible.

Not all Scots were happy with the Union of 1707. As early as 1715 an uprising was attempted, aimed at restoring the Stewart monarchy. That year the Earl of Mar raised the first Jacobite rebellion. The Jacobites were so called because they adhered to James II after his abdication: "James" in Latin is *Jacobus*. That rebellion failed for lack of substantial Lowland support. The Jacobites had been promised help from France, but the death of Louis XIV led to withdrawal of French support. The uprising was a failure and the reprisals were moderate, although thirty Jacobites were executed and hundreds were transported to the

American colonies. A generation later came the great uprising of 1745, known later simply as "the Forty-five." France now seemed ready to send troops. In 1744 some actually assembled, but a bad storm prevented the planned invasion. The movement was now focused on the romantic figure of "the Bonnie Prince," Charles Edward Stewart, the Young Chevalier, who had been born in Rome on December 31, 1720, grandson of James II and elder son of James III (the "Old Pretender") by whom he had been at birth created "Prince of Wales."

Everything relating to Jacobitism is in some circles even today likely to arouse the most irrational passions. At the time, Charles received fanatical loyalty from his followers. He can hardly be said to have deserved it. At any rate, with merely nominal support from France, he led the new and final rebellion with contingents of such soldiers as he could pick up, mostly untrained. At first the Jacobite progress was astounding. Their forces made their way to Edinburgh, where the Bonnie Prince actually took up residence in Holyrood, still hoping for French help. He then resolved to march on London, and in fact reached Derby in the English Midlands. By this time the English had gathered their forces under the Duke of Cumberland and General Wade. The decisive battle was fought on a tract of moorland near Inverness. This, the Battle of Culloden, was Scotland's greatest defeat since Flodden.

Not only was Prince Charlie's army ill-trained and ill-equipped, it was also hopelessly outnumbered: five thousand men against Cumberland's nine thousand mostly well-trained soldiers. The previous night the Jacobites had made an abortive attempt to surprise the enemy, and they were still weary and hungry when the battle started with an artillery duel the following afternoon at one o'clock. Despite a plucky attempt, the Jacobites suffered an appalling defeat. On the English side were even some Highlanders playing the pipes from the enemy lines. Surrounded and demoralized, the Jacobites fled, leaving twelve hundred dead while the English lost only fifty. The wounded crawled as best they could into neighboring woods and farms. Cumberland's search parties relentlessly pursued them, hunting them down and killing them with their bayonets. Even casual bystanders were slaughtered. The Provost of Inverness, because he had protested against the barbarous cruelty, was kicked downstairs on the orders of Cumberland's general. The English even slaughtered the Highlanders' cattle and feasted ostentatiously while the vanquished starved. Some of the Highland families, maddened with hunger, crawled to the English encampments and begged to be allowed to drink the blood of their own slaughtered animals. But Cumberland's orders were clear: any of his soldiers found supplying food to the enemy would be court-martialed and punished by flogging or death. Eighty known Jacobites were executed.

Cumberland's treatment of the rebels and their families ranks among the most brutal acts in human history. Well he deserved the nickname "The Butcher." Among Jacobite sympathizers, far more numerous than those who openly espoused the cause, the English were held in infamy such as that in which Greeks have held Turks. For Cumberland's victorious return to London, Handel composed "See the Conquering Hero Comes."

After Culloden, Highlanders were forbidden to carry arms, to play the bagpipes, or to wear the kilt, three points on which Highland pride had focused as of right. Not till 1782, six years after the American War of Independence, was the right to wear the kilt restored. Scottish Episcopalians were suspect of embroilment in Jacobite plots. Such of their clergy as were permitted to officiate at all were required, under an Act of the British Parliament of 1746, to pray for the King *by name* when they did so. Punishment for the first offense was six months imprisonment. For the second, no mercy was shown: banishment to America for life!

Jacobite sentiment has enriched Scotland's lore. Every Scot with a drop of Highland blood warms to the old songs celebrating the exploits of the Bonnie Prince. From a commonsense standpoint, the whole episode of the Forty-five was folly; from a military standpoint it was pure madness. Yet it was ennobling folly of which no Scot could ever be ashamed, as no Scot shall ever forget the inexcusable barbarity of the attempted genocide. Culloden, by bringing Lowlanders into sympathy with their Highland compatriots, actually helped to solidify national Scottish sentiment. English action at Culloden was as stupid as it was cruel. Nevertheless, the Union was giving Scotland such advantages, both cultural and economic, that by the early nineteenth century the Jacobite cause had already become largely sentimental. Yet it persisted. When in 1821 my own great-grandfather, a MacKinnon and a Jacobite, born in 1795, proposed to marry my great-grandmother, a Grant and a Hanoverian, *his* father at first refused to come to the wedding. When, through feminine wile, he was at last persuaded to do so, he ostentatiously drank the health of "the King over the water," an act of defiance performed by raising one's glass of whisky with a tumbler of water between one's heart and the whisky. It was perhaps only for that reason that Highlanders in those days ever thought of having water on a festive table.

In the nineteenth century the railways (made possible through a Scottish invention) revolutionized transportation and communication between the two countries. Industries boomed—including coal, shipping, textiles, and minerals—as did trade overseas. By the end of Victoria's reign in 1901, the economic growth of Scottish cities, notably Glasgow and Dundee, had been fantastic, as we shall see in a later chapter. Amid such prosperity, few among the beneficiaries could have had the gall to decry the Union openly, whatever murmurings they heard in their own hearts.

Scotland's role in the United Kingdom had become, under Victoria, increasingly important. In 1884 a Scottish National Convention held in Edinburgh demanded the creation of a Scottish Office. The following year a Scottish Secretaryship was created, which in 1926 became a Secretaryship of State, further dignifying Scotland's position in the Union. Yet the psychological wounds of Flodden, Darien, and Culloden have bitten deeper into the Scottish mind than modern inhabitants of Scotland are willing to recognize. Less still are they willing to admit what has been in fact the most effective instrument of subjugation: participation in England's modern welfare state, with all its notorious disincentives for work and especially for enterprise. Never did even Culloden dispirit the Scots as has this seemingly pacific weapon, which has crushed the old Scottish spirit of independence, thrift, and enterprise without shedding a drop of blood. Not all Scots have been lulled into slumber. The political scene today, however, belongs to a later chapter.

3

Kilt, Clan, Tartan, and Bagpipe

He'n clo dubh, ho'n clo dubh,
B'f hearr leam am breacan.

(Hey, the black clothes; ho, the black clothes;
I'd rather have the plaid.)
—Alasdair MacMhaighstir Alasdair,
Captain in the army of Bonnie Prince Charlie

T HE kilt, with all its appurtenances, is known all over the world as a symbol of Scotland and one of the most spectacular forms of dress to be seen on our planet. At one time it was merely the traditional dress of the Highland Scot. Its proscription in the eighteenth century intensified Scottish pride in it. The tartan or pattern woven into a kilt is nowadays related to the clan or family of the wearer. Before we consider clans and tartans, let us look at the general principle of Highland dress, how it evolved, and how it should be worn today.

Before the seventeenth century, the ordinary dress of the Scottish Highlander was a large, full, saffron-colored shirt, over which was worn a thick woolen garment somewhat like a priest's cassock but reaching only to the knee. We know this from reports by foreign visitors to Scotland. After about the year 1600 that costume went out of style. Two alternatives came into vogue: the *breacan-féile* and the *féile-beag.* (The latter is anglicized as "fili-beg.") The *breacan-féile* was worn in togalike fashion, the twelve yards of tartan secured around the waist with a belt. The lower part was the kilt; the upper, fastened at the shoulder with a brooch, covered the torso and hung down behind. It would require a good deal of arranging for neat appearance. The *féile-beag* was to the *breacan-féile* somewhat as a made-up bow tie is to a regular one. It was made of at least six yards of tartan, pleated, sewn, and fixed at the waist with straps. It was substantially the kilt as we know it today.

Nowadays a kilt is worn with an ordinary white shirt for everyday attire, a tweed jacket and a waistcoat, brogues or other heavy shoes, plain knitted woolen hose secured by garters usually adorned with "flashes" (red or green strips), and a bonnet of either the Balmoral or Glengarry style. The sporran, a kind of shield originally intended to protect the male genitalia in battle, is worn hanging from a chain or a strap at the waist. It also serves as a purse, for there are no pockets in a kilt. For ordinary day wear the sporran may be a simple leather pouch with a few decorative tassels, or a grander affair made of sterling silver and fur, often fox or badger. If the "plaid" (pronounced *playd*), which is really the counterpart of an overcoat, is to be worn, it should be about four yards long, one and a half yards wide, and fringed at the ends. Today the plaid is rarely worn as ordinary dress, having been replaced by the Inverness cape, designed somewhat like a regular overcoat but with a cape. For everyday wear a tweed jacket of short, military cut is customary, with a plain rather than a tartan tie.

The correct length of the kilt may be ascertained by kneeling on the ground, body and head erect. The front of the kilt should not quite touch the ground. The six to eight yards of pleated material make the kilt very heavy at the back, so that it will stay put even in a high wind. In front a simple or a decorative pin adorns the kilt on the right side. To the perennial question, "What is worn under the kilt?" the answer is simple. In the old days probably nothing, but today always briefs, preferably of a dark color and best of all of the same tartan as the kilt. In the stocking should be worn a *sgian dubh,* on the outer part of the right leg. The *sgian dubh* is a knife in a simple sheath. The bonnet may be adorned with a brooch showing the clan crest of the wearer or else the clan badge. One must always wear the badge with a representation of a belt and buckle, to show one's tie to the chief of one's clan. Only the chief of the clan wears it otherwise.

So much for everyday wear, such as one would use for a walk across the moors or on the golf course. The full-dress outfit can be and usually is very resplendent. Many clans have a special "dress" tartan as well as the ordinary "hunting" tartan. The hose should be made of the web of the tartan or knitted in a check of its predominant colors. (For everyday wear any color hose, such as gray or green, will do.) The doublet or jacket should be of velvet with lozenge-shaped buttons, usually silver. There are various forms of the doublet. Black velvet is usual; green is also used. Ornaments may include shoe buckles, which may be of silver; if the wearer is entitled to armorial bearings, these may adorn the mounting of the sporran and the belt. The cairngorm is the customary jewel used to fasten the plaid. For formal dress wear the lace jabot and lace sleeves are customary.

The kilt is strictly a male garb. It is often said that the test of a true Scot is: does he feel more masculine in a kilt than in trousers? Unless he does he cannot be authentic! At any rate, the kilt is definitely not to be worn by women. To Celtic eyes, a woman in a kilt is as ridiculous a spectacle as a man in a bra. For ordinary day purposes, ladies wear a tartan skirt. It may be pleated, but not with the heavy pleating used in a kilt, which is designed for the male figure. She wears a tweed or other jacket, brogues, and stockings covering the knees. For reasons already made clear, a woman in a sporran is accounted indecent.

Appalling caricatures of Highland dress flourished in Victorian times and well into the twentieth century, especially for little boys and girls. Common sense and informed opinion eventually prevailed, bringing about a revulsion against such atrocities as women or girls in masculine attire. Instead, a beautiful modification of the ancient *arisaid* was devised and offered as an alternative at the Aboyne Highland Gathering in 1952, which forbad the use of male costume by female dancers. The ancient *arisaid,* which will be presently described more fully, was a one-piece garment. The modern adaptation for dancers, worn over a white undergown with wide sleeves usually ornamented with little tartan bows at shoulder and elbow, consists of a very full, gathered tartan skirt, designed to billow when the dancer is in action, and a separate piece of the same tartan material attached at the waist from the back and fastened to the right shoulder with a brooch. A velvet bodice, low cut and laced through with silver buttons, is worn with the skirt. The ensemble is extraordinarily beautiful, giving the wearer an air of feminine vitality and grace.

To understand the principles behind *formal* dress for ladies, a little historical background is helpful. The principal garment for women in ancient times, the *arisaid,* was of light tartan, always on a white ground. It fell from the neck to the heels in one piece, tied in front by the two upper ends and clasped to the breast by a silver or other buckle or brooch. The *arisaid* was pleated all around and was fastened with a silver and leather belt at the waist. The headdress might be a fine linen scarf tied around the head and hanging tapered down the back. Sleeves might be of scarlet cloth closed at the end, with gold lace encircling them. The stones used in brooches and other adornments would vary with the taste of the wearer. The *arisaig* may be worn today, but for evening or other formal occasions ladies generally wear a white dress with a tartan scarf over the shoulder.

Some controversy attends the question: which shoulder? According to some knowledgeable authorities, the sash is a curtailed version of the tartan cloak a woman in former times wore to support and cover her baby. She would hold the baby in her left arm, so as to leave the right arm free, and would therefore drape the cloak over her left shoulder. On this theory, the sash should be worn over the lady's left shoulder. The Lord Lyon King-of-Arms, who is the supreme authority in Scotland over heraldic and other such matters, gives no formal, judicial opinion on the subject. Nevertheless, Sir Thomas Innes of Learney, a former occupant of that office, personally approved the following styles: (1) clanswomen wear the sash over the right shoulder across the breast to the waist, then across the back over the right shoulder where it is secured by a pin or brooch, with the rest of the sash hanging down in front to just above the right knee; (2) wives of clan chiefs wear a somewhat fuller sash (about twenty-four inches wide with a twelve-inch fringe) over the left shoulder across the breast to the waist, then across the back over the left shoulder, where it is secured with a pin or brooch, with the rest of the sash hanging down in front to just above the left knee; (3) ladies who have married out of their clan but wish to use their original clan tartan may wear a longer sash over the right shoulder, secured there with a pin and fastened in a large bow on the left hip. Ladies who are wearing chivalric orders or decorations or the riband of an order would wish to keep the front of the dress clear. According to the same authority, they may attach the sash to the back of the dress at the waist and with a brooch at the right shoulder, so that both ends fall back and hang behind the right arm. For ballroom dancing, moreover, it may be inconvenient to have the right shoulder encumbered by the sash, and therefore ballroom dancers may prefer the second style, with the sash over the left shoulder. The basic rule is that the sash should be worn over the right shoulder as in (1), unless the wearer has good reason to do otherwise. Most ladies are not carrying babies when they appear in formal attire, so that consideration need not affect practice today.

In all matters of Highland dress, as indeed in any form of clothing, the wearer should both look and feel comfortable. This is far more important than attention to minutiae, not least when the rules are the subject of historical controversy. As we shall see presently, the whole concept of tartans as distinguishing clan badges is comparatively modern, although the use of tartan in Highland dress is of great antiquity. Thus no rules or conventions about detail are likely to have any absolute authority behind them or to merit any strict obedience. Informed common sense and innate good taste are the best guides of all. Formal Highland dress, properly worn, is certainly one of the most beautiful garbs in the world. A well-attired lady and gentleman in Highland dress complement each other. As they enter a room together they create a feeling of warmth, confidence, and grace. Anyone, man or woman, with a drop of Highland blood will feel happy, confident, and self-fulfilled in his or her dress. No one who does not should wear it. We shall presently consider who is entitled to wear it.

The word "clan" comes from the Gaelic word "clann," which means "children." A clan is a family, but more than a family in the modern sense. The central idea of the clan is kinship. In theory, the chief of a clan is the father of the clan; at any rate all members of the clan belong to the same kin. The clan system in Scotland has very ancient roots. The founders of the clans, which may go back to as early as the eleventh century, were sometimes incomers. For instance, the Gordons and the Frasers had Norman beginnings, the Stewarts Breton origins, the Murrays and the Sutherlands, Flemish, the MacNeills Irish, the MacLeods Norse. These incomers, when they acquired land either by conquest or by charter—or sometimes through marriage—took over people living on the land, who might often be already a family unit. By the sixteenth century the patriarchal system of clanship had fully developed. Precedence was rigorously observed. The chief himself preceded all others, of course. Then came members of his immediate family, his younger sons and grandsons, who founded "cadet" or landed families of their own. These cadets inherited their lands and granted long-term leases or "tacks" to middlemen, who were known as tacksmen. They, in turn, gave short-term leases to their tenants. All, however, whether strictly connected by blood or not, owed a common loyalty to their clan. The chief, who *par excellence* enjoyed the loyalty of the rest of the clan, was in return their leader in battle, their arbiter in peace, and their judge. As the monarchy strengthened, the chiefs acquired a sort of vice-regal authority and status: they were responsible for the good conduct of their clan.

Nowadays we think of clans in terms of surnames: "he is a MacLeod" (pronounced *maklowd*) or "she is a Colquhoun" (pronounced *cahoon*). The use of the surname is comparatively modern. It was certainly not generally used till at least the seventeenth century, and it was long after that till it became universal. In the Middle Ages a member of a clan would be called, for example, the Gaelic equivalent of John macJames vicDuncan. His son Robert would then be Robert macJohn vicJames, and so on. Eventually many families adopted as their surname the name of their chief; others used more arbitrary methods. Anyone, of course, can adopt any surname he chooses, so the name in itself is no proof of Scots ancestry, let alone membership of the clan whose name he or she bears. Nevertheless, if a person named MacDonald or MacPherson, for example, can trace his or her lineage back to a Scottish ancestor early last century, he or she can be reasonably sure that his or her claim to membership in the clan is very well founded.

What, then, is a clan? It is based on a mixture of tribal tradition and the organization of families upon land. Title to land consisted of descent from him who first "raised smoke and boiled water" on the land. The clan made for a very broad-based society. The same blood flowed in humble folk as in grandees. The determining factor was the land. This is reflected in modern clan maps showing areas supposed to represent clan "countries." You will see an area around Killin, Perthshire, for instance, marked as MacNab country, and another in the far north as the country of the MacKenzies. Such maps give a general idea of the traditional whereabouts of the clans; but bear in mind that there was never any neat delineation of territory, so that at no time could one ever have drawn a map of clan lands as one could nowadays draw one of counties or the like. The fact that land is the basis of the clan system explains two traditional features of Scottish life and outlook: (1) the absence of class distinction as understood in England and other countries, for the highest and the lowest, the richest and the poorest, rubbed shoulders; and (2) the immense sense of family pride. True, the Scots also have pride in titles and rank, but such pride relates to family more than to rungs on a social ladder stretching from a lower class to a higher. Scotland always thought "clan warfare," never "class warfare," till quite recent times, and then only under English and other alien influence. From this basic fact about Scotland springs her ready development of democratic ideas. In the medieval tenements of Edinburgh's Canongate, noblemen and humble tradesmen came to live together on the same stair, greeting each other as they passed up and down, recognizing the difference in their functions but lacking that intense class consciousness that has bedeviled English and other societies.

The Golden Age of the clans in Scotland was already beginning to decline about the time of the Union of the Parliaments in 1707. The Jacobite risings finished it. Clan sentiment continues, however, throughout the world. It is indubitably stronger abroad than in Scotland. The first clan society was that of the Buchanans, founded in 1725. Like most of these societies in the past, it did important charitable work, especially in educating its young members by providing various scholarships to help them go to college or to learn a trade. Today clan societies flourish in America, often vigorously fostering loyalty and promoting clan spirit. Some such societies in Scotland continue their work faithfully, usually in a modest way. Others have become moribund. The chief of one important clan, in an effort to revive its society, wrote three hundred letters in his own hand to members of his clan who seemed to be in fair circumstances or better. Only a very few even took the trouble to respond. This may well be an extreme case. But clan fervor is nowadays generally more lively outside Scotland than in it, and it is better that Americans visiting Scotland should be forewarned than that they should be disappointed.

The tartan is unquestionably ancient, going back to at least the thirteenth century, probably earlier. The Highlander loved bright colors and loved cloth of a checked or a striped material, called *breacan.* Whether clans used distinguishing tartans such as we know today is much more questionable. According to a romantic opinion, the Highlanders wore distinguishable tartans so that in battle they could recognize friend from foe. That is unlikely, since in fact much evidence shows that they generally discarded the *breacan* and fought in the shirts already described, which would give them more freedom.

At least as early as the seventeenth century, the weavers of each locality tended to develop their own particular weave, somewhat as farmers develop distinctive methods pertaining to the region and as each Italian town has its own distinctive way of cooking spaghetti. Clans were associated with regions, not very exactly, as we have noted already, but by the sixteenth century the connection was growing. Even by the time of the Union of the Parliaments it is highly doubtful that you could have pointed to a figure approaching from the crest of a hill and have been able to say: "There's a MacLeod coming over to see us," or "I wonder what this MacDonald wants." Yet anyone well versed in the local weaves could no doubt say, "That's not one of our tartans, that's how they weave in Sutherland," or something of the sort.

The more clans came to be associated with definite regions, the easier it would be to say, "That's the way they weave and these are the colors they use in MacKenzie country—he'll be a MacKenzie, no doubt."

All that is only in the realm of probabilities. It may well be that many Highland ladies and gentlemen before 1745 chose their tartan much as we today choose our suitings, simply because they liked the pattern. This is suggested in *Common Errors in Scottish History,* edited by Dr. Gordon Donaldson and published for the Historical Association, London, in 1956. The author of the relevant article admits, however, that "certain dyes would prevail in different regions and that traditional types of pattern might be followed in various parts." The whole topic is controversial, except that we do know tartan to be ancient. What is in question is only the notion that distinctive tartans "belong" to individual clans as their exclusive badge. We do have some evidence, however, that when tartan was proscribed after the failure of the 1745 rebellion, the weavers kept the patterns on their frames, many of which broke or wore out in the course of the long period of proscription. The old people often could not remember exactly what the patterns had been, so there was confusion arising from necessary dependence on a sometimes shaky oral tradition. Imagine how difficult it would be for women today, if there were no books or pictures in existence, to remember the details of fashions that nobody had ever been allowed to wear for nearly forty years. To recall individual patterns would be even more difficult. Probably only people with excellent powers of observation as well as accurate memories could have given reliable accounts, and then of only a limited number of designs. If, as seems to have been the case, the relation between clan and tartan had been still not entirely constant even by the time of the risings, that would add to the difficulties.

In the early nineteenth century, the Highland societies tried their best to collect patterns and research the authenticity of their traditional relationship with the respective clans. Their efforts were only partially successful. The demand for tartan grew rapidly about this time, aided by the appearance in Edinburgh of King George IV arrayed in the kilt and other habiliments of Highland Scotland. What were the manufacturers of tartan to do in meeting the demand? They used such knowledge as oral tradition had provided, supplemented with creative imagination wherever tradition failed. Books appeared with plates showing the tartans attributed to each of the clans. All we can say now is that the degree of authenticity must have varied from clan to clan. Some tartans were probably as nearly authentic as they could have been in the circumstances; others might deviate considerably from past tradition; some might be entirely fanciful, the arbitrary inventions of an imaginative designer.

Nothing in all this affects the fact that the tartan is of great antiquity. What happened was not fundamentally different from what happens when an ancient statue or building is restored or a manuscript that has been partially destroyed is edited and printed. The restorer does the best he can with the material and facts available to him. During the past century and a half, the exact recording of the patterns has become a very technical business, almost like the "limning" of heraldic arms. In the execution of the design, however, some latitude is allowed; hence there may be slight differences in matters of fine detail such as shade of dye and thread count. What is called "ancient" as distinguished from "hunting" tartan for the same clan is done with faded dyes. "Dress" tartans are sometimes of a pattern quite different from the one used for other-than-dress occasions. The dress Stewart, for instance, is predominantly white, while the hunting Stewart is green and the royal Stewart—the tartan King George V adopted as his own—is red. The clergy have a tartan, which was used at one time as the regular weekday dress of clergy in the Highlands. It differs slightly from the tartan assigned to Clark, the Gaelic form of which is *cleireach,* meaning "cleric." The name MacChlery has the same derivation; there is an analogy in the French name Le Clerc.

Clans have their own mottoes, badges, and war cries. The badge of the MacGillivrays, for instance, is the red whortleberry *(lus nam brolleag).* Clan Gregor uses for its motto the proud affirmation "Royal is my race" *('S rioghail mo dhream).*

The clans also have their respective chiefs, the recognized representative of the ancestor who founded the clan or family. He embodies the race. By its nature the chiefship is hereditary. Wherever the line of succession is accounted clear, this is the method of succession that prevails. In default of hereditary succession, a chief may be elected or acclaimed by members of the clan. In Scots Law, the chiefship, like other rights and property, descends to heirs of line, not necessarily males only. Where the chiefship passes to or through a woman, however, her husband is recognized as "Chief by the courtesy of Scotland," and he and his children must take her clan name. All such matters, as well as the use of personal coats of arms, are regulated by the Court of the Lord Lyon, the principal heraldic officer in Scotland, corresponding to the Earl Marshal in England. The chief of a clan may possess no other dignity or title, although in many cases he may happen to have a military rank or title of nobility. In some clans the chief has also a special designation, for example, "The Mac-Donald of MacDonald," "The Chisholm," "The Macneil of Barra," and "MacFarlane of that Ilk."

We have seen how deeply entrenched in Highland tradition is the clan system and that the use of tartan is ancient. No less ancient and traditional is the instrument so much associated with the Scottish Highlands: the bagpipe. The use of pipes in one form or another is obviously of extreme antiquity, antedating ancient mythological lore about Orpheus and the great god Pan, and as universal in the history of music as the use of strings. In Scotland the pipe was improved to serve the development of traditional Highland music. The "variations" played on the bagpipe are historically associated with the MacCrimmons, who were hereditary pipers to Clan MacLeod. They were probably the first to form a school of piping, which they did at Borreraig on the Isle of Skye. The pibroch (Gaelic, *piobaireachd*), as this traditional music is called, was probably for long the basic pipe music of the Highlands. After the failure of the 1745 rising, certain British military regiments eventually took over the instrument. New forms were then developed for martial purposes by regiments such as the Scots Guards and the Seaforths. About the time of the Crimean War, in the middle of the nineteenth century, official pipe bands were introduced and became an essential appurtenance of those regiments. Civilian pipe bands were developed later and are now found all over the world, wherever people of Scottish ancestry reside.

Bagpipes are not easy to play. Apart from the technicalities of the instrument, the lung power it demands is not a universal human endowment any more than are the sturdy calves and knees without which the kilt looks so ridiculous. Some might cynically suggest that not only is the playing difficult, so also is the listening. That depends. When, as often happens today, the pipes are played by the dozen in a room so small that a dying girl's voice could be clearly heard without mechanical aid, the decibels inflicted by a pipe band would make rock music in a discotheque sound by comparison like compline in an under-staffed convent of nuns. The pipes are essentially for outdoors. You have not heard them till you have heard them coming toward you over the summit of a distant hill. It is then that they will stir your heart with love of and loyalty to all that is right and good in the human race. But first make sure that the hill is distant. After all, Washington Cathedral's organ would not move you to religious devotion if you brought it into your living room, so there is no reason to expect better of the bagpipes. To understand their meaning, first listen to the words of "Scotland the Brave":

> Hark, when the night is falling,
> Hear, hear the pipes are calling,
> Loudly and proudly calling down through the glen.
> There where the hills are sleeping
> Now feel the blood a-leaping
> High as the spirits of the old Highland men.

CHAPTER

4

Golf, Dances, Sports, and Highland Games

Golf . . . is the very epitome of the elements which have given the Scottish character its strength and individuality. It is the game of the patient, self-reliant man, prepared to meet whatever fortune may befall him.
—Garden G. Smith, *The Royal and Ancient Game of Golf*

SOME call golf Scotland's national sport; others call it her national religion. Such is the number of golf courses that probably no one has ever taken a complete inventory. Of the 250 best, fifteen are internationally famed. These are, in alphabetical order: Carnoustie, Cruden Bay, Dornoch, Gleneagles, Gullane Number One, Muirfield, Nairn, North Berwick, Prestwick, Royal Burgess, St. Andrews Eden, St. Andrews New, St. Andrews Old, Troon, and Turnberry. Glasgow has eight golf courses within the city bounds, Edinburgh fifteen—and both cities are within easy reach of many more. Sometimes one almost gets the impression that the entire country is one enormous golf course interspersed with buildings and other scenic interruptions.

Many American and other golfers wonder at the incontestable fact that Scotland, despite being the golfer's Mecca, has produced no really great international champions such as Jack Nicklaus and Arnold Palmer. The reason is simple: the Scots do not work at it; they enjoy it. Of course they do have professionals, but even some of the professionals have no idea how much work it takes to attain international stature.

Almost everywhere you go in Scotland you will see people playing golf. It is not only a game for the well-to-do as it is in England and the United States. Even many private clubs are comparatively inexpensive, while public courses are available to all. Golf is a very popular way of spending Saturday after a week cooped up in factory or office. In the cities and larger towns little putting greens may lie along the way home; workers will sometimes stop to practice a few putts to keep their hand in for the coming Saturday, when they will go farther afield to a course on the outskirts of town. Or in the long summer evenings they may saunter out to enjoy such practice games in the "gloaming."

The quality of courses varies a great deal. There are two principal types: the links, which are close to the sea, and the inland courses. Gleneagles, for instance, is a course, Muirfield a links. Not all courses are close to being as grand as the famous ones, and none is manicured as are golf courses in the United States. Most are somewhere between the great courses and the one described by a visitor to one of the islands who had been attracted to an inn by the promise of facilities for boating, fishing, and golf. In the morning, refreshed by sleep and a hearty breakfast, he asked the landlord about the golf course. The landlord looked thoughtful. "Yess indeed, there iss a golf," he murmured at last. "I will be showing you the place." They set off till they reached a hillside with growth a foot deep. "Yess, yess," he went on, "there wass indeed a golf and I will be finding it for you." After poking about with his cane, he stopped short with an air of triumph. "I *knew* there wass a golf—and here indeed is the hole."

Such may be the state of affairs in some very remote places, but it is certainly far from being so in most places the visitor is likely to encounter today. In the village of Gullane (pronounced *gillen*, hard *g*), eighteen miles from Edinburgh, are no fewer than three eighteen-hole courses, with the Luffness course adjoining them to the south; east of the village is Muirfield, headquarters of the Honourable Company of Edinburgh Golfers, a venerable institution. An Edinburgh man once boasted that he had played on thirty-seven courses on thirty-seven consecutive days without ever once sleeping away from home. It *could* be done, providing you had the fortitude that is the fruit of that religious fervor with which so many Scottish golfers pursue their avocation.

Even those who never play golf should see Gleneagles, much as one might say that even an atheist should surely see St. Peter's when in Rome. The name "Gleneagles" means "Glen of the Church" ("church" in Gaelic is *eglais*). It was a virtually unknown place till 1923, when a magnificent hotel, brain child of some railway magnate, was opened with two superlative golf courses, called "the King's" and "the Queen's." The well-known Scottish golfer James Braid had a part in planning both courses.

St. Andrews is to golfers what Mecca is to Muslims. There are four full-length courses and five putting greens. The four courses are the Old, the New, the Eden, and the Jubilee. The Old, which is the most venerated in the world, has two of the most famous holes anywhere, the short eleventh or "sea" hole and the seventeenth or "road" hole. Both are stern yet beloved schoolmasters, the terror and the wonder of every votary of golf who has made the pilgrimage. Golf was played on this terrain four hundred years ago or more, although the Royal and Ancient Golf Club was not founded till 1754. Antiquity is, however, no more than an ingredient in its fame. Of greater significance is the fact that it was never planned or designed like a modern course. It was a natural course on which nobody ever built a bunker. Nobody ever would have thought of building a bunker such as the celebrated natural one known as Hell Bunker. Tall tales abound of golfers having been lost in it for days. No doubt somebody patted the earth down here and there to make something like a green around the holes, but otherwise this course is as much Nature's handiwork as are the sandy beaches that are among the many other attractions of this unique little town. St. Andrews houses also the smallest, oldest, and most picturesque of the four ancient Scottish universities. Moreover, in the Middle Ages the town was the ecclesiastical capital of Scotland, to which the ruins of its once splendid cathedral and other relics of the past stand witness today. The present clubhouse, which dates a century later than the club itself, is a handsome Victorian structure housing an interesting collection of pieces relating to golf in early times.

Although the essentials of golf have not changed over the centuries, a typical round of golf on a modern course differs considerably in some respects from a similar outing in bygone times. For one thing, the modern golf ball has been developed with such technical skill that it flies much farther and truer than its more primitive precursors. Golf was played with wooden balls in the seventeenth century and later. Feather-stuffed leather-covered balls were also used. Resourceful Scots sometimes made their own of whatever material came to hand and could serve the purpose. Nor is there anything sacrosanct about the number of holes in a golf course. At Leith Links in 1744 there were five holes; in some places where space was more restricted, perhaps only one at either end of the course. According to a picturesque legend, the number eighteen was determined by a Scot who found that with a "wee dram" of whisky at each hole, eighteen was as far as a standard bottle would go.

Hugo Arnot, writing two hundred years ago, describes the game of golf as "commonly played on rugged, broken ground, covered with short grass and bents in the neighborhood of the seashore. . . . The game is generally played in parties of one or two on each side. Each party has an exceeding hard ball, somewhat larger than a hen's egg. This they strike with a slender and elastick club, of about four feet long, crooked in the head, and having lead run into it to make it heavy. The . . . game is gained by the party who puts his ball into the hole with the fewest strokes."

No doubt modern golfers would feel more comfortable with

the description provided by Robert Browning, who edited the journal *Golfing* during the first half of the present century: "The combination of hitting for distance with the final nicety of approach to an exiguous mark."

Golf is indeed a very ancient game. Older spellings are "goff," "gouff," and "gowff." Scots still occasionally pronounce the word exactly according to this last spelling. The word comes from the Dutch *kolf* and the German *kolbe,* which mean "club." Dutch pictorial representations of the game and Scottish complaints about the cost to the Scottish economy of importing golf balls from Holland strongly suggest a Dutch origin for the game, although it would be most unwise for any visitor to Scotland to let anyone know that he or she had even heard such a theory. In some circles, at least, the view that golf was invented in Scotland is an article of religion that one should not dare call merely an article of faith.

Be that as it may, it is likely that the Scots many centuries ago gave the game much of the distinguishing character that it has had ever since. As early as the middle of the fifteenth century, the Parliament of Scotland under James II decreed against playing golf, which the rulers of the country felt to be an unprofitable expenditure of time that could be better spent practicing the use of the bow and arrow and other martial arts. Legislation of this kind was repeatedly enacted, being repeatedly disregarded. Not till 1502, under James IV, is there any evidence of acceptance of the game as something not necessarily against the national interest.

In all this, however, two points should be noted: (1) Scotland was not alone in condemning ball games. France and England did so too, and for the same reason. Football had been condemned in Scotland in 1424 and ball games in general in France in 1319. (2) The objection had no religious basis, such as might be expected had it come two or three centuries later under English Puritan influence. It was solely a matter of national concern. Archery was the approved sport because it had obvious national usefulness. Golf, like football, was deemed useless. What could it do for the country? Anything that could be said in its favor (fresh air, exercise, cultivation of eye-hand coordination, and other such merits) would seem to apply at least equally to archery. The high approval of the latter and the low esteem for golf are understandable.

From early times golf was known as "the Royal and Ancient Game of Goff." That the old Scottish kings enjoyed the game is clear. Some evidence exists to suggest that Mary, Queen of Scots played it; her enemies charged, as proof of her indifference to her husband's murder, that a few days after that event she was seen playing golf. Charles I and James II were also golfers. In 1834 William IV became patron of the Royal and Ancient Golf Club and three years later presented a splendid gold medal to be played for annually. Not till near the end of the last century, however, did golf become a fashionable game in England. In America at that time it was still little known, although American enthusiasm for it among the well-to-do has since outrun that of any other people in the world. As in so many other activities, Americans have scored many triumphs in international golf and have established many world records. It was an American (Haskell) who, in 1899, invented the rubber-cored ball that soon became standard. American expertise and successes in golf are of course galling to Scottish pride, so if you go golfing in Scotland you will do well to talk, rather, about the invigorating air. Or, if you prefer to be more technical, you might allude to the use of the smaller ball, which Scotland favors because of its greater carrying power in a high wind.

The east coast of Scotland, where many of the most famous courses lie, is indeed windy. Hence the old Scots jokes about carrying your own clubs to keep from being blown off the course and into the sea. The west is rainier. Neither wind nor rain, however, nor any other condition ever likely to occur in Scotland this side of doomsday, will deter a Scot on a golf course. Golfers habitually return from a round with the rain still bulging their pockets even as they are recounting what an enjoyable game they just played. This hardy disregard of water is expected. I remember once standing with another man of about my own height beside a flagpole near the clubhouse of a golf course. After he had engaged me in conversation for about ten minutes in drenching rain that was falling on already soggy ground, I glanced at the pole and at him only to find that we had both lost about two inches in height. So varied and so fickle is the Scottish climate that one might well meet the opposite. Perhaps the longest recorded drive on level ground in the history of golf occurred in June 1933 on the Old Course, St. Andrews, when the American Craig Ralph Wood, on the 530-yard fifth hole, drove 430 yards, assisted by parched ground and a strong following wind.

Before the present century women were already playing golf. They did not play on the regular courses, however, which were still exclusively male preserves. Scotswomen played on the short links at North Berwick and the like. Nowadays they often play on the same courses as the men and have attained much prowess in the game.

Before the present century, rules were minimal. The internationalization of the game brought not only highly developed equipment but extensive rule-making. Professionalism in golf, as in other games, has naturally accelerated such developments and raised playing standards to formerly unheard-of heights. But it has not made the game any more enjoyable than it was a hundred years ago, and it is surely arguable that one of the greatest merits of the game lies in providing healthy and enjoyable exercise in the open air. It also suits the individualist side of the Scottish temper and does not lend itself, as do tennis and football, to spectatorism.

Americans at a Scottish golf resort who find the conversation veering toward potentially explosive topics can usually clear the air with a Texas story such as the following. A Scotsman did a business favor for a Texan, who asked how he could repay the Scot. The Scot replied: "Well, if you insist, I wouldn't mind having one of these clubs you make over there." The Texan said, "Sure, I'll see you get a couple." Nothing happened for nearly a year. Then at last the Scot opened a letter with a Texas postmark. It read: "As promised I've found you a couple. The reason for the delay is that I wanted to make sure they both had swimming pools." It will go down better than the one about the Scotsman on the golf course who broke the bottle in his hip pocket, felt a trickle down his leg, and murmured hoarsely, "Oh michty, Ah hope it's only blood." If the first story sounds corny in Texas, the second will sound even cornier in Scotland.

No golfing story will be accounted as objectionable on any course in the world as Churchill's definition of golf: "a game designed by the Devil and played with instruments ill-adapted for the purpose." That is the ultimate blasphemy. You would probably be safer throwing eggs at the Black Stone the Muslim pilgrims circumambulate in Mecca than to repeat that definition in St. Andrews just as someone is readying for a crucial putt.

Scotland has long been known for its outdoor sports. Preeminent among these is hunting, which in Scotland, except in the case of deer, is almost always called simply shooting. Today the vast majority of Scots live in cities and, apart from those who are in principle opposed to blood sports of any kind, comparatively few Scots can afford to shoot, at any rate not officially. In rural areas a sport known as poaching is not unknown, but we shall consider only the more legal forms of shooting. Large areas of moorland and forest abound in game, a category that includes grouse, pheasant, wild duck, blackcock, goose, pigeon, and capercaillie, as wild turkey is called. The grouse season begins on August 12, a date most Scots somehow know even if they have never seen a grouse in their lives. Enthusiasts call it "The Glorious Twelfth." By that date most of the birds are fully grown and it is legal to shoot them, except for small birds that may remain, known as "cheepers."

Deer stalking is generally accounted the sport of kings. The cost, if you are to use the virtually indispensable services of an experienced ghillie, tends to be as lofty as the prestige of the sport: at the least several hundred dollars a week. The season for red deer begins on July 1 and continues till October 20.

For those who prefer fishing, Scotland is a paradise. For only a few dollars you can rent a rod and reel and go fishing. Trout and salmon are the fish most generally sought after in Scotland's beautiful rivers. In the sea, however, many other fish are caught, including halibut and skate. I once took a picture of a skate caught off the northwest coast near Ullapool by a teenager from England who displayed it for me. Its size and weight were that of an average-to-large man. To his great disappointment, local regulations apparently precluded his taking it home with him in his station wagon. I suspect that his parents, thinking of the hideous mass being conveyed hundreds of miles by road in mid-summer, must have been indeed grateful for the regulations, whatever they were, that prevented his bringing it home. I photographed the boy with the skate to provide him with the necessary evidence that the story he would tell was less fishy than it would sound. Such episodes are not part of the day-to-day joys of angling in Scottish waters. Generally speaking, if you obey the usually reasonable local rules, you will find your fishing proclivities not only successful but welcomed.

Mountain climbing is obviously a sport that can be practiced in Scotland very easily, with climbs to suit every degree of expertise. Skiing is also available at the proper season. In the cities, most of the larger public parks have tennis courts. Many of the parks have bowling greens. Bowling on the green is very popular in Scotland. Till fairly recent times it was widely accounted a game for elderly men who had lost the nimbleness and fleetness of foot necessary for tennis and other fast games. But nowadays it is played by men and women of all ages, a pleasant and relaxing way to spend an hour or two without engaging in violent forms of exercise.

Among urban dwellers in Scotland, by far the most popular spectator sport is soccer. It dominates the outlook of the masses, especially in Glasgow, more than any other form of outdoor amusement. Dog racing has also enjoyed a good deal of popularity. Both afford opportunities for small-time gambling. Rugger (rugby football) and horse racing tend to be favored by those who look down on these other spectator sports as plebeian, for in modern Scotland, alas, class consciousness, through English influence, enters almost every aspect of life. That is why golf is such a refreshing aspect of Scottish life, since it seems to be the exception, being everybody's game: the game of the individual rather than the class.

The tradition of Highland games is very ancient. More than a thousand years ago chiefs were using games to test the capabilities of those who seemed to hold promise for positions of military leadership, which required both agility and strength. What had been at first serious competition for such positions developed later into a festive occasion in which the display of physical prowess played a leading part. Traditional feats are tossing the caber (Gaelic, *cabar*), weight throwing, hammer throwing, the shot put, and the beer-keg toss.

A caber is an enormous heavy pole, which can be as much as eighteen feet long, about nine inches in diameter at one end and five at the other. It weighs typically between 80 and 140 pounds. The competitor begins with the caber set on the ground vertically with the thick end in the air. To judge the quality of the performance, imagine a huge clock face to which the competitor runs with the caber, stops at six o'clock, and tosses the caber to land in the center of the dial. In a perfect toss the thin end of the caber is at twelve o'clock.

In weight throwing, the competitor stands under a bar, over which he must throw the weight. Weights are either twenty-eight or fifty-six pounds. In hammer throwing, the competitor swings the hammer several times around his head and lets go so that the hammer flies behind him. In a perfect hammer throw the hammer flies straight back. The hammer, which is developed from the old blacksmith's hammer, has a round head and a stiff shaft. In shot-putting, which originated in the sport of putting a stone from a river, the weights now used are standard: either sixteen or twenty-two pounds. The beer-keg toss is a free-style event in which a standard aluminum one-quarter keg is used.

The atmosphere at Highland games is generally very pleasant and, for the spectators, relaxing: an enjoyable way to spend an afternoon when the weather is clement. There are often other events such as dancing competitions.

One must distinguish carefully between Highland dancing and Scottish country dancing. Dances such as the sword dance and the Highland fling are ancient in origin, possibly a thousand years old. These are traditionally male dances, although for long now women have danced them too. Such dances demand a great deal of energy and develop a high degree of coordination, not least the sword dance. Nowadays these dances and the competitions that are held all over the world are very formally regulated by the Scottish Official Board of Highland Dancing. The most prestigious championship is held at Cowal, Argyllshire, every August.

One of the most interesting Highland dances is the Shantruse, which celebrates the return of the kilt after the long decades in the eighteenth century during which it had been prohibited. In the course of the dance the dancers mimic kicking off imaginary trousers, the hated symbol of oppression.

Scottish country dancing has a different origin and is a radically different art form. It is progressive dancing, with set formations. It should not be thought of as folk dancing in any ordinary sense; it has more the character of ballroom dancing. The term "country dance" may derive from the French *contre danse*. These dances, when well performed, are extremely graceful. Of course they may be sometimes danced informally just for fun or exercise. Only when you have seen them formally danced can you appreciate their beauty and their true character. Nowadays the Royal Scottish Country Dance Society, formed in 1923, regulates the steps and other details of the performance.

All Scottish dancing is delightful. If you fail to thrill to it, the reason cannot be merely that you have no Scottish blood in your veins. It must be that you come from another planet.

CHAPTER

5

Education

Education makes a people easy to lead,
but difficult to drive; easy to govern,
but impossible to enslave.
—Lord Brougham, Scottish-born British states-
man and Lord Chancellor of England, in a
speech in the House of Commons, 1828

THE Scottish educational system has a very distinctive history.
In the middle of the last century and even later, while public
elementary education in England left much to be desired and
higher education was still very much a preserve of the upper
classes, Scotland had a remarkably comprehensive system that
was admired in continental Europe. It was a system strictly without frills and Spartan both in concept and in practice at every
level. It was thorough and efficient. It did not go out of its way
to nurture brilliance, for according to the prevailing theory, brilliant minds would shine later on, no matter what kind of education they received. The aim was strictly a meat-and-potatoes education, although in fact many of the recipients were more likely
to be eating herring and oatmeal porridge to sustain them as they
plodded from the "three R's" (reading, 'riting, and 'rithmetic) to
their Latin and perhaps some Greek.

Above all it was a democratic system. Almost any boy with

genuine ability could get financial help to go beyond the regular schooling and even up to the university, especially after Andrew Carnegie's benefaction in 1901, which provided funds to send any boy otherwise qualified to one of the universities by paying about half or, in approved cases, even all the tuition fees. As we shall see later, Scotland was also in the vanguard of the movement to admit women to higher education, providing a university degree for them before they were admitted to any university in England and at a time when strictly academic colleges for women (as opposed to mere seminaries for young ladies) were at only an embryonic stage in the United States.

The system of elementary education in Scotland dates from 1696, when the Act of Settling of Schools was passed. One of the plans of John Knox during the Reformation in 1560 was to provide a school in every parish in the country. This plan was substantially what the Act of 1696 implemented. These schools were under the control of the national Kirk. The schoolmaster, who held office for life, enjoyed considerable local esteem, next after the parish minister. Not a few schoolmasters were, indeed, men who had entertained hopes of going on to the ministry but whose aspirations had been unrealized. Although the Kirk ran the schools, they were in theory, at least, nondenominational. The Church-State question that has been so important in pluralistic societies such as the United States scarcely affected the Scottish scene at all. In any case, so rigorously was the program focused on the "three R's" that management of the schools by the Kirk signified little more than does the management of American hospitals by Presbyterian, Lutheran, and other such bodies today. The students were taught the Scottish Shorter Catechism. That document was so widely accepted by the vast majority of the population that its inclusion in the curriculum was almost as unquestioned as is today the teaching of United States history in American schools. Boys and girls were taught together.

This system, with some modification, prevailed until 1872, when the Education Act took away management of the schools from the Kirk and placed it under the control of school boards, with members elected regularly by the taxpayers. Until 1889, the parents of children had been expected to contribute token payments toward the cost of educating their children, on the principle that people never value anything they get for nothing. In many cases the contribution was a penny a week; hence the phrase "a penny teacher" that was still remembered a few generations ago. In 1889, however, all school fees for what we now call grade school were abolished. The Education (Scotland) Act of 1918 brought more sweeping changes in administration of the school system.

So much for the elementary, primary, or grade school education. What of the ambitious student who hoped to go further? Knox's scheme had envisioned a complete system of education from first grade to university. In several towns excellent high schools, such as those at Edinburgh and Glasgow, had been founded at an early date. Many schools of this type emerged, sometimes called high schools and sometimes academies, corresponding roughly to the English "grammar school," which is not to be confused with a grammar school in the American sense. Such schools were intended to prepare students in Latin and in other subjects necessary for admission to a university. They charged modest tuition fees. Once again, they were no-frill schools offering very sound training in the essentials.

An able student, diligent in his or her studies, can go through such a school and be as ready to gain admission to a university as by any other means. Such a student may lack the graces that might be acquired at an expensive school, and also (more important) the self-confidence, maturity, and capacity for leadership that are emphasized in the more socially prestigious schools. But the student at the high school or academy graduates knowing what mental discipline is, ready to compete with his or her peers at the university. A student who plans to do a science degree at the university, for example, will have been thoroughly grounded in physics, chemistry, and biology, and will have been trained in mathematics up to calculus. A student proposing a university program directed more toward the humanities will have a somewhat lower standard in the sciences but will have the necessary languages up to a considerable level of competence, at least from a literary if not a conversational standpoint. In French, for instance, the student will have had at least an hour a day with correspondingly heavy homework for about six years, culminating in the ability to read material such as Molière's plays and to write straightforward French prose composition correctly if without literary distinction. In short one may go from such a school to take one's place as a university freshman without injury to the standards of the institution for which one has been prepared.

Matters were not quite the same two hundred years ago, although Henry Mackenzie, who attended Edinburgh's High School in the mid-eighteenth century, read Latin up to Virgil and Horace, Sallust, and parts of Cicero before being admitted to a more senior class that also read Livy. The first morning class was from seven through nine, followed by an hour's interval for breakfast, then another two hours of class. After a two-hour interval for the midday meal, students returned for the last two of the daily stint of six hours of class. Annually in August they had not only to take examinations but also to declaim passages from the Roman poets. Greek was not taught at this time at that school, but it was introduced in 1772.

In Scotland, as in England, is another class of school at the same level that has produced many famous men: the liberally endowed schools of the Merchant Companies. George Watson's, in Edinburgh, is one of the best-known examples of these, standing high in general repute. It was founded in 1741. Older, and with a magnificent seventeenth-century building, is George Heriot's School, begun in 1628 but not completed till 1659, when instruction first began. Such schools were originally intended for children of parents belonging to the merchant class who either had fallen on hard times or had died, leaving their offspring orphaned, and for descendants of such families. Nowadays, like their counterparts in England, they rank high in public esteem. Girls' schools of this class also flourish. Perhaps the best known is the Mary Erskine School for Girls, named till 1944 the Edinburgh Ladies' College, although more generally called simply "Queen Street" from its location. Originally founded toward the end of the seventeenth century as the Merchant Maiden Hospital, with special assistance from Mrs. Mary Erskine, it was intended for the daughters of merchants.

Scotland has yet another principal class of school: boarding schools on the English model, called "public" schools in England, although in American terms they are just the opposite. These charge higher fees than others and have much social prestige. Some scholarships are available, but generally they are for the well-to-do. Since they are not indigenous to Scotland in any traditional sense, they are generally regarded as alternatives rather than as an integral part of the Scottish educational system. To say this is merely to recognize that they are imports from England, geared toward admission to Oxford and Cambridge, although many of their products go to the Scottish universities or elsewhere. Glenalmond, Fettes, Merchiston, and Loretto are among the best known for boys, and St. Leonard's for girls. All were founded in the nineteenth century and in many ways are similar to America's "preparatory" schools such as St. Paul's and Phillips Exeter. They are designed to provide a "rounded" education, usually with a strong emphasis on sports and definite training in the qualities one looks for in a leader, whether in public service, business, the army, or elsewhere. Since the system is still so closely geared to Oxford and Cambridge, they must also provide first-class academic preparation, at least for those students who aim at proceeding to a British university. The quality varies, naturally, from school to school and also from time to time, as in all systems; but they must keep up standards, for maintenance of their status depends, among other things, on their success in competitive examinations for scholarships to the two older English universities. Nevertheless, admirable and necessary as may be their function, they are alien to the mainstream of the Scottish educational system and tradition. They are as English as the cliffs of Dover, yet they play a most important part in modern Scottish life.

The difference between Scottish and English educational tradition is expressed in subtle and not-so-subtle ways. One of the latter is the form of corporal punishment. All British schools have a remarkable faith in the rod. In England this takes the form of a long, flexible cane applied to the trouser-clad buttocks of the victim, who first bends over to receive the appointed number of "cuts." In Scotland the leather strap (called in older times the "tawse"), applied to the extended palm of the hand, is no less venerable. Although the use of the tawse may be less copious today than in the past, when it was prominent in the daily scenery of the classroom, it is still sacrosanct. With rare exceptions one can still tell, from whether the tawse or the cane is used, whether the school is of the pure Scottish tradition or (like Loretto and Fettes) an English import.

The tawse, terror from kindergarten onward of every Scottish boy and known also to some girls, is a leather strap varying in size but typically twenty inches long, about an inch and a half wide, and sometimes as much as a quarter inch thick, very flexible and often cut at the receiving end into two or more thongs. The skill of the executioner (every qualified teacher) varies also; even the least expert can produce a remarkable degree of pain with one stroke, while what an athletic and experienced male teacher can accomplish with three or four strokes is truly fearsome. The pain has a peculiarly memorable quality, which makes the instrument a very effective deterrent. It has the great advantage, from a public relations standpoint, of leaving almost no noticeable mark or visible bruise at the end of the day, although for an hour or so the recipient's hand feels as if the inhabitants of a whole beehive simultaneously attacked it. The intensity of the pain, which does not reach its climax till one has returned to one's seat, is considerably enhanced by an unwritten rule not to show any sign of suffering—none, at any rate, that would call attention to oneself. The punishment is administered for a vast variety of offenses. Typical is the crime of whispering in class. It was also, at least in my time, administered energetically as a matter of routine for failure to respond with the correct Latin equivalent for an English noun or verb. Almost unlimited faith is placed in its curative and educational properties. Its presence in a drawer or closet naturally produces almost perfect classroom behavior. By tradition, tawse are manufactured in Lochgelly, a town in Fife. The industry still exists.

Perhaps nowhere except in the Law and the Kirk is the difference between Scotland and England so marked as in their universities. Till the nineteenth century England's two ancient universities, Oxford and Cambridge, were her great academic glory; they still dominate British university life, all changes and developments notwithstanding. They are peerless. Scotland's ancient universities came later and were different in conception, character, tradition, and outlook. Like the schools just described, they were developed along Spartan lines, with a minimum of frills and a maximum of basics. More democratic in spirit and in organization, they welcomed the impoverished on the same terms as the well-to-do. This spirit is commemorated in the institution of "Meal Monday," still observed as a sort of midterm holiday. This was originally provided to enable poor students from outlying crofts and the like to return home to replenish their sacks of oatmeal, the staple diet with which they nourished themselves during term, having no money for more substantial meals, let alone for luxuries. It is a noble memorial to the industry and rugged resolve of the Scottish student of bygone days, who was prepared to make all kinds of sacrifice in cooperation with his parents so that he might attain the degree that would qualify him to serve as minister, lawyer, doctor, or schoolmaster. It was a long struggle: seven years to be a minister, three or four to be a teacher, and for the other professions somewhere in between. When looking at the old stones of these venerable institutions, save a word of praise in your heart for those students of olden time and their families who so greatly valued the opportunity to learn.

Of Scotland's four ancient universities, St. Andrews is the oldest and Edinburgh the youngest. St. Andrews, Glasgow, and Aberdeen were all papal foundations. Edinburgh came later, in 1583, after the Scottish Reformation. It has no motto, for at that time mottoes were out of fashion, being accounted "popish." St. Andrews was founded in 1412, Glasgow in 1451, and Aberdeen in 1494. The four modern Scottish universities are all twentieth-century foundations: Strathclyde, Heriot-Watt, Dundee, and Stirling, all founded in the Sixties.

St. Andrews is certainly to this day the most picturesque (more will be said in a later chapter of its unique atmosphere). Apart from monstrous recent accretions, it preserves much of its ancient physical charm. It is by far the smallest of the old universities and has had a more checkered history. In the eighteenth century it declined alarmingly in almost every way. In 1730 the number of students at all three of its colleges had dropped to about 150 and the quality of the faculty was by all accounts grievously low. A visitor relates that nobody seemed to bother even keeping out the rain or fixing the windows. Thereafter the fall in numbers became catastrophic. Not until the middle of the next century were reforms made to save the university from total collapse. Gradually the tide turned and Victorian St. Andrews became an attractive and esteemed place once again.

Originally St. Andrews had been founded as an attempt to provide university education for those who wanted one but, because of the difficulty, if not the impossibility, of going to Oxford or Paris at the stage of the Hundred Years' War that was then raging, were glad of the chance to study in their native land. The basis of the curriculum was Aristotle: the regent (professor) would dictate from a set book (printing had not yet been invented in Europe) and then discuss what the students had noted. Examinations took the form of defending theses: a modest ancestor of the modern American Ph.D. All teaching was in Latin, which the students were expected to speak even in their leisure hours. In all this St. Andrews was simply following, as best it could, the practice of the great universities of the day. It developed some interesting traditions. Freshmen were called *bejauni* (from the French *bec jaune,* yellow-beak, presumably signifying a little bird's mouth open to seek food), and to this day they are called "bejants." The use by undergraduates of the red stuff gown, which has fallen into disuse at the other Scottish universities, is still a picturesque feature of St. Andrews. This gown is very heavy and serves as an overcoat, a much-needed appurtenance.

The University of Cambridge instituted special examinations for women in 1869, and successful candidates received a certificate. Edinburgh followed with a somewhat similar arrangement in 1874. At St. Andrews in 1877, however, women could aim at a special degree designed for them, carrying the formidable title of Lady Literate in Arts. The recipient was entitled to wear a special silver pendant suspended by a green ribbon around her neck, like an order of chivalry. From a strictly technical standpoint it was probably not a degree, but for all practical purposes it was as near to a regular degree in Arts as any woman in those days could hope to obtain. Candidates had to follow a course similar to the one taken by the men but were allowed a wider range of subjects, on the theory (widespread at the time) that subjects such as Greek and Latin might be too arduous for their frailer constitutions. That not all took advantage of such relaxing provisions I can personally attest, for two of my aunts were in the first or nearly the first vintage of these daring ladies, and both were alarmingly learned. One of them married and even after many years would occasionally rouse her husband in the morning with a little Greek ode she had composed. The other never married. As a little boy I well remember how her extraordinary eloquence at the dinner table would be interlarded with learned allusions and French and German asides. Nor was she entirely a "blue stocking," as such ladies were then dubbed. I recall that when I was eight she gave me a long talk on how to secure feminine admiration, an ambition which at that age I had not yet developed. This title of Lady Literate in Arts (L.L.A.) continued to be available till 1931, although of course by that time it had fallen into disuse, since regular degrees had long been open to women on exactly the same terms as men.

Glasgow and Aberdeen had similar pre-Reformation beginnings. The old buildings of Glasgow University were demolished and the present handsome Victorian structure erected in 1870. It stands on a spectacular site, an eminence in Glasgow's West End. Aberdeen, which calls its freshmen "bajans" and, if they are girls, "bajanellas," boasts two colleges: King's in Old Aberdeen and Marischal in New Aberdeen. King's is a charming old building; its chapel, completed in 1505, contains probably the finest extant example of Scottish ecclesiastical woodwork from the Middle Ages. The crown tower is very distinctive. The long, lofty hall in which the University library is housed dates only from 1885 but is probably the grandest physical setting of any university library in Scotland, except for those who prefer Edinburgh's more modern twentieth-century structure. The charm of King's is enhanced by the delightful old streets, such as the Chanonry, that surround it, much of which it owns.

The other college, Marischal, is an old foundation, dating from 1593. The present buildings are early Victorian and, in their way, among the most remarkable in Europe. When built in 1844 they constituted the largest granite building in the world with the exception of the Escurial in Spain. The fretted pinnacles in glistening white granite shimmer in the sunshine after a shower of rain like the turrets of a fairy-tale castle. Only one stone of the old Marischal building remains. On it is an eloquent inscription of the individualism of the Scot of bygone times: "They haif said. Quhat say they? Lat thame say." In English: "They have said. What do they say? Let them say." It is believed to have been placed there by the Earl Marischal, who wished to express his disdain for critics who had scorned him for his spoliation of one of the abbeys in the county. It has been found as a Greek inscription on rings in Pompeii.

The University of Edinburgh had its origin in a decision of the Edinburgh Town Council in 1581 to build a college for the town. On April 14, 1582, James VI of Scotland (as he then still was) granted it a royal charter. The following year money was provided and the college was built. So many students flocked to it from outside the city that they had to sleep "twa in ilk bed" (two in a bed) and to pay forty shillings a year for their room. The Town Council also appointed the "maisters." The threat of plague caused the entire student body to flee the college in May 1585. That was but a temporary setback, and the college prospered so well that after the King became James I of Great Britain (1603) and returned on a visit to Scotland in 1617, he invited the Principal and the Regents (professors) to conduct a public disputation in his presence at Stirling. The result pleased him so well that he expressed his desire that the college thenceforth be known as King James's College. But the name "Tounis College" (Town's College) had by then gained such a hold that it continued to be so called. In early documents, however, it was designated sometimes *Academia* (Academy), sometimes College, and sometimes University. The terms seem to have been used synonymously till the Universities (Scotland) Act, 1858, after which it came to be known always officially and almost always also in popular usage as "the University."

The present building of what is now called Old College dates from 1789, when the foundation stone was laid, although the building was not completed till 1834 and the dome not till fifty years later. The architect was Robert Adam, who also designed the Register House at the east end of Princes Street. Erected at a time when the university had already attained some international repute and Edinburgh was in the midst of a feverish building spree, it was a remarkable accomplishment. It is a handsome building of noble aspect, although a little heavy for most tastes. Yet it suits the northern skies and accords with the massiveness and fortresslike quality of so much of the Scottish capital's late eighteenth- and nineteenth-century building. The present Medical School and other buildings scattered over the city are of later date; the new buildings on two sides of what was once the handsome eighteenth-century George Square emerged only in recent decades.

The Medical School, dating from the seventeenth century, has brought international fame to the University of Edinburgh. The site of many important discoveries and of famous professors of medicine and surgery, it has attracted students from all over the world, as have the Royal College of Surgeons and other great medical institutions associated with the university, although not part of it. At times the number of students in the Medical School has almost matched the number in all other parts of the university. Edinburgh's medical graduates have served all over the world, both as practitioners and as teachers.

These four ancient Scottish universities have never developed the expensive tutorial system of Oxford and Cambridge, in which undergraduates are assigned to a tutor whom they see regularly and who guides them to such lectures as he deems suited to the particular needs of each. The Scottish system has been in this respect more like that of many American and continental European universities, with large lecture classes sometimes supplemented by additional instruction in smaller groups. As in the French universities, and very different from the situation in England and America, the standard at all four universities has been traditionally the same. Of course one university might be particularly reputed for its work and its teaching in a certain field because of the distinction of a particular professor or department; but the examination for admission has for long been uniform. So far as practicable, uniformity has been sought in the conduct of the degree examinations, so that a degree from one institution has been always accepted as of much the same value as that taken from another within the system.

One of the most unusual features is the office of Lord Rector. This person is *not,* as one might well suppose, the administrative head of the institution, who is the Principal and Vice-Chancellor. The Lord Rector is elected by the students every three years and holds office for that period. Till some recent exceptions, he was almost always a person of extraordinary distinction, such as Churchill, who had already received all the formal "Establishment" honors a man could wish but who was pleased to be honored, for a change, by the rising generation. Theoretically he is supposed to look after the students' interests. In practice his duty has generally been to deliver one major address.

The week of election campaigning among the students is very roughly the counterpart of hell week at American universities and colleges: an opportunity to give vent to the boisterousness of youth. Bags of flour and sacks of soot are scattered copiously over the opposing party as a matter routine. Sometimes, of course, things get out of hand, as when students once burst into the dressing room of a neighboring vaudeville theater and kidnapped one of the actresses without giving her sufficient time to dress. Both the lady and the university authorities took a dim view of that one. Generally speaking, however, wide latitude is allowed students that week. A venerable student tradition also prescribes that at the Lord Rector's speech every possible effort must be made to give him as much annoyance as possible. Boos, catcalls, pigeons, toilet paper rolls, even hens and turkeys—all are among the equipment used to ruffle the speaker, who, if he is wise, does his best under such trying circumstances to smile, appear unflappable, and endeavor to impart at least a few of his intended words of wisdom, which have sometimes been much wiser than the occasion demands. The performance is usually picked up by some newspaper or other and transmitted abroad whence it tends to return under captions of horror and disgust at what is taken to be the day-to-day behavior of Scottish students. Alas, with changing times these sacred saturnalia may be in some danger of losing their pristine fervor.

Formal lectures are conducted much as they would be at any other university, except for one exhilarating custom borrowed from Germany long ago. When an announcement is made that pleases the audience, such as that classes are to be canceled for a day or that a class test will be postponed, applause takes the form of vigorous stamping of feet, which in winter are somewhat heavily shod, causing an impressive din. If, on the contrary, the news seems unwelcome or the professor affirms something that is generally disagreeable or produces a hostile reaction among the students, the approved method of comment is a no less vigorous shuffling of feet. This foot talk, which has the advantage of anonymity as well as clarity and loudness, is singularly eloquent in its way.

Each university has its own special traditions, such as the annual Kate Kennedy pageant at St. Andrews, which dates from the 1840s but was suppressed after a particularly riotous one in 1881, which happened to coincide with a nautical disaster and a heavy snowstorm. The pageant was restored in 1926. Another tradition at St. Andrews is the students' walk after Sunday morning church service to the pierhead. This is said to commemorate John Honey, who in 1800 rescued seven men single-handed from a wreck in the East Bay.

The other four Scottish universities are playing an important role in Scottish education. Though lacking the long history of the four more ancient foundations, their histories, in at least three cases, antedate their attainment of university status. Dundee had been a college affiliated with the University of St. Andrews from the late nineteenth century, housed in a building in Perth Road. When Dundee attained academic independence as a university it drew from St. Andrews, besides much else, its clinical medical school. Heriot-Watt University and Strathclyde University, in Edinburgh and Glasgow respectively, were both developed out of former "technical colleges" that had for long served important functions. Stirling University enjoys a unique setting in the heart of Scotland amid some of the most historic monuments and sites in the nation. The development of these newer foundations, as of their English counterparts, is essential for the future of higher education in Britain.

6

Religion

The cheerfu' supper done, wi' serious face
  They round the ingle form a circle wide;
The sire turns o'er, wi' patriarchal grace,
  The big ha'-bible, ance his faither's pride:
  His bonnet reverently is laid aside,
His lyart haffets wearin' thin and bare;
  Those strains that once did sweet in Zion glide
He wales a portion with judicious care,
And "Let us worship God!" he says with solemn air.
                    —Robert Burns, *The Cotter's Saturday Night*

To understand the religion of a people is to understand the people. For their religion expresses what they take to be the ultimate values of human life, underlying their whole attitude to everything else. As everyone knows, only a minority in any society are in fact noticeably devout in or dedicated to their religion. Nevertheless, the national religion does affect the national outlook and attitude. If there be some truth in the old witticism that a French atheist is a Catholic atheist while a Greek atheist is an Orthodox atheist and a Swedish atheist a Lutheran one, then it is most certainly true that every Scottish atheist must be a Presbyterian atheist.

Since the Reformation led by John Knox in 1560, the vast

majority of Scots have been very definitely, not to say self-consciously, professed partisans of the Reformed Church. Knox did
not establish that Church in Scotland in a specifically Presbyterian form. That may be said to have been accomplished by Andrew Melville toward the end of the century. Yet Presbyterianism
came to be so basic to the religious life of Scotland that the
popular image of Edinburgh as the Presbyterian Jerusalem is not
far off the mark, although like all popular images it needs some
modification. Scotland and Presbyterianism seem to have been
made for each other. Even to this day, when the old dogmatisms
have softened and sometimes all but evaporated, a thoroughbred
Scot who for one reason or another is not a Presbyterian tends
to feel somewhat ill at ease about it, even a little embarrassed,
almost as might an American who preferred cricket to baseball
or an Englishman who liked Cervantes better than Shakespeare.
For Presbyterianism is the civil religion of Scotland more than it
is expressive of any body of religious doctrine to which the Scottish people give their interior assent.

Considerable sections of the Scottish people today give their
religious allegiance elsewhere. Scotland is not as monolithic in its
Presbyterianism as is, say, Denmark in its nominal adherence to
Lutheranism. Scottish Episcopalianism, although numerically
small (about 3 percent of the population), has a respected place in
Scottish history. The number of Roman Catholics with deep ancestral roots in Scotland is not large, but Irish immigration in the
last century and a half has introduced to Scotland a substantial
Roman Catholic population. Baptist, Methodist, and other religious bodies that play a large part in the religious life of England
and the United States do exist in Scotland. Their role is very
limited, however, and they never seem at home, being popularly
regarded as English imports, which indeed they generally are. No
doubt you can find Quakers in most Scottish cities, as you might if
you looked hard enough in Italy or Greece. When all that is said,
however, the Kirk (as the Presbyterian Establishment is called)
dominates the scene. It is Scotland's religious face.

Historically, Scotland has known other options. The notable corruption of the pre-Reformation Church in Scotland is generally taken to be the major factor accounting for the extreme hostility of the Scots to anything suggesting even a hint of what earlier generations than ours called "popery," although even without that special circumstance Scotland and Rome would never have liked or understood each other. By and large the majority of Scots seem by temperament singularly incapable of understanding the spirit of Catholicism and are ill disposed toward what they find in it. Indeed, the average Scot may feel more affinity toward the Jews, in whose history the Scots sometimes see, consciously or otherwise, a counterpart of their own. Hence the traditional popularity of Old Testament themes in the Scottish pulpit and also the extraordinary development of a reverence for the Sabbath which, often described in nineteenth-century literature, could match even the most strict Jewish orthodoxy. Many Scots of a few generations back would not have mailed a letter on a Saturday if they had reason to believe it might be picked up on Sunday, thus encouraging what they took to be sinful sabbath-breaking. Shoes had to be shined the night before and meals prepared so far as possible ahead of time, so that no work would take place on the day set apart for religious observance. People walked miles to church rather than take any kind of vehicle. That the Presbyterian Sunday became too often a sort of caricature of the Jewish Sabbath is expressed in the story of a minister who, being tired of the lamentations of one of his parishioners about the increasing desecration of the Sabbath, pointed out to her that, while he agreed in principle, she must remember that Jesus himself broke the Sabbath by eating grain in the fields as he and his disciples passed through them.

"Aye," she snapped back, "and I never thought any the better of him for it."

The Episcopalian Way was a clear alternative for the Scots during the seventeenth century. That century was, in Scotland as elsewhere, a period of fierce religious strife. In the end, however, Presbyterianism emerged as unquestionably the victor both politically and in popular sentiment.

Far more important for understanding the religious face of Scotland today is the fact that the most bitter theological and ecclesiastical disputes Scotland has ever known took place within the Presbyterian framework. The story of the schisms is too complex to be usefully described here in detail. It is a sad, though sometimes edifying tale. One example may be helpful by way of illustration.

During the eighteenth century Scotland, like England and France, was affected by a general distaste for religious dogma, a distaste that had naturally supervened on the vitriolic quarrels of the preceding century. The new spirit was expressed in sermons designed to be ethically edifying or uplifting and socially constructive, rather than biblical or theological. The preacher, in accordance with tradition, would take a verse from the Bible, but soon would be talking about matters of the day rather than about anything that could be called specifically religious, such as grace and sin, repentance and salvation, faith and the life hereafter. While some liked that style of preaching, others saw it as traducing and eventually killing the Church. The former came to be known as the Moderates, the latter as the Evangelicals.

The cleavage between the two parties came to a head on May 18, 1843, when the General Assembly of the Established Kirk of Scotland met in St. Andrew's Church, George Street, Edinburgh. When the retiring Moderator (Dr. Welsh) had taken his seat, he announced that, on certain specified grounds, he felt it was impossible for him in conscience to continue in that assembly. Having read and laid on the table a lengthy document, signed by most of those who concurred with him, in which they claimed to be the true and rightful General Assembly of the Kirk, he left the building, being instantly followed by practically the whole of his party, who walked three abreast downhill to the district of Canonmills, where a large hall had been prepared to accommodate them. Dr.

Thomas Chalmers, one of the most eminent churchmen of his day as well as one of the greatest preachers in Scotland, was elected Moderator.

So was the Free Church of Scotland born. The organizers of the Disruption, as this particular movement came to be called, saw very well what courage was needed for the success of the movement. Out of the 1,203 ministers that had composed the Kirk at that time, 451 had walked out, thereby giving up their livelihood, their tenure, and their position, which in those days was socially very prestigious indeed.

The response of the laity was overwhelming. They rallied around their pastors and for the first time in the history of Scotland gave magnanimously to support the "Free" Church. Till then people had been accustomed to expect the Church to be supported through the legally enforceable "teinds" (tithes), with an occasional benefaction from a local bigwig for anything special that was needed from time to time. Now they had to build from the ground up. And build they did: a rival church building in almost every parish in the land, often on a grander scale than the existing one. Moreover, in time the Free Church went far to outdo the "Auld Kirk" in scholarship and in the quality of preaching. Rivalry, by no means unhealthy, was fostered. Differences developed. The Auld Kirk ministers were generally reputed to be not averse to a "wee nip" of whisky. In some tragic cases the "nip" became a copious draught, for alcoholism was a widespread phenomenon in Victorian Scotland. The Free Kirk, by contrast, made a fetish of abstemiousness. Many a story was told to symbolize the gulf between the two main branches of Presbyterianism. For example: a local church elder went to the railway station to meet a visiting minister who was expected for the weekend. Seeing a man in clerical garb, he inquired if he were the Free Church minister who was expected.

"No," replied the clerical stranger mischievously, "it's indigestion that makes me look like this."

In Scotland's tempestuous religious history, the divisions and cleavages have been far more varied, of course, than can be illustrated in any such story. But throughout all the acrimony, everybody seemed to take for granted that the Presbyterian form of church government was above question. It is relatively simple. Each parish is ruled by the Minister and his Kirk Session, consisting of elders who traditionally assist the Minister in supervising the moral and spiritual welfare of the flock and attending to cases of want and to families in any kind of trouble. This body constitutes the lowest court of the Kirk. Immediately above it is the Presbytery, which corresponds roughly in function to the bishop and his committee in Episcopal and similarly governed churches. The Presbytery consists of all the ministers together with an approximately equal number of lay representatives. Finally, the General Assembly of the whole Church is the highest ecclesiastical court, although it can function as a court of first instance as well as an appellate court. Such is the theory. In practice government is by a pyramid of committees.

Although the average American Presbyterian might find many churches in Scotland that would not strike him as notably different from his own, he is often surprised to find considerable pageantry associated with the General Assembly of the Kirk, which meets every year in Edinburgh in the month of May. The Kirk is established by law, but some claim it is the least established of Christian Churches, since the Sovereign or his or her representative comes only as an official guest of honor, not in any way as an officer of the assembly, and the emphasis is on the independence of the Church from the State. Nevertheless, the procession of the dignitaries on their way to the opening of Assembly (a procession that may include contingents of cavalry), the *levées* at the Palace of Holyroodhouse, and other festal accompaniments of the week-long gathering, and the general air of commercial expectancy among the shopkeepers of Edinburgh, might all give the impression of a Church very much established indeed, even in these days when religion plays far less part in the life of the people than was the case a few generations ago.

The fact is that the General Assembly was for long a very important national conclave, having become, after the Union of Parliaments in 1707, the nearest thing to a parliament that the Scots had at their disposal for expressing in public debate whatever was on their mind. It received a shot in the arm in 1929 through the union of the Auld Kirk and the Free Kirk, thereby increasing its numbers and unifying it as the undoubted arena of Scottish debate on all matters believed to be of national importance and having any kind of spiritual or moral dimension that might justify inclusion on the agenda.

The Episcopal Church in Scotland, which tends to encourage all the pageantry of Catholic ritual and practice, is distinctly apart from the mainstream of Scottish religious life. Its position is very special. Small yet influential, desperately poor although in full communion with the Established Church of England, it claims to be the "true" Church in Scotland. Extremely self-conscious of its historical position in the life of the nation yet also of its atypical character *in the eyes of many Scots,* it tends to look (and, despite valiant efforts, to feel) the oddity that it is. In our pluralistic American scene its peculiarity would go more readily unnoticed among so many other "mainline" churches. In Scotland many people cannot get away from thinking of it as a quaint little bonbon on the side of a plate of ecclesiastical porridge.

The position of the Roman Catholic Church in Scotland is very different. In some of the remoter islands its adherents still dominate the local scene, the presence of a Presbyterian parish church notwithstanding; but these are exceptionally remote places that the Reformation never touched or did so ineffectively. In the cities the Roman Catholic churches have an almost universally Irish flavor and are traditionally administered much as are their counterparts in Ireland, although this, like all else in Scottish religious life, is changing.

Not so very long ago the Presbyterian children used to sing in a mocking staccato rhythm after the Episcopalians in the street:

> Piskie, piskie, A-men.
> Doon on yer knees and up again.

To this the Episcopalian children retaliated with a mischievous pun on the first question in the Presbyterian Catechism ("What is the chief end of man?"):

> Presbie, presbie, dinna bend,
> Sit ye doon on man's chief end.

Such altercations as might have occurred in those days between Presbyterians and Roman Catholics were likely to have been much less printable and not always free of bloodshed. Today, altercations of any kind between one religious group and another in the street would be unlikely.

An American visitor to Scotland who happens to be active in his home church will usually find, on visiting one of the corresponding denomination in Scotland, some unexpected differences. If he is a Presbyterian, for instance, he will find, in many places, the use of the common cup in communion. Some of the parish churches will be very ancient, having been built long before anybody had ever heard of Presbyterianism. No matter what his denomination, he is likely to be surprised by the meager provision in many churches for social activities and other gatherings for purposes other than worship. In the rural areas there is often no provision at all, and even in the larger city churches it is often minimal compared with what an American would expect in churches of that importance or size. Attendance is also astonishingly thin. Some churches in Edinburgh and Glasgow were, within living memory, so well attended that people queued up on the street for the evening service. It is hard to imagine that or anything at all like it in any church in Scotland today. Till the turn of the present century the Kirk was still an extremely powerful institution, with not only well-attended churches but also a clergy who commanded widespread popular respect and who were in some cases theological or biblical scholars with a prominent place in the intellectual world of their day, participating in international scholarly inquiry. Their discourses were long and tedious by modern standards, but they were often (if not usually) substantial in terms of the knowledge of the day. The clergy were often devoted pastors who knew every family in the parish almost as intimately as their own. All that has sadly changed; the Kirk today is at best only a faint shadow of her former self.

The causes of the decline of the Kirk are complex, and theories about them are controversial. It is easy to point to changes in lifestyles and to the fact that people today have so many other interests and preoccupations that did not exist a hundred years ago. In bygone times the Kirk exercised numerous functions now taken over by the State and other agencies. For many it was also a chief source of adult education and entertainment, the only respectable relief from the drudgery and boredom of daily toil. All that is true enough, but it cannot be the whole story. The Kirk was always, in theory at any rate, a democratic institution. Unlike the Church of England and other Churches abroad, it received genuine public support and remarkable popularity. Many preachers and leaders of Church opinion fostered that support in many ways; some openly resorted to making their sermons a sort of entertaining spectacle. Yet everywhere in Scotland was evidence of a solid ministry and a creditable attitude on the part of clergy and people alike toward recognizing what great service the Kirk could perform for both social and individual life, and how awesome was the ethical responsibility of those entrusted with the moral and spiritual training of the young. The Kirk, for all its well-known faults, was indubitably a great moral force in the formation of the Scottish character. By repute, Scotland was one of the most theologically literate nations in Europe. People walking home from the Sunday sermon discussed the theological points in it with an enthusiasm that may have been amateurish but was by no means ill informed.

That all that should have virtually evaporated in less than a hundred years needs more explanation than is commonly off-ered. The isolation of Scotland from the great currents of Euro-pean culture may be part of the explanation, yet it is unlikely that it is of any great importance in itself. Perhaps there was some-thing profoundly wrong with the Kirk from long ago, even before Milton pointed out that "New Presbyter is but Old Priest writ large."

The best religious awareness in Scottish tradition was devel-oped and nurtured in the family rather than in church. Family worship in a peasant's cottage, as described by Burns in *The Cotter's Saturday Night,* for instance, was often a profoundly mov-ing devotion. Such was the Scottish love of family that through family relationships the Scot of bygone times learned to know the mysteries of the unseen world and came to look on God as his friend. Burns, having described such a scene, goes on to reflect:

> Compared with this, how poor Religion's pride,
>   In all the pomp of method and of art,
> When men display to congregations wide
>   Devotion's every grace, except the heart!
>   The power, incensed, the pageant will desert,
> The pompous strain, the sacerdotal stole;
>   But haply, in some cottage far apart,
> May hear, well pleased, the language of the soul;
> And in His Book of Life the inmates poor enrol.

The real religion of Scotland was nourished at its deepest level in the home. The family would quietly gather around the fireside and, amid a reverent hush broken by the occasional flickering of a lamp or candle, the father would open the well-used Bible that had come down with immense pride from generation to genera-tion as the Ark of their family's Covenant. In a voice strangely different from any ever used at work or at play, he would read a chapter, perhaps sometimes sharing the reading with one of the older boys. The others in the family would listen, not always understanding all the words but somehow seeing beyond them to the eternal verities of loyalty and love they were learning through family life and to which the Bible language always seemed to point. Then, as the father gave the signal by the solemn closing of the Book, all would fall to their knees, faces half-buried in their hands, while the father put into words, as best he knew how, a prayer for the fulfillment of the inmost longings of each: for happiness at home, strength and contentment at work, that Jean's lad she hoped to marry might be worthy of her gifts and grace, that Jock's broken arm would mend well, and above all that they all might thank God every day of their lives for the joy of life and the knowledge of salvation, with perhaps a word about all meeting again one day in the "land of the leal," the life beyond, where loyal hearts beat even more clearly and families love even more dearly.

That was the source of much of Scotland's greatness and of what made her, as Burns said, "revered abroad." Although this has largely disappeared from Scottish life, you can occasionally find echoes of it. When you do, pause; look and listen hard, for you will be in the presence of something more Scottish than Loch Ness or Edinburgh Castle, the bagpipes or the kilt. You will be looking right into loving eyes and listening to the very beat of Scotland's heart. It was in such simple family worship that our Scottish ancestors, even in early childhood, met God face to face. When that happens to people, they never afterward attach much importance to the paraphernalia of institutional religion even when, for one reason or another, they happen to like or approve of it. When George MacDonald, a profoundly spiritual Scottish Victorian, wrote, "There is nothing more deadening to the divine than a habitual dealing in the outsides of holy things," he was expressing in that single observation the quintessence of all authentically Scottish religion. Only men and women who knew the inside of religion could have gone forth like Abraham, as did our Scottish forefathers, "not knowing whither they went," yet confident of standing honestly on their own feet wherever they might go.

7

Edinburgh

The moon passed out of Holyrood, white-lipped to open sky;
The night wind whimpered on the Crags to see the ghosts go by;
And stately, silent, sorrowful, the lonely lion lay,
Gaunt shoulder to the Capital and blind eyes to the Bay.
    —Will H. Ogilvie, "Holyrood"

EDINBURGH'S physical grandeur is incomparable. Such is her natural situation that even from earliest times she must have been striking. Much has happened since Robert Burns called her "Edina, Scotia's darling seat." If she so impressed the Ayrshire poet in his time, before the ambitious architectural schemes that later transformed her, what can we say of her now? Perhaps the churlish might grumble that the darling has become a spoiled darling. The fact remains that her skyline is theatrical, her scenic wonders overwhelming, her vistas breathtaking, her antiquarian riches inexhaustible. One moment she is romantically as Gothic as the castles of the Rhine, the next as coldly classical as the Panthéon. Now you are looking at the chaste dignity of Charlotte Square, gracious cold stone encompassing, in spring, a sea of dancing daffodils (they really do dance in the Edinburgh wind) and the magnificent Georgian squares and crescents beyond. Soon you are looking over the Dean Bridge to the picturesque little village in the great forested chasm below, where runs the Water of Leith on its way to the sea.

Within the bounds of the city, whose area is large for her population, are endless surprises for even the superficial observer: not only nobly distinctive streets (Ann Street is a good example) and quaint closes and wynds but whole villages of striking character such as Cramond, and more sights than even history-conscious residents can hope to see in a lifetime.

Many industrious sightseers miss unobtrusive glories such as the sixteenth-century Magdalen Chapel, which lies deep down in the Cowgate underworld that runs like a ridge in one of Dante's infernal circles below the Holy City of Jerusalem. It contains the only important medieval glass in Scotland. After the Reformation it was used for centuries by the hammermen's guild. It has become in modern times the chapel of the new Heriot-Watt University. Innumerable treasures of this kind lie hid from vulgar gaze, some inevitably unmentioned even in standard guidebooks and likely to be missed among the plethora of more visible grandeurs.

The allusion to Jerusalem is more than casual. The Scots have something in common with the Jews. They see their history as paralleling that of ancient Israel. That is why the Old Testament is traditionally so popular in Presbyterian pulpits: the people have always readily identified with the heroes of the Bible and their struggles. They believe in their hearts that for good or ill they were at their noblest when they were true to their own ways and that they have deteriorated in proportion to their "whoring after other gods," notably English ones. As Jerusalem, not least since the dispersion of the Jews, has been a magnet for world Judaism, so Edinburgh has been the Holy City of the Scottish Diaspora. Edinburgh is not only the Presbyterian Jerusalem; even to the most un-Presbyterian of her sons and daughters she remains the Holy City, as does the other Jerusalem to even the most unbelieving Jew. Jesus has not been alone among Jews in lamenting the propensity of Jerusalem for killing her own prophets, and here the analogy with Edinburgh is positively macabre. Edin-

Charlotte Square, Edinburgh: north side. Designed by Robert Adam, 1792.

burgh is kindly disposed to almost everybody other than her own sons and daughters. She is also in an odd way the most English city in Scotland, while remaining as Scottish as Glencoe and the Braes of Balquhidder.

Most visitors head straight for the Castle, which is standard procedure and enjoys the blessing of the Scottish Tourist Office. It is indeed a must for everyone; but if you like to get first impressions without so much noise and bustle of buses, rent a car and drive up Arthur's Seat which, though its summit is only 823 feet, looks immense and, to the imaginative eye, was constructed by Nature in the form of a couched lion to provide a more pacific alternative to the rampant one that has the imprimatur of the Lord Lyon, Scotland's supreme heraldic authority, for the royal arms of Scotland. At one end of the park containing it is the Palace of Holyrood House, which, except for Glamis, is probably more full of ghosts (including that of Mary, Queen of Scots) than any other castle in Scotland. That is not an easy win. It serves as the Edinburgh residence of the Sovereign. At another end is Duddingston Kirk, with its "loupin' stane" (a step to help riders into the saddle) and the "jougs" or "jugges" hanging from the outside wall: an iron collar in which the Kirk, in the heyday of her power, put persons whose conduct the Minister and Kirk Session officially disapproved. The recognized qualifying norm was fornication. Culprits had to ask the forgiveness of each worshiper entering the church.

From the road that encircles that hill you can have Edinburgh at your feet, spreading herself comfortably below you in a sort of ladylike yawn, her innumerable spires aglow (if you are lucky) under the placid northern sun. You will see nearby, slightly to the west, the green dome of the Royal Observatory on Blackford Hill. The lovely crown tower of St. Giles' and other landmarks will come into view, with the Castle and the old medieval town on the ridge that runs from the Castle Esplanade down through the "Royal Mile" to Holyrood. The steep rocky ridge known as Salisbury Crags will stare gauntly at you. And sometimes to the north,

in the far distance, you will be suddenly surprised by the Firth of
Forth leading out to the North Sea.

I recommend this little drive for first impressions partly because it is astonishing that Edinburgh lets you look at her from
above. One would suppose that, like the former Emperors of
Japan, she would insist on being always above her subjects. That
would be to underestimate Edinburgh's pride. She feels so secure
that she allows people to look at her from any point. Look at her
from below; she will stare haughtily down on you. Look at her
from above; she will peer serenely up at you. Wherever you look
she will rebuke you silently for your dabbling with vulgar ideas
of progress and your preoccupation with unrealities such as time.
If you wish to avoid being written off as an ignorant foreigner
wholly bereft of taste, take warning now: *never praise Edinburgh in
the presence of any of its inhabitants.* They take it for blasphemy. It
is like paying a compliment to God. Belittle her if you will, for
they will extend to you the charity and compassion they feel they
can well afford and will generously use to assist in your education. But if you praise her they will account you hopeless. One
does not, in good Edinburgh society, attach any predicates to her
at all. Edinburgh is not this or that. Edinburgh IS.

Edinburgh pride is beyond anything that an outsider can con-
ceive. If you are only a casual visitor you may not notice at first
that everybody is treating you as though you were a protectorate
applying to the Queen for temporary status as a Crown colony.
After all, the citizens themselves hardly notice they are doing it,
so why should you? If you did happen to notice, you might think
them arrogant; but you would be much mistaken. There is not a
hint of arrogance in their mind, only generosity and compassion.
Such is Edinburgh's pride. It is much buttressed by the fantastic
advantages she has inherited, partly by geographical location,
partly by historical accident, partly by the industry of forebears,
and most of all by the fact that almost nobody in living memory
has felt the impetus or even the need to contribute anything
significant to her splendor. Contributions to her glory would

generally have seemed unnecessary, not to say in bad taste. She simply stares away from the cheap modern excrescences imposed upon her in these current times, ignoring them as beneath her notice.

Attempts were made in the nineteenth century by some adventuresome spirits to have her nicknamed the Athens of the North, and old books sometimes have that phrase. These attempts eventually failed, however, largely because the pride of the inhabitants is such that most of them could not understand why Athens should not be dubbed the Edinburgh of the South.

A New Englander's map of the United States is supposed to show New England twice the size of all the rest. Although Edinburgh has been noted as a center of professional cartography, its citizens in practice take it to be the pivot of all galaxies in the universe, which constitute, in effect, The Wilderness contradistinguished from The Where. If a camel, whose flaming pride is proverbial, were to be seen walking along Princes Street, it would look positively cowed. From Edinburgh's pride flows much of her conservatism, which sometimes borders on ideophobia. Her smugness would embarrass the Sphinx of Cheops, were he not safely exiled in Cairo. Before I could take a degree at the University of Edinburgh, I had to promise in writing to persevere in loyalty to the institution till my dying breath *(ad extremum vitae halitum);* but that is because academic people are trained to skepticism and so recognize the formal possibility that one might conceivably be disloyal. Only Edinburgh intellectuals, however, go so far. Most of the inhabitants would not be able to entertain so theoretical a possibility.

Take all the Bostonian stories you have ever heard—you will still know nothing of Edinburgh's self-assurance. Bostonians, when asked "Are you going somewhere today?" are supposed to reply with politely concealed astonishment, "Why no, I am here." Such a response, however, implies a degree, however minuscule, of reflection, a horrid doubt, however dim, that identification with deity might not be taken for granted. Edinburgh, by contrast, basks forever in the sunshine of unwavering and unquestioning awareness of divinity.

Once you establish a circle of friends there, you may leave and return after twenty years only to be greeted with a discreetly averted glance and a query such as: "Haven't you been away for a little while?" Edinburgh people are polite; they would not wish to allude publicly to your having been in exile. Those who have traveled approve of cities such as Venice, San Francisco, and Quebec that have a distinctive character marking them worthy of notice; but they are only, after all, mere eminences in the hierarchy of cities. They stand to Edinburgh only as the archangels Michael and Gabriel stand to God.

Edinburgh takes precedence over the other principal cities of Scotland not because of population or size, but because she is The Capital. That is not an unusual state of affairs. New York and other American cities are larger than Washington, D.C., and in many of the individual states the capital is notably insignificant in population. There is nothing intrinsically remarkable in the fact that Edinburgh is the capital while Glasgow, forty miles to the west, has more than twice its population, infinitely more up-and-go, and was in Britain's imperial heyday the second largest city in the whole Empire on which the sun never set.

What is remarkable is the number of times you are likely to be told in Edinburgh that she is The Capital. I can't remember anyone's having mentioned to me that Washington is the capital of the United States. It is the sort of thing one learns in school books and then seldom ever again hears mentioned. I can hardly imagine a Londoner's reminding an American visitor that London is the capital of England. It would be like telling you the Atlantic is the Atlantic Ocean. A Frenchman who kept on reminding you that Paris is the capital of France would be in danger of civil arrest by his compatriots and removal to a place where his sanity could be investigated. Yet this is exactly what the citizens of Edinburgh do with impunity. How come?

The name of the city is pronounced *Ehdinbruh,* unless you want to sound either a peasant or a foreigner. The city, however, is more ancient than its name. The name means "Edwin's borough," from Edwin, King of Northumbria, who in 617 held the fortress that is now the Castle. The older Celtic name for the city before Edwin's day was Duneiden or Dunedin; hence the adoption of the latter name by the New Zealand city that was settled by Scots in 1848.

Edinburgh's origin in the mists of prehistory lay, no doubt, in the natural advantage its rock seemed to provide for establishing an impregnable fortress, to which could be added many other natural assets such as the presence of an estuary (called in Scotland a "firth") leading to the nearby North Sea. It became the capital city of Scotland in the middle of the fifteenth century, by little more than historical accident. James II of Scotland liked it and held his parliament there. Edinburgh's claim to be the capital, although unsupported by any specific charter or other official document, has been unquestioned for centuries. Perth, smallest of Scotland's larger cities, very beautifully situated and the gateway to the Highlands, seems to have been an earlier capital of Scotland, although some obscurities attend that claim.

Some think cities have sexual characteristics: London is certainly a masculine city, Paris a feminine one. If so, then Edinburgh is indubitably an old lady: stately, irrational, unrepentantly obstinate. Her slums and, till comparatively recent years, the absence of a proper modern sewage system are among the circumstances that have caused uncouth critics to suggest that she is not only an old lady but an old lady who flaunts her flamboyant figure and, having powdered her nose, has forgotten to press her skirt. Yet when all that is said about her Olympian smugness, Edinburgh as a city has few notable shortcomings.

The climate is certainly not a shortcoming. Of course, if you live in California or Bermuda you may think Edinburgh fit only for polar bears; but as climates go Edinburgh's is not bad at all. The annual rainfall of about twenty-five inches is slightly less than that of Honolulu, about half that of Washington, D.C., and about a yard and a half less than that of Vancouver, B.C. The impression of raininess that some visitors get arises from the fact that, as elsewhere in the British Isles, you may get a shower or two any day without notice, then call it a rainy day in the sense that rain has occurred. That is like calling a day sunny because the sun briefly emerged from the clouds once in the late afternoon. The east wind can be fierce and the "haar" (a wraithlike white hoarfrost) that often accompanies it in winter can make the cold penetrate to the marrow of your bones; but the actual temperature does not often fall more than a few degrees below freezing and is more usually above that point. Subzero Fahrenheit temperatures are completely unknown anywhere in Scotland; even in winter the *average* temperature in no month falls below freezing; and in two thousand square miles or more the annual rainfall is less than thirty inches. Only in the mountainous regions is rainfall heavy, sometimes exceeding eighty inches a year.

Edinburgh's inhabitants have a reputation for being spiritually cold all year round. The charge is probably derived from a jibe made by James Bone in a book on Edinburgh that attained a good deal of fame just after World War I, *The Perambulator in Edinburgh*, in which he called her "east-windy, west-endy." According to legend, the notoriously hospitable inhabitants of Glasgow, when you call on them casually, greet you with, "Oh, you're just in time for tea," no matter what hour it is. Those of Edinburgh, although the grandfather clock be melodiously striking four in the hall, say, "Oh, you'll have had tea." Perhaps there is some truth in such aspersions, but remember that Edinburgh and Glasgow indulge endlessly in such gibes, somewhat as would, say, Los Angeles and San Francisco, or Boston and New York, were they also situated in a country that had the time for them, having retired from the regular pace of life on our planet.

The parallel between Edinburgh and San Francisco is indeed even more apposite than might at first appear. Not only are both cities steep; long after other Scottish cities had acquired very efficient tramway systems, Edinburgh clung to her old cable cars till 1920 or thereabout. Toward the end they were slow and unreliable. The cable would frequently break, holding up traffic, while huddles of Glaswegians grinned nearby, remarking that it did not matter, since nobody in Edinburgh is ever in a hurry anyhow. Till about the same time Leith, Edinburgh's seaport town, was still a separate burgh. There was a pub with a brass arrow down the middle of the counter to mark the dividing line between the two municipalities, which happened to have different licensing hours: closing time was ten o'clock for one and nine for the other. When the bell rang at one end and the solemn proclamation, "Time, Gentlemen, please," was uttered, the customers gravely moved over to the other end of the counter for the remaining hour. Edinburgh people are a happy breed so long as they are allowed to remain unhurried. Try to accelerate them and they turn vicious.

Edinburgh, like Rome, claims to have been built on seven hills. The ridge from the Castle to Holyrood constitutes the medieval town, which the upper classes left toward the end of the eighteenth century for the "New Town" that had been made possible by building bridges over what was then the "North Loch." This "New Town" consists of truly magnificent squares, streets, and circles, in the classical manner, to the north of the incomparable Princes Street, once the most elegant street in Scotland and one of the most beautiful in the world, but now snobbishly lamented by the cognoscenti as having been destroyed by the tourist trade and the general deterioration of taste. Indeed it may be wise to carry in your pocket a picture of the street as it was around 1830, with its genteelly low buildings on the north side and the then as now magnificent gardens on the other. Whisk it out when expedient to prove to the inhabitants that you know how much more patrician it once looked and that the presence today of Woolworth's and other affronts to its dignity is to be understood as the concession that an aristocratic nature grants to inferiors. It would be well, however, not to carry a picture showing what it looked like fifty years earlier still, for Edinburgh does not like you to think that anything has actually had to be built.

Princes Street still remains an astonishing street. It is about three quarters of a mile long, running from east to west with the great sloping Gardens and the Castle Rock on the south. Little but the Scott Monument and the dignified if somewhat heavily classical Royal Academy of Art interrupt the sweep of sward and flower beds leading up to the lovely old seventeenth-century houses above, the spectacularly situated neo-Gothic twin towers of New College, and the domed Bank of Scotland. On a summer evening during the International Festival in August, when the Castle and other buildings are floodlit, the grandeur will catch the breath of even the most sullen.

According to recent legend, the International Festival is the result of a slip of the tongue Edinburgh made in the aftermath of World War II. As legend has it that the British Empire was established in a fit of absentmindedness, so it is said that Edinburgh, which habitually says "no" to every idea ever proposed, momentarily forgot herself and said "yes," a word she had never before uttered. Having said it, Edinburgh could not go back, and so the habit of the annual International Festival took root. Although never a financial success, it does bring to the city millions of people who otherwise might not be so readily attracted. Edinburgh is just a little out of the way for many who visit Britain and find so much to see and do in London and the south of England that they often get no farther north than Stratford-on-Avon. The Festival has brought to Edinburgh many of just the people who ought to see her glories. Typically, of course, as little as possible has been done to provide really good modern auditoriums, and inadequate provision has been made to house people. Thus at the height of the season improvident visitors may have to lodge in a neighboring county. It is very unfashionable in Edinburgh to recognize that the influx of visitors can convey any benefit. Well-bred inhabitants greet each other in September with chirps of relief: "Isn't it lovely they've all gone? I suppose it's nice for *them* but wasn't it awful?" Edinburgh has an infinite capacity for assuming that everything it does is by way of conferring an unappreciated benefit on noncitizens.

The Calton Hill, to the east of Princes Street, is the site of the City Observatory (older than the Royal Observatory) and several monuments, including one to Dugald Stewart, a Scottish philosopher. The sculptor William Playfair copied it from the monument of Lysicrates in Athens, the oldest extant building of the Corinthian order, aptly epitomizing the ideals of the "New Athenians." Looking down you can see the severely classical buildings of what was once the Royal High School, now a museum, and nearby the monument to Robert Burns. In the Calton cemetery, a little way off, are found many Scottish notabilities, and also a fine statue to the memory of Abraham Lincoln. Few people—and not even all guidebooks—will tell you about the latter, because Scots are easily alarmed by their dread of being charged with "buttering" Americans, a fear that does seem singularly unwarranted. Yet such is Edinburgh's addiction to paradox that in Princes Street Gardens, not far from the famed floral clock, is an enchanting war memorial, a tribute to the friendship between Scotland and the United States. Nor is it only Americans that Edinburgh is afraid to praise. Some years ago, when a resolution came before the City Council to honor the widely popular Prince Charles, their future King, with the freedom of the city, they turned down the proposal.

Behind the uncompleted building on the Calton Hill lies an interesting story. About the turn of the century an effort was made to raise a million pounds (an enormous sum in those days) to substantiate further Edinburgh's claim to the title "Athens of the North" by building a replica of the Parthenon atop the Calton Hill. The project was halted for lack of funds when only a little of the projected Acropolis of the North had been completed. Nevertheless, the uncompleted building gives a noble aspect to that hill, enhancing the already magnificent skyline. It is popularly called "Pride and Poverty" or "Edinburgh's Disgrace." Edinburgh is, of course, entirely undismayed by gibes of this kind, most of which she has invented herself. No blemish on the brow of the Buddha could diminish the serenity of his countenance. Time was when John Ruskin and others raged at the rather self-consciously neo-Gothic Scott Monument; but Edinburgh knows how Parisians once fumed at the Eiffel Tower, which has now become the very picture-postcard symbol of Tout Paris. Surely, then, Edinburgh can afford to have her divinity represented by even such crude anthropomorphisms as the Scott Monument. This magnificent hauteur is part of what endears Edinburgh to her sons, among whom I am glad to be numbered. You can tell our authenticity by the love-hate relationship we have for our exasperating but irresistibly endearing mother.

I suspect that there is some connection between Edinburgh's flaming pride and her stupendous powers of procrastination. The word *mañana* does not exist in this beautiful city, because it would suggest indecent haste. Should you want to do some shopping, you might consider zooming over to Glasgow or Dundee, for you will sometimes get better prices and you will almost always get better service. In other cities people see nothing demeaning about conducting business. True, Edinburgh's individualism can result in the discovery, in some remote nook, of an oasis of moderate efficiency, for in Edinburgh you need never be surprised by anything you find. But since it may take months to make such a discovery, you may prefer the procedure I suggest.

Among the treasures of my *mañana* file is a letter from an Edinburgh firm dated November 14, 1957, which opens in a crisp, matter-of-fact, seemingly businesslike way: "With reference to yours of April 12." The letter ends: "We shall be glad to hear from you at your earliest convenience." In the interval, not only had I been to Edinburgh for the summer; the matter about which I had written in April became within a month as topical as the Battle of Waterloo.

Edinburgh always has a built-in excuse for all her manifestations of the principle of inaction. In early summer nothing can be done because of the impending two-week Trades' Holidays. During the period itself, obviously nothing can be done. Then, for a longer time than you could imagine possible, the alleged backlog of work it has brought in its train provides excuse for inaction. That takes care of the summer and most of the late spring and early fall. For the rest of the year they must rely on bad weather to avoid exposure to the danger of undignified involvement in the conduct of business. Business is offensive to the soul of a city that thinks itself, like Aristotle's god, a magnet that draws all things to itself in such a way as to make shocking even the idea of the conduct of business. On Olympus the gods did not so demean themselves, so why should they today on the slopes of Arthur's Seat and the Braid Hills?

Behind incomparable Princes Street and its lovely gardens lies George Street to the north, a spacious thoroughfare that uniquely preserves its dignity. It is so wide that cars are nowadays parked in the middle of it, although as elsewhere in old cities you will never find a slot unless in a previous life you were a tiger with a special aptitude for stalking prey. Between the two great thoroughfares nestles Rose Street, a narrow rift lined with comfortable pubs and here and there an interestingly sinister-looking nook. If you continue north beyond George Street you will encounter the severe grandeurs of Queen Street and Heriot Row (more gardens). Then Edinburgh suddenly descends toward the quaint old quarter of Canonmills, where in the Middle Ages the Canons of Holyrood ground their meal, and toward Stockbridge, where Raeburn spent most of his life. You can wander past the unexpected stately façade of Edinburgh Academy and on to sip the healthful waters of St. Bernard's Well.

This north side of the city has a curiously different feel from the south side: it is danker and even more dour. If you go on to 21 Comely Bank you may see where the ill-matched Thomas Carlyle and Jane Welsh set up house before they moved to Craigenputtock. Or you might go instead to Robert Louis Stevenson's house in Heriot Row. Farther north lie the extensive Royal Botanical Gardens. From the Gardens you can see a panoramic view of much of the city. Within the Gardens is housed in an old mansion a contemporary art collection with outdoor sculpture. Stevenson's *birthplace* is a thatched house in picturesque Swanston, a village on the fringes of Edinburgh.

We must not say more here of the dwellings of Edinburgh's famous sons and daughters, for there are markers at almost every turn, and in the guidebooks are at least partial inventories of those whom the Fates favored with an Edinburgh home or birthplace. Many are unmarked, however, and indeed the inhabitants tend to wonder why any should be singled out, since the presumption is that everyone with any Edinburgh connection is bound to become famous unless he or she lives there long enough to learn how to avoid such an undignified destiny. Perhaps, however, one should at least mention the house of David Hume, Scotland's greatest contributor to modern philosophy, where Adam Smith and other old friends often dined with him as they had done in their younger days in sleazy old taverns in the medieval town. It is the corner house on the southwest side of St. Andrew Square and St. David Street. Legend insists that the latter street was named after him and that the sign writer was so accustomed to writing "St." before given names that from sheer habit he used it for this one, ignorant of how singularly inapposite the designation would be for one accounted by some an enemy of God and the Kirk.

In the Castle one is surfeited with history: Argyll's Tower, Mons Meg (a fifteenth-century cannon), and on the ledge below the little graveyard for soldiers' pets that moistens many a dog-lover's eye, the spectacular Scottish War Memorial, the Old Palace, the Banqueting Hall, and the Naval and Military Museum. Also there is the Scottish Regalia (including the crown refashioned by James V in 1540, the great Sword of State given by Pope Julius II to James IV, and the scepter he received in 1494 from Pope Alexander VI, the Borgia father of Lucrezia and Cesare), and the tiny chapel (sixteen and one-half by ten and one-half feet) of St. Margaret, oldest building of all on the Castle Rock, almost the only surviving example of Norman work in Edinburgh, and indeed one of Scotland's most endearing shrines. Near one o'-clock get ready (with earplugs) to stand by a great gun that is fired daily to announce the hour. In my boyhood days elderly gentle-men who prided themselves on the accuracy of their gold watches would slip them out of their waistcoat pockets, gravely explaining that it was their custom to check on the gun's accuracy as a timekeeper: an eloquent symbol of the unimpeachable self-confi-dence that rubs off on the citizenry of this maddeningly lovable city.

From the Castle one crosses the drawbridge on to the Espla-nade (scene of the Tattoo, a highlight of the annual Festival), and down the Royal Mile, whose treasures not even a special volume could fully catalog. The Outlook Tower, brainchild of Sir Patrick Geddes, a pioneer in civics, with its camera obscura and fascinat-ing exhibits, should not be missed. All must visit St. Giles', of course, the focus of much of Scotland's story. The anecdote about Jenny Geddes, the applewife who is said to have thrown a stool at the Dean during service, is shopworn. There is so much more to tell about St. Giles', whose checkered history epitomizes that of all Scotland. In the Royal Mile are innumerable vendors of antique silver and jewelry, and also more fabulously historic courts and "closes" (narrow passageways) than anyone could fully explore in a lifetime's residence in the city. The closes in-clude Lady Stair's, Milne's, Monteith's, Advocates', Bakehouse, Brodie's, Whitehorse, Warriston's, Weir's, Old Fishmarket, and Carrubber's. The courts include Chessel's, Boswell's (where Dr. Johnson's biographer lived), Riddle's, Wardrope's, Mylne's, James's, and Patterson's.

These eerie haunts have been the scene of many strange hap-penings and fearsome crimes, such as those perpetrated around 1828 by Burke and Hare. They set up a profitable partnership that entailed murdering vagrants and others whose disappear-ance would be unlikely to be noticed and callously selling their bodies to the surgeons, who in the days of the rising fame of Edinburgh's Medical School in the early nineteenth century needed bodies and were not inclined to ask any searching questions about them. Burke gave a new verb to the English language, duly listed in Webster: "to burke."

Double-life characters also seem to have flourished in this multifaceted northern city. Deacon Brodie, who provided Stevenson with the idea for *Dr. Jekyll and Mr. Hyde,* was but the most famous. The Deacon, an exceptionally well-respected citizen and pillar of the Kirk, noticed that his storekeeper neighbors, when they went out for their little midday visit to the tavern, left their doors open and the keys hanging in place. He would deftly take the impression of the keys on a piece of clay or putty in his hand, which he later gave to a blacksmith in his pay. The numerous nocturnal burglaries that ensued long puzzled Edinburgh, till a special inquiry followed a particularly shocking burglary. Suspicion at last fell on the Deacon. He had disappeared but was traced to Amsterdam; he was arrested and hanged at the Tolbooth prison, also in the Royal Mile.

Behind St. Giles' stands Parliament House, with its handsome Great Hall (1632–1639) in its original condition. Two great libraries are housed here. And around the corner, in adjacent George IV Bridge, is the National Library of Scotland, which has the right, like the British Museum and a few other British libraries, to receive a copy of all books published in Britain. The handsome City Chambers and the partly ancient so-called Mercat Cross are nearby. A little farther is historic Old St. Paul's, a holy shrine for Episcopalians. It is entered from an unpromising close on the north side of the High Street. John Knox's House and the Huntly House Museum are much visited. Farther still are the seventeenth-century Canongate Kirk and its historic kirkyard and contemporary manse, and finally Holyrood House.

No matter how many "musts" you note, there are scores of others that will cause people to look at you with that mixture of contempt and pity that only an Edinburgh eye can convey as its owner sadly intones: "Surely it cannot be that you missed . . . ?"

Probably no city of Edinburgh's size in the English-speaking world has so many statues. Not counting innumerable merely architectural ornaments and the like but only genuine, independent, three-dimensional figures, I know of at least forty. And I know, too, that there must be more. Most were erected in Queen Victoria's reign, and many are of considerable merit. Not very many citizens know where Queen Victoria herself sits, although she is not inconspicuous atop the Royal Scottish Academy in Princes Street. Fewer still could tell you where to find George III, who is tucked away in a recess under the dome of Register House, one of the finest buildings of its period in Scotland and the place to go if you wish to conduct a search into your family history when you have some clues to start you out. The oldest statue is that of Charles II in Parliament Square.

The scale of some of the statues is impressive: the largest of the blocks used for George IV weighs fifteen tons. Although science, literature, and the Kirk are represented, the tendency to honor political and military figures drew the remark of one observer that Edinburgh gives highest honor to "the memory of men chiefly remarkable for banging other men on the heads." That seems hardly warranted.

Still, Edinburgh does appear to favor the dead over the living. The number of cemeteries, sepulchers, and mausoleums could disappoint not even the most ardent epitaph buff. Preeminent is Greyfriars, where Allan Ramsay, George Heriot the elder, and John Kay are among those commemorated in this kirkyard in which the National Covenant was signed in 1638. The names of some of the signatories were written in blood. In the Canongate kirkyard are the graves of Adam Smith, Horatio Bonar, Dugald Stewart, as well as the simple stone raised by Burns to his friend and fellow poet, Robert Fergusson.

Among those laid to rest in Greyfriars is a poor and lonely man whose faithful Skye terrier, Bobbie, was so grieved by the death of his master that he accompanied the body to its grave and refused to move from the spot. The year was 1858. The caretaker, in obedience to regulations, had to turn him out, but next day there he was again. Day after day he lay cold and hungry on his master's grave. At last the caretaker could bear it no longer and undertook to shelter the dog in his cottage at night; a neighbor who owned a tavern promised to give Bobbie his dinner every day. By an exception made to the rules of the kirkyard, Bobbie was permitted to stay by his old master's grave during daytime, which he did faithfully for many years, except that at the sound of Edinburgh's one o'clock gun he took off briefly to the tavern for dinner. When eventually he died, he was buried beside his master in the kirkyard. Outside in George IV Bridge is a statue and fountain erected in much deserved tribute to Bobbie's fidelity. This memorial, through ignorance or barbarism or both, was vandalized some years ago but was duly restored. American lovers of Bobbie also erected a red granite stone near the grave itself, which is on the left side of the walk leading north. The story of dear Bobbie is true and infinitely touching. Nobody who knows and appreciates animal friendship will visit Edinburgh without paying homage to Bobbie's memory, and many quietly shed a loving tear into that little fountain.

Perhaps the most handsome sepulchral monument in Scotland is not in a cemetery but stands on a piece of ground in Craigentinny now surrounded by pedestrian twentieth-century bungalows. William Henry Miller, who raised the elegant monument, was born in Paris in 1789 and died in Edinburgh in 1848, both dates for other reasons memorable in European history. A lifelong bachelor born to much wealth, he was a member of Parliament, cultured, the collector and owner of one of the most sumptuous private libraries ever amassed in Britain. He was an eccentric. His request that he be buried in a grave at least forty feet deep, together with his general eccentricity and the fact that the funeral was postponed till six weeks after his death, gave rise to various rumors such as that he was a hermaphrodite.

Rather than attempt even a judicious selection of Edinburgh

"musts," I prefer to convey enough of the atmosphere to show that no such selection is really possible. Of course one should see George Heriot's School and Donaldson's Hospital, two educational establishments of very different periods. Each is remarkable for its beauty, although the alumni of a dozen other great Edinburgh schools must be expected to frown on such a singling out, even for the purpose of merely architectural praise.

Toward Corstorphine is the attractive hillside site of the Royal Zoological Society's park, with its very handsome clubhouse for members. It was one of the first zoos in the world to have lions, bears, and other such animals in open-air, natural surrounding; its penguin collection is famed. The old parish church of Corstorphine, founded in 1376, with its octagonal spire and partly flagstone roof, is one of the most charming medieval churches in Scotland.

I have hardly even mentioned Leith, one of the chief seaports of Scotland and included within Edinburgh since 1920. It has a very distinctive character. Nor have I said anything of the delightful country walks on hills and water's edge that one may take within the city's bounds. A summer evening stroll that is refreshing to those who do not mind the wind and want to see yet another aspect of the city is along the Granton breakwater. And nearby Newhaven still preserves something of the character associated with the traditional striped dresses of the fishwives.

After morning service at an Edinburgh church, a visit on Sunday evening to the square at the foot of the Mound is instructive, for there is Scotland's nearest equivalent to London's Hyde Park. The vitality, vehemence, and venomous humor of the orators, as well as the wide spectrum of their topics and the revolutions they propose, can be as invigorating as the evening air. And if you want to hear our mother tongue as it is spoken in the Edinburgh streets, this is your safest bet. It is often the most entertaining show in town, and it is free. Moreover, if you care to mention that you are American, you will likely have leveled at you forthwith a battery of prejudice so rich, so varied, and of such nuclear power and vast sweep that if it were weaponry and ammunition it would totally demolish the United States from California to Maine, except that the warheads would have been mostly turned the wrong way around.

The endlessly fascinating places of interest that lie only a half hour's drive from Edinburgh are likewise too numerous to catalog, but three of them must be noted. Just across the Forth Road Bridge lie Dunfermline and Culross (pronounced *kyoorus*), both of immense interest. Culross is a small town that has been almost totally preserved and restored by the National Trust for Scotland. Despite its much smaller scale, it is a sort of Scottish Williamsburg. Culross Palace is a delightful example of a late sixteenth-century Scottish mansion. Along with the partially restored Cistercian abbey, whose early fourteenth-century choir is now the parish church, and the little houses and paved causeways, one gets a good idea of what an old Scots town was like. Dunfermline, of great historical interest, should not be missed. More Scottish kings and queens (including Margaret and Malcome Canmore) have been buried in Dunfermline Abbey than anywhere else, Iona excepted. Dunfermline is also the birthplace of Andrew Carnegie (1835–1919), who was especially generous to his native city.

South of Edinburgh lies Rosslyn (or Roslin) Chapel, begun in 1446. It is the burial place of the Sinclairs who, till 1650, were buried in full armor. The flying buttresses and possibly Portuguese influence in the profusely decorated sculptures give the chapel a very distinctive flavor. At the east end of the south aisle is the lovely "Prentice Pillar," of special interest to members of Masonic orders. According to tradition, a master mason was charged with ornamenting the pillar but felt he needed to learn more before undertaking the task, so he went abroad to improve his knowledge. On his return he found that his apprentice had gracefully completed the work. Such was the master's jealous rage that, instead of felicitating the young man, he clobbered him to death. No doubt the story has been ornamented as richly as the pillar; but it does symbolize the curious streak of negativity that is the dark side of Edinburgh and stands in strange and gloomy contrast to the glories of her fantastic heritage.

No one who knows Edinburgh can deny she is exasperating. Yet no matter how much you fume, if you fume long enough and with competence to match you will end up falling in love with her. It is not difficult to fall in love with a woman who can be now Florence Nightingale, now Zsa Zsa Gabor; easily Katharine Hepburn, yet as readily a rosy-cheeked dairymaid; Glenda Jackson acting out Elizabeth I and at the same time Emily Dickinson; Lily Langtry one minute and Queen Victoria forever. Indeed, you *must* fall in love with her unless, of course, you happen to be yourself a woman, in which case the versatility of this other woman must at least arouse your envy. She is the only woman in the world who has never once thought of competing with any other.

8

Other Cities

*It is this colossal opportunity to escape
from life that brings yokels to the cities,
not mere lust for money.*

—H. L. Mencken, *Prejudices*

APART from Edinburgh, Scotland's major cities are Glasgow, Dundee, Aberdeen, Perth, and Inverness. Glasgow, we have already noted, is by far the largest and commercially most important city in Scotland. In the nineteenth century, Dundee and Aberdeen became close rivals, being roughly the same size after Dundee's mid-Victorian jute trade had brought it quick prosperity. But Aberdeen, always historically important and geographically unique, has acquired a new role in the last decade as the center of North Sea Oil developments, bringing the sound of American and English voices to one of the most northerly cities on our planet. Perth and Inverness are both smaller. Perth must be included if only for its beauty and historical significance, while Inverness must be counted in since it is generally recognized as the unofficial capital of the Highlands.

Glasgow, despite her antiquity, has comparatively few historical places. She does have some very important ones, but nothing of the historic riches of Edinburgh. In Glasgow they are fewer and unobtrusive. Yet Glasgow, although it does not attract the average tourist, has much to commend it, including a Victorian grandeur that comparable English cities lack. It is worth visiting for its extraordinarily distinctive flavor and above all for the special outlook on life and attitude of its inhabitants that are found nowhere else. The uniqueness of the Glasgow character and atmosphere is no doubt due to the peculiar blend of history, commerce, and peoples that gives the city an indefinable but pervasive aroma, like that of a special blend of the tobacco that was once such an important part of its trade. The warmth of the people is world-famed, and their hospitality is beyond compare. Since the Industrial Revolution it has been a center of heavy industry. The river Clyde, on which it is built, long was synonymous with the highest standards of shipbuilding in the world. Before planes were invented and the automobile was still a novelty, Glasgow was Queen of the Seas. "Clyde-built" spelled quality.

That is one of the factors that have given Glaswegians the self-assurance that cannot but strike the most casual visitor. Glasgow breathes an atmosphere of success such as not even her darkest tenement poverty, though fearsome in its magnitude and devastating in its squalor, can erase. Even during the worst depressions, the air of success lingered on through soot and fog. During the potato famine in Ireland, Glasgow absorbed an enormous influx of Irish, and today probably at least one Glaswegian in five has some Irish ancestry. Poles, Lithuanians, and Italians all came in large numbers also, at first alarming the native population and then being gradually assimilated. It was almost the American scene in miniature.

Much of the alarm was on religious grounds. Glasgow was strongly Protestant. Many stories are told of cultural clashes. A favorite concerns the boy who was arraigned before the magistrate for having been caught writing "To hell with the Pope" on a door. The kindly magistrate admonished him, telling him that it was very offensive to many people, and asked why he had written the words. The boy replied: "Please Sir, there wasn't enough room to write 'To hell wi' the Moderator of the General Assembly of the Church of Scotland.' "

Glasgow likes to do things "big." Her business magnates built themselves showy mansions, each grander than the one last erected, as though anything less would have diminished their repute. Wealth still enjoys showing itself off. Yet any arrogance that might elsewhere rear its ugly head in such circumstances is quickly neutralized by Glasgow's extraordinarily jovial spirit. If you simply cannot believe the friendliness to be genuine, you are wrong. It is. It is also found among all classes. The reason is simple: Glaswegians love people. They also like parks, of which the city has seventy. Most beautiful among them in Rouken Glen, which lies to the south of the city.

Snooty critics of Glasgow were saying a hundred years ago that her warm-hearted love of success and her tendencies to megalomania had infected even her ancient university. That historic seat of learning, founded in 1451, a long generation before Columbus sailed, was housed for centuries in comparatively modest surroundings in the High Street. In 1870 it moved to a spectacular pile of buildings erected on Gilmorehill, the finest site in Glasgow. Those who sneered (Ruskin was among them) may have been hiding a little natural envy, for the work by George Gilbert Scott was indubitably one of the greatest masterpieces of that famous Victorian architect. In recent times critics have taken a second look at all the neo-Gothic that their elders so religiously affected to despise. Nothing could help more to incite reevaluation of it than Glasgow University. Fortresslike when inspected nearby, when viewed from a distance in the valley below it has an air of almost dreamy lightness. That in itself is a remarkable achievement for any architect, for lightness does not come easily in Glasgow, which is perhaps the most solidly and heavily Victorian city in the world, a vast monument to the Victorian era. If you admire Victoriana you will love Glasgow; if you don't you probably won't. I was trained from my youth to perform the then fashionable sneering chuckle at every reference in words or images to anything suspect of being Victorian, and I have thoroughly repudiated that indoctrination. If you want to see what the Quattrocento could do, go to Florence or Rome; if you would see the Victorian ideals in full splendor in handsome stone, go to Glasgow.

Nor should we suppose all the architecture of this period to be merely various varieties of mock-Gothic. One of the best-known architects of the mid-Victorian period was Alexander Thomson, whose passion for imitating Greek models earned him the nickname "Greek Thomson," by which the Glasgow cognoscenti still call him. A good example of "Greek Thomson's" work is the St. Vincent Street church. The local stone, hard and gray, lends itself remarkably well to this treatment, although it could not shine laughingly in the sun like the Pentelic marble of Greece—but then there is not all that much sun in Glasgow. The rainfall of Glasgow is almost twice that of Edinburgh; such is the difference between a North Sea coast and a quasi-Atlantic one even though only forty miles or so lie between the cities.

There are churches and other buildings that reflect Egyptian influence. Although Glasgow lacks the vast, well-planned Regency and late Georgian squares and crescents of Edinburgh's "New" Town, she does have some examples of these styles. The trouble with Glasgow is that all such points of interest tend to be smothered and occluded by the exuberant bustle of life that is so characteristic of this ebullient metropolis. Even the kindliest Glaswegian cannot help thinking of Edinburgh as a sort of cross between a cemetery and a mausoleum. Glasgow is, after all, the New York of Scotland. You can hate it, you can love it, you can mock it, you can call it a depressed area, you can declare it bankrupt, you can rage at its vulgarity, you can envy its opulence, you can howl with holy indignation at its poverty and filth. But when you turn around the next minute it is grinning with inexhaustible vitality and the will to pursue the next buck.

The fervor of local patriotism is intense. One of the poorest sections of Glasgow is Bridgetown, known to its inhabitants as "Brigton." During World War II an American GI wandered into a pub in that area and, getting himself well plastered, began shouting, "To hell with Britain." A wee "keelie," as the riffraff of Glasgow are called, took up the challenge with a bellicose gesture and a loud-mouthed demand for repetition.

"Whit's that ye said?" he growled, beginning to remove his jacket in anticipation of a fight.

"I said 'To hell with Britain'," grunted the American GI defiantly.

"Oh," retorted the Glaswegian in a conciliatory tone as he replaced his jacket. "That's all right. I thocht for a meenit ye said 'To hell wi' Brigton.' "

So strong is the self-confidence of Glaswegians about their city's place in the world that they feel they can afford such local patriotism within its bounds. It is a self-confidence that relies little, if at all, on history or ancestral pride, although it does not exclude these. It is a self-confidence born of an inner awareness of merit: "a man's a man for a' that." Not all the bureaucrats in London have been able to destroy it.

To see something of the earlier history of Glasgow, begin at the Cathedral. Glasgow was built around a cathedral, as Edinburgh was built round a castle. It is mostly fifteenth century, although parts go back to the twelfth. The vaulted crypt is the finest of its kind in all Europe. You can also see the well in which St. Mungo, patron of the city, did his baptizing in the sixth century. There is a curiously religious element in the Glasgow air. Perhaps the Scottish Highland element in the racial mix introduced it long before the Irish arrived. At any rate, Covenanting Presbyterian or Roman Catholic, the Glaswegian has a kind of instinct for religion, whether he is for it or against it. Glasgow's official motto, usually contracted to the flamboyant "Let Glasgow flourish," is, in full form: "Let Glasgow flourish by the preaching of the Word." All this is symbolized in this great medieval church. To see it apart from the rather dingy surroundings to its normal approach, go up to the Necropolis (across the Bridge of Sighs). This cemetery built on a hill is where the Glasgow merchants aspired to be buried, each tomb in the style of the country where he traded or in which he made his money. It is a sort of Glasgow Père-la-Chaise. Look out at the Cathedral from that eminence, in the company of a statue of John Knox who will gaze down with you. I hope yours will be the more tolerant gaze. Tolerance, however, is no stranger to Glasgow. When that cemetery was opened in 1832, the first person to be interred was a Jew.

In Cathedral Square stands Glasgow's oldest house: Provand's Lordship, a fifteenth-century structure. Mary, Queen of Scots, is said to have lived there; but then, like George Washington, she seems to have been very mobile. In the same general neighborhood you can also see the Tolbooth Steeple and the Tron Steeple, both early seventeenth century, and also the Gallowgate, formerly the road to the gallows and in more recent times a notorious slum. "Gate" means "gait," that is, "walk" or "road."

In recent years the face of Glasgow has changed much yet remains remarkably the same. High-rise buildings and fly-overs should have ruined the Victorian atmosphere of the city, but they have not. Glasgow can no more be changed by a few innovations than could the Atlantic Ocean with a few oil spills. Glasgow has been changing so much for so long that changes do not change it. She is happily less afraid of them than is her sister Edinburgh to the east. Glaswegians like to recall that wise men always come from the east, and they add: "Aye, and the wiser they are the quicker they come."

Glasgow has five museums and art galleries, among which Kelvingrove and Pollok House are especially worth visiting. No provincial city in Britain has been a more ardent patron of the arts. When the Kelvingrove Galleries were opened in 1902, their cost was half that of the city's municipal buildings. The Glasgow merchants in their heyday had money to buy extensively from continental Europe, and they spent it liberally. They specialized in the French Impressionists. A Glasgow school of Impressionism arose, with Lavery and Hornel among the best-known exemplars. The collection also includes some of the most interesting works of Whistler, Turner, Rembrandt, Salvador Dali, and others, such as Corot's *Souvenir d'Italie* and Rubens's *Boar Hunt.* About the time of the opening of the Kelvingrove Art Galleries, Charles Rennie Mackintosh, a pioneer in modern architectural design, had given Glasgow, in its School of Art, a remarkable example of work far in advance of his time: a landmark in the development of twentieth-century architectural concepts.

Glasgow is the base for several first-rank British orchestras. It also has the Mitchell Library, which, with about four million books, is one of the major municipal reference libraries in Britain and perhaps the largest of its kind in Europe. It contains, among much else, some three or four thousand volumes on Burns, a collection begun within a few years of his death. Students at the University of Glasgow, as well as other citizens, are certainly fortunate to have at their doorstep "The Mitchell," as it has been called by generations of readers.

During the depression in the Thirties, Glasgow acquired some ill repute for its hoodlums, mainly young delinquents who formed gangs and tried to emulate the Chicago gangsters who were at that time making international news. The sartorial vogue among them included extremely pointed shoes and a coiffure of hair brushed straight back and plastered down with Vaseline or the like. They often wore a row of safety-razor blades inserted into the peak of their cap, although an old whisky bottle broken at the bottom or middle occasionally served their purpose. They did succeed in terrorizing many homeowners into silence, to say nothing of some of the magistrates before whom they were sometimes arraigned. Today all this would seem hardly newsworthy, but at the time it gave Glasgow a bad reputation among many people who were already prejudiced against it. The Chicago model these hoodlums revered is noteworthy, for Glasgow has in several ways more the feel of Chicago than of any other American city.

Both Glasgow and Dundee, although essentially commercial and industrial cities, have almost immediate access to some of the finest scenery in Scotland. Glasgow is the gateway to the Western Isles, the beauties of the Clyde, and the celebrated "bonnie, bonnie banks of Loch Lomond." Dundee, too, has treasures all around it: the beautiful and fertile Carse of Gowrie that stretches between Dundee and Perth; the rich farmlands of Angus from whence come the world-famed cattle; lovely Glamis Castle (pronounced *glahmz*), ancestral home of the Earls of Strathmore, the pleasant Sidlaw Hills; Broughty Ferry, once probably the richest suburb in Britain; Carnoustie, with its famous golf course; ancient Arbroath; the lovely eighteenth-century streets of Montrose; and all this with the spectacular estuary, the Firth of Tay, running along Dundee's shores, opening into the wild North Sea.

Dundee lies just far enough up that estuary to provide its important docks with shelter from the ferocious North Sea winds. Like Glasgow and Edinburgh it is ancient, with many remains of the sites of Roman encampments. It was the headquarters of Kenneth MacAlpin when he set out to conquer the Picts and to become, as we have seen in an earlier chapter, the first King of Scots. Like Glasgow, Dundee's prosperity came in the Victorian age. Situated on a sloping stretch of land whose summit is the 572-foot Law Hill, the city had been for centuries a rather mean little medieval town. It had always enjoyed trade with the Low Countries (what are now Holland and Belgium), mainly in wool. It was a weaving town and very much a Lowland town, although geographically on the threshold of the Highlands. By the dawn of the nineteenth century it had become a flax town and was hurt by the Russian flax crop failure in 1835.

A whaling port from the twelfth century, it became one of the great whaling ports in the world—perhaps the greatest of all, Canada's not excepted. When I lived in Dundee as a boy, I heard vivid descriptions of whalers' homecomings that had occurred in the lifetime of my parents when the whaling industry was still going strong: incredible scenes when a whaling boat would arrive back after many months in the Arctic. By the time the local tavernkeepers and ladies of the night had attended to them, there was not a single penny of the wages of the voyage left in many a sailor's pocket. One of the perils was scurvy, and the seamen entertained a superstition that if, en route to Greenland, you stopped off in Iceland and collected a plant which you then cultivated aboard and the leaves of which you ate, you would stay free of scurvy during the entire voyage. Today we know that Vitamin C in any form would have done the job, but the whalers did not know that. Whale blubber was used for many purposes, including street lamps. Talk of gas lighting alarmed the whaling industry's leaders. They need not have worried, for somewhat miraculously a new use for whale oil was coming in the context of the hitherto unimagined prosperity for Dundee.

To understand what the new jute trade meant to Dundee and the world, we must glance at the town's economic history. It is a romantic tale. Dundee had been frequently attacked by the English before the Union of the Crowns in 1603, but the old weaving trade had kept the little town going. In 1651, however, under Oliver Cromwell's General Monk, the town was sacked so savagely that the weaving industry, which had always been Dundee's lifeline, came to a standstill. It could not be revived without local capital that the town did not have. Dundee's economic depression lasted more than a century. The weavers turned to spinning only the lowest quality of Russian flax, leaving the finer linens and woolens to other, better equipped towns. The plantations in the American South provided Dundee with a market for this coarse fabric.

In 1822 a sample of a new material from India came to Dundee. It was called jute. The weavers tried it out but could make nothing of it at first. Then they hit on using whale oil in the batching process, with promising results. Meanwhile, the Russian flax crop failure in 1835 left the weavers short of their customary raw material. They turned more and more to jute. Imports of it from India rose rapidly: four thousand bales in 1836 but more than a quarter of a million bales fourteen years later.

Jute transformed Dundee from a miserably depressed little town to a city of prosperity beyond even the wildest Victorian dreams. In many ways jute was to the nineteenth century what plastics have been to the twentieth. Its cheapness commended it for an endless variety of purposes. It was shipped to every corner of the earth. Where a cotton factory in Manchester might get an order for a few bales of cotton, Dundee would be as likely to get an order for a score, a hundred, or even a thousand bales of jute. The jute lords could not build mills fast enough to fill the orders that came pouring in from all over the globe—and with practically no advertising costs as we understand them today. Jute was used for the covered wagons that went to the American West. American railroad workers often slept with partitions of jute between them, and even received their pay in little jute bags. Jute was the answer to thousands of questions, including many that people had never known to ask. When the trade was in full swing the American Civil War held up cotton supplies to the Manchester mills, so that while Manchester and other English towns languished for lack of raw materials, shiploads of raw jute from India came steadily into the booming docks of Dundee to be quickly unloaded so that the ships could go back for more.

Labor was the most obvious problem. It was solved with the ruthlessness of the age, an age that was unfastidious about ethical niceties such as human rights. Dundonians, who had seen generations of the children of honest parents go to bed hungry with an Arctic wind howling at their ears, had a strong stomach for seizing opportunity. The denizens of preponderantly female workers who poured into the town were somehow squeezed into the squalid little medieval tenements of the old Overgate (now demolished) and other sleazy quarters of the town. Some came from poor Highland crofts, lured by the new trend. A great many were starving Irish lassies who came over by the boatload from their famine-stricken homeland, shawled and barefooted, priest-shriven, desperate for a shilling or two. They received just about that: four to six shillings a week at most, the equivalent then of a dollar to a dollar and a half. A mill girl, if she eventually became a forewoman (which must have often seemed as unlikely as her priest's becoming a cardinal), would earn more. With six or seven women to every man in Dundee, a girl's chance of marriage was sometimes almost as slim as her priest's of becoming pope. A native Dundonian foreman was placed in charge of a group of them. These foremen were a unique class in Dundee. The girls came unskilled, many never having seen the inside of any sort of mill. The foreman was often no less inexperienced in handling personnel as it is understood today. Intoxicated with power, he often developed the mien of a more or less benevolent dictator. I knew by sight one who, even after his retirement, still walked with his chest stuck out like a pigeon, his left hand on his kidneys, palm turned outward, his spine curved so far inward as to make one fear he might break in two. He was not much more than five feet and was obviously fantasizing himself as seven.

The mills could not be called dark or satanic in Blake's sense. Jute is light industry, and Dundee's air, jute notwithstanding, is fresh and clean. Nevertheless, life in the mills must have been the nearest thing to slavery that could exist where slavery had been abolished. The mill girls constituted a definite caste. The shawl was their caste badge. No girl dared appear at work wearing anything but the shawl and skirt of her caste. On Sundays only might she don a blouse and suit, pin a hat on her head, and sally forth to show herself off to the world. A few boys were hired when they left school at twelve and were used as messengers till they were about seventeen, when they were thrown back on the street as completely untrained for anything as when they entered and generally accounted, in those days, too old to be apprenticed to any respectable trade. No doubt many joined the army or went to sea. An adolescence of lunch breaks on the mill steps munch-

ing their sandwiches and "kidding around" with the girls would
have done nothing to develop initiative or responsibility. The
mill girls, by contrast, had a lifetime job. The demand for their
labor was rarely lacking at their price, and among all but a small
minority of work-shy women, work was highly valued at any price.

When I was a very small child, the factory whistle went off
before six o'clock in the morning. Six was the hour when the
gates were closed. A woman who was not inside the gates before
then was locked out for the day and her pay correspondingly
decreased: a severe punishment indeed when you were living on
subsistence wages, with "subsistence" very broadly interpreted.
Only when I was a little older was the severity of mill discipline
relaxed by a controversial innovation. Hours had been six to six
daily, six days a week, including Saturdays, with fifteen minutes
off for breakfast and half an hour for lunch; but now a decadent
move provided for a starting hour of seven thirty, though of
course breakfast was presumed to have been consumed by then.
The final decadence came sometime around the mid-Twenties in
the form of a Saturday afternoon off every week, a move accompanied by the prediction of many of the clergy and other respectable citizens of Dundee that the collapse of society was at hand.
Was not this a preamble to a widespread decline in morals? With
so much free time, what mischief might not ensue? The moral
decline certainly came; but perhaps the cause was more complex.

The jute nabobs who owned and operated the mills reaped
enormous profits in an age in which income tax either had not
been invented or was still a negligible factor. The equivalent of
half a million dollars a year was by no means an unusual income.
They built fantastic mansions. The country gentry often sniffed
at these nouveaux riches, whose taste by no means always
matched their wealth; but at least one of them sent to France for
skilled artists to paint the walls and ceilings of the public rooms
in the most elegant style of the day. Many spent their wealth on
expensive dresses and diamond rings and necklaces, as well as

lavish furnishings for their homes, with of course a large staff of servants, including footmen and coachmen as well as the staff of the servants' hall. The ladies in those days not only wore their best jewelry even in trains and in the street but carried a supply of gold sovereigns and half-sovereigns in the little net purses that happened to be in style. Such was the safety of life and property in those days, when Scotland's standard treatment of youthful offenders consisted of judicially ordered liberal application of the birch to their bare buttocks, while the threat of the *Mars,* a training ship that lay in the Tay estuary, where even worse punishment was the order of the day, was also vividly before the minds of potential delinquents. The jute lords were generally disinclined to contribute anything much to their communities, although they were often generous to the Kirk, tossing handfuls of gold coins into the plate on Sunday. Some, however, notably the Caird family, gave munificently to Dundee.

The evil conditions under which the mill lassies worked were not their only form of enslavement. They were also victims of their own tribal customs and superstitions. For instance, when a girl did find a young man and became engaged, the other girls worked off their envy by observing a tribal custom that dictated various ritual indignities to be perpetrated on the prospective bride on the eve of her wedding day as she left the mill at night, such as making her wear a chamber pot on her head while she ran the gauntlet of lines of jeering workers to the tune of obscenities flung at her by onlooking men. Thomas Hood, who spent some years of his childhood in Dundee, published in the Christmas 1843 issue of *Punch* a poem destined to become famous: *The Song of the Shirt.* It was about the sweatshops of London, depicting the thoughts of a seamstress:

> And it's oh, to be a slave
> Along with the barbarous Turk
> Where woman has never a soul to save,
>   If this be Christian work.

In Dundee conditions could hardly be said to have improved much by the time of World War I, when I can remember first beginning to take notice of them as a child. Even as late as the Twenties the jute workers' pay was still the lowest in Britain. What would amaze many today is the amount of happiness that prevailed among the poor, their hard lot notwithstanding. Part of the reason lay in the cheerful situation of Dundee and the fact that lovely seashore with sandy beaches and beautiful walks through parks and woods were all yours if only you had a penny for the tram or a pair of strong legs. So those who knew, as do most Dundonians, what are really the best things of life did not have so much bitterness toward the rich as is so often elsewhere the case.

The most conspicuous ancient landmark in Dundee is the Old Steeple in the Nethergate. It is 156 feet high (roughly the height of Oxford's Magdalen College tower) and contains a lovely little hall with a lofty groined roof and some finely carved figures. Other places of considerable historic interest abound and are well worth exploring. The sooner they are explored the better, for Dundee has an evil repute, richly deserved, for the stupidest forms of civic vandalism. The beautiful old Town Hall, an eighteenth-century work by William Adam that for two hundred years was the trysting place of generations of lovers as well as the symbol of Dundee as much as is Independence Hall that of Philadelphia, was peremptorily demolished in the early Thirties to show off a pedestrian sort of auditorium, the belated gift of one of the jute lords, and to create an even more pedestrian city square.

The Royal Arch, built in 1844 to commemorate the visit of the young Queen Victoria, stood till a few decades ago at the docks. It was not one of the great architectural triumphs of mankind, but it was handsome and pleasing enough in its way, a place where the whalers rested their stout hulls between whaling seasons. That, too, was demolished for not even a passably good reason. According to legend, when the young queen arrived in Dundee for the occasion, she held her script somewhat nervously in her hand and began: "My Lord Provost." This was a little error, because at that time only the provosts of Edinburgh and Glasgow enjoyed the courtesy title of "Lord" ("provost" is the Scottish counterpart of the English and American "mayor"); but the Provost of Dundee took it as a royal act. Nudging one of the bailies (councilmen), he whispered: "Did ye hear whit she called me? It's a great honor for Dundee!" The story symbolizes the fact that even as early as 1844 Dundonian hopes were rising high.

Dundee is such a hard, matter-of-fact town that it inevitably produced a few eccentrics. Notable among these was a worthy who, although Edinburgh-born, spent most of his life in Dundee and all of it in miserable poverty: William McGonagall, whom literary critics have now for long acclaimed as the world's "best worst" poet. The doggerel verses that he prolifically composed and recited in pubs and to all who would give him a few pennies earned him mocking plaudits in late Victorian Dundee and worldwide notoriety after his death. After a brief visit to the United States to seek his fortune, he left without having made a cent. But he celebrated his visit with an effusion that will illustrate the irresistible character of his Muse:

> Oh mighty city of New York, you are wonderful to behold—
> Your buildings are magnificent the truth be told—
> They were the only thing that seemed to arrest my eye,
> Because many of them are thirteen stories high.

The Dundee students laureated him, purporting to bestow on him, at the command of King Theebaw of the Andaman Islands, the title of *Sir* William *Topaz* McGonagall, Knight of the White Elephant, Burmah. McGonagall gravely accepted, no doubt shrewdly ignoring the hoax, for misfortune had taught him to turn insults to his advantage. A convenient introduction for aficionados is provided by David Phillips, a Dundee writer, in *No Poets' Corner in the Abbey,* published in 1971.

When the Tay Bridge was opened in May 1878, it was one of the engineering wonders of the world. Spanning the estuary from Dundee to Wormit on the shores of Fife, it was more than two miles long, the longest bridge built to that date. It still is the longest cantilever bridge, since bridges are no longer built that way. So secure was it believed to be that in June 1879 Queen Victoria's royal train passed over it. On the Sunday night after Christmas of the same year, however, the train that was expected from Wormit did not come into Dundee. The night was pitch dark and a terrible gale was blowing. The Dundee stationmaster eventually crawled along the footbridge to see what had caused the delay, for there were of course no telephones then. He came back with the fearsome news: the bridge ended about a third of the way across. Next morning, at daybreak, all Dundee knew the worst. The train had indeed left Wormit according to schedule; but the middle third of the bridge had been blown down and the train, with its occupants, passengers and crew, all plunged into the icy waters. Only one living thing survived: a little spaniel who somehow escaped and swam to shore. In those days when disasters of that magnitude were practically unknown, it was a world-shattering event. Many studies, including more than one book, recount the tragic details. Dundee was at the height of its prosperity. A few months before the opening of the bridge, General and Mrs. Ulysses Grant had visited Dundee, and the Scots had been delighted that a man with such a good Scottish name had made such a name for himself in America. The Tay Bridge had seemed a celebration of the renaissance of Dundee and of its important place in the world. Its collapse and attending tragedy now seemed like a rebuke from heaven.

The preachers of the day were quick to take the opportunity that the disaster provided. Proposals to run trains on Sundays had already been attacked from many a Scottish pulpit. Here, then, was plain proof of divine vengeance for the sin of sabbath-breaking. Images of the engineer being hurled into the furnace before even reaching the water were solemnly waved at terrified congregations along with the inevitable interpretation that that furnace was but a token of the everlasting fires of hell in store for all who had broken the commandment to keep holy the sabbath day. Sermons were delivered also about the mercy of God who had spared his elect: the few who had missed the train. In the Scotland of those days, however, the pulpit was by no means always or even usually a source of such solace.

The engineering of the bridge had been obviously deficient, yet it might still be standing but for the exceptional gale of that night: exceptional even for the wind-swept east coast of Scotland. Masonry toppled from houses. Fallen chimney pots danced about the streets. My uncle, who had been in Dundee that night as a young man, told me he had been lifted off the street and into the air like an old newspaper in the wind. A locomotive foreman reported to his incredulous boss what turned out to be perfectly true: three wagonfuls of coal, each weighing up to ten tons, had been blown *up* a gradient! A naval report estimated the strength of the gale at 12 on the Beaufort scale.

Today the bridge, duly repaired and strengthened (you can see the middle third higher than the rest) is still very much in use, carrying the important daily railway traffic from London to Aberdeen. In 1966 was added, a mile or so down the estuary, a road bridge that immensely shortens the journey by automobile from Aberdeen and Dundee to Edinburgh and the south. The importance of jute has long since waned, its place taken by other light industries such as cash registers and computer parts. Jam and marmalade, long also products of Dundee, continue to be manufactured. Journalism (represented by popular magazines such as *The People's Friend*) is traditionally added to Dundee's special industries, making "the three J's": jute, jam, and journalism.

The city now, with modern shopping malls and some high-rise buildings, has greatly changed since the palmy days of the jute boom. Vast areas of old tenements have been torn down. Dundee cannot claim many fine buildings. The High School is one of them, however, and there are some handsome churches. The

Wishart Arch, so called because the Scottish Reformer preached there to the plague-stricken people beyond the walls of the city in the sixteenth century, is worth seeing, not least since like all else of historic importance in Dundee it is at the mercy of the Dundonian passion for demolition. All this may make the city sound far drearier than it is. Climb or drive up the Law Hill and survey the city below, the graceful old Tay Bridge, the wide firth leading out to open sea, Broughty Ferry Castle in the distance and on a clear day even Carnoustie, pleasant-looking new towns to the north, the Sidlaw Hills and even the Grampians beyond them, the lush and tidy patchwork of the farmlands of Angus and the woods and hills of Fife to the south across the water—you may well wonder how many cities can claim a finer situation. The inhabitants are a very special breed: hard, independent, un-ceremonious, yet by no means lacking in human compassion. The motto of the city is "Prudence and Candor." Dundee has for centuries demonstrated her fidelity to both.

Aberdeen, the most northerly of Scotland's four largest cities, is, despite the recent developments connected with oil, in some ways the most Scottish of all. She mysteriously retains the unique essence of her past. The special charm of her atmosphere lies in a curiously old-fashioned quality that seems to pervade the air. Aberdeen was never, till recently, invaded by Irish and other extraneous elements as were Glasgow and Dundee. Aberdeen is commonly accounted the chief locus of the thrift attributed to Scotland in general. The reputation is no doubt well founded, for Aberdonians are a careful people. They are also eminently clear-headed and sane. There is a Scots word that well describes the traditional Aberdonian: "pawky." Unfortunately it is an untranslatable adjective. It includes, however, notions of shrewdness, boldness, caution, and artfulness, with hints of mischievous but not unkindly mirth.

The city itself is so solidly built that it is said that during the war when the Nazis bombed it from their Norwegian bases, the walls of some houses that were directly hit still stood when their entire contents had been blown through the roof. Be that as it may, Aberdeen is built solid even by Scottish standards. The local stone happens to be a blue-gray granite. After a shower of rain it glistens and shines from the mica that is among the crystals of quartz and felspar in the granite. Yet that is not by any means the whole story. Well to the north of the fifty-seventh parallel, Aberdeen is one of the most northerly cities in the world, yet it looks as though it had been there forever. The people are hardy, seafaring, and seem to be made with the same qualities as their granite. Aberdeen was doing business in the Baltic centuries ago in little ships tossing their way on the wild sea to Sweden, Russia, and the Baltic ports.

Aberdeen lies mostly within two miles of undulating land between the mouths of the rivers Dee and the Don, stretching about four miles inland. It is really two towns: the university and cathedral town on the one hand and the fishing and commercial one on the other. The former is called Old Aberdeen and the latter New Aberdeen, though in fact they are both ancient. One very handsome street, a mile long and seventy feet wide, takes unquestioned precedence above all others. It is Union Street, so straight that you can see from end to end, so stately that no amount of commercial development seems available to destroy its queenly assurance. The simple grandeur and unity of the whole is accented here and there by a decorous church steeple breaking the line of granite frontages, many of which are in the Regency style of the early nineteenth century in all its noble dignity.

In the middle of that incomparable street is the single, 130-foot span of Union Bridge, from which one looks down on impressive scenery. In an attractive little park in the Denburn Valley below you can see players with long poles moving pieces on gigantic checker boards. Nearby is a range of buildings that include a library, a church, and a theater, cheek by jowl, which in more puritanical days were jocosely called "Education, Salvation, and Damnation." In the Aberdeen Art Gallery is a fine collection of paintings, mostly representative of Scottish work but with many others too, and some fine bronzes by Epstein. In this general area, called Schoolhill, from the old school where Byron was taught, you can capture much of the flavor of New Aberdeen, besides visiting the two churches of St. Nicholas, an early medieval foundation. St. Nicholas is the patron saint of New Aberdeen. Marischal College, even if you were to see nothing else in Aberdeen, must be visited. It has been already briefly described. In Bon-Accord Square and Crescent you will find, on a smaller scale than Edinburgh's New Town, and slightly later in date, Aberdeen's counterpart in architectural dignity. ("Bon Accord" is the motto of Aberdeen.) There are statues almost everywhere in the city, many of them splendid ones that enhance the pleasure of sightseeing.

Aberdeen has a long tradition of fishing. A visit to the Fish Market near the harbor is indispensable, for it is the old breadbasket of the whole region as well as the very vivacious focus of much of its traditional trade. The smell of fish should not intimidate even the most squeamish visitor, for in the cold fresh air of Aberdeen it does not lie stagnant and oppressive as in warmer climes.

Many fishy stories are told. A typical one is of the ventriloquist who asked a fishwife whether the huge cod she was carrying was fresh. Being a ventriloquist, he was also something of a Pygmalion. He put the question in a fairly authentic Cockney.

"Fresh!" screamed the fishwife. "I've just brocht it in fae the sea."

The cod, in full hearing of the local crowd, piped out in unmistakably Aberdonian accents: "She's a lee-ar. I've been here for a week!"

If you get in the way of others who look to the salesmen to be more likely customers, you may be told: "Keep back, mannie (or wifie) and let the fish see the folk!"

Old Aberdeen is another world and a very lovely one indeed, almost all of it belonging to the University of Aberdeen. In the

Chanonry you can get a marvelous sense of bygone Aberdeen. The oldest inhabited house in the city is here, dating from 1519. King's College, founded by Bishop Elphinstone in 1494, has a square-buttressed tower with a fine lantern spire surmounted by crown and cross, built in 1515 and rebuilt the following century. The canopied stalls in the chapel with their beautiful carvings escaped the iconoclastic activities of the less respectable agents of the sixteenth-century Reformation. There is also a sixteenth-century pulpit, and the library contains important treasures.

Half a mile away is St. Machar's, the only granite cathedral in the world. Over its entrance rise twin towers with short conical steeples. The site was consecrated in the sixth century by St. Machar, a missionary from Iona, and the church was founded in the twelfth century. The twin towers were added to a central one, which later collapsed, by Bishop Gavin Dunbar, whose emblazoned paneled oak ceiling is the most striking feature of the interior of this handsome church. Can one wonder that Lewis Grassic Gibbon called Aberdeen "the one haunting and exasperatingly lovable city in Scotland—its fascination as inescapable as its shining mail"?

Less than a mile to the northeast of St. Machar's is the celebrated and beloved Bridge of Balgownie, sometimes called the Auld Brig o' Don. Its picturesque single Gothic arch, sixty-two feet wide, spans a deep pool of the river and is backed by lovely woods. Built by Bishop Cheyne about the beginning of the fourteenth century, it became the subject of an old superstition expressed in the lines:

> Brig o' Balgownie, wight's your wa';
> Wi' a wife's ae son an a mare's ae foal
> Doon ye shall fa'.

Byron alludes to this in *Don Juan*. Being an only child, he is said to have been observed dismounting before entering the bridge and then leading his pony across. The Bridge of Dee, built by

Bishop Gavin Dunbar in the early sixteenth century, has seven ribbed arches decorated with coats of arms and inscriptions. It, too, is worth seeing.

Within easy driving distance of Aberdeen is some of the finest scenery in Scotland, including lovely Deeside and Balmoral Castle, Scottish home of the royal family. Purchased in 1852 by Prince Albert, Queen Victoria's consort, for £31,500, it is a splendid mansion in the Scottish "baronial" style, of white granite and beautifully situated. Nearby is Crathie Church, which the royal family attend when at Balmoral.

Perth, smaller than and different from any of the cities so far considered, is beautifully situated on the river Tay and is a convenient center for the Perthshire Highlands. It offers some of the best scenery in Scotland. Traditionally called the Fair City, its setting is even fairer than itself. It is also historically important as a place (probably an ancient capital of Scotland) in which parliaments and councils met and kings resided. Nearby is Scone (pronounced *skoon*), where royal coronations took place. Perth is first mentioned in records in the twelfth century, but some evidence suggests that it may have grown out of a Roman encampment in the first century.

The most striking view of the city and its surroundings—woods, bridges, hills and the river—is from Kinnoull Hill, 729 feet, a spur of the Sidlaw range. It is a compact city with a comfortable air about it. Its industries, which have quietly thrived even in times of depression elsewhere, included dyeing, printing, insurance, and confections. Dominating the life and outlook of the city is its function as a center for the sale of livestock from neighboring farms. The bull sales, which have been conducted since 1864, are world-famed and attract buyers from many nations.

Two parks, or commons, give an impressive air of spaciousness to the otherwise compact city. They are the South Inch, formerly used for archery (also for witch burnings), and the North Inch, about a hundred acres, with golf course, cricket grounds, and bowling greens. Of the several handsome churches, by far the most important is St. John's, a thoroughly restored medieval church, consecrated by David de Bernham in 1243. The present choir dates from the fifteenth century. Much history attaches to this church, in which John Knox preached a sermon in 1559 that led to iconoclasm beyond his intent. Otherwise, not many important historic buildings remain.

Scone, associated with the Stone of Destiny, the dramatic theft of which from Westminster Abbey in 1950 will be considered in a later chapter, is about two miles from Perth and was once the ancient capital of the Pictish kingdom, and probably also an important center of the Celtic Church. As a result of Knox's preaching, the Abbey of Scone was sacked; within a few generations it had become a ruin. The present Palace of Scone, which dates from the early nineteenth century, contains a magnificent collection of china, open to the public at appointed hours. It replaces a sixteenth-century palace destroyed with the abbey.

We come finally to Inverness, the royal burgh generally accounted the capital of the Highlands and for that reason included in this chapter. Situated on a plain through which the Ness River flows, it is the focal point of road and rail systems in the north of Scotland. A small and somewhat congested town, it is of great antiquity, with evidence of a settlement here long before recorded history. The castle that St. Columba is said to have visited to meet King Brude in the sixth century was probably the predecessor of Macbeth's castle, destroyed by Malcolm Canmore in the eleventh century. Inverness was the scene of much carnage and destruction throughout the centuries. The castle was frequently rebuilt only to be destroyed. The present early Victorian red stone building may occupy the same commanding position as did the ancient castle. There are splendid views of the Black Isle and other regions. Little remains of the old buildings. Queen Mary's House in Bridge Street is the oldest. Abertarff House dates from the early seventeenth century; a clock tower from Cromwell's fortress survives.

Although Inverness has some well-established industries, it is a marketing and administrative center rather than a manufacturing town. Despite its long history, its chief significance today lies in its function as the focus of contemporary Highland life.

Inverness is an excellent center for making excursions to beautiful Highland scenery and famous places. Of these none is sadder or more romantic than Culloden Moor, about six miles from Inverness. A simple cairn erected in 1881 commemorates those who fell in battle.

9

Some Scenic Glories and the National Trust

Scotland small? Our multiform, our infinite Scotland small?
—Hugh MacDiarmid, *Lucky Poet*

W HY go to Scotland? If you live in the United States, you need not even cross the Canadian border to see spectacular scenic beauty: the magnificent national and state parks; the awe-inspiring Rockies; the wild Oregon coast; the astonishing California combination of forest, mountain, coast, and colorful desert; the Great Lakes, the incomparable dogwood in Virginia and other eastern States—all without even getting a passport. And these but hint at America's scenic splendors.

Nor do we lack either the antique or the picturesque. Santa Fe, New Orleans, San Francisco, and the little New England towns: what more need we ask? We certainly do not lack great museums and libraries. What, then, does Scotland have that we cannot find at home? No use saying it is "different": so also are Kashmir and the Alps. There must be a better reason for going to visit so small a country as Scotland. Is it the mountains? Not really. Certainly not their size, for we have already seen that Scotland's highest peak is less than a third of the height of California's Mount Whitney. Then is it the picturesque cities and towns? Hardly, since few cities in the world are more picturesque than Quebec, which by American standards is almost at the doorstep of New Yorkers. There are so many things to see without the hassle of travel to a foreign country. Why, then, Scotland? What can it do for us? What balm can it bring to jaded eyes? What solace to weary hearts?

For a quick answer I would suggest: variety and propinquity. Everything, including the sea, is always nearby, and the variety is astonishing. To that answer you can add what you please: beauty, romance, ghosts—anything. And if because of even a slight claim to ancestry you can call Scotland in any sense The Homeland, then comes the most important reason of all: love.

Scotland is many-faceted. Her countenance, like many a human face, changes as you look at it. Now it smiles, now it frowns. Scottish scenery is like that. Here it throws you a sad, wistful glance as though mindful of a tragedy it would like to forget; there it breaks out into a sunny smile, perhaps even a rippling laugh, as though it knew the secret of the universe. In a face, every feature counts. What would a face be without eyes or mouth or nose? Yet even lesser features play their role, each in its way an indispensable glory.

Take, for instance, Scotland's old stone bridges. You can no more imagine Scotland without her bridges than you could imagine a habitually bespectacled old lady without her granny glasses. And what bridges they are! Not many of them are merely ways of getting across. The Bridge of Balgownie (the "auld Brig o' Don") and the Bridge of Dee in Aberdeen have already been mentioned. Because of Burns, almost everybody knows of another romantic bridge in a very different region, the Brig o' Doon, across which Tam o' Shanter rode at breakneck speed when the witches were pursuing him. It is a lovely little bridge near Alloway, birthplace of the poet, two miles south of Ayr.

What of the scores of other stone bridges, no less romantic, that span little rivers here and there all over Scotland from the borders to the Highlands? And what of the great ones, the engineering feats that span the estuaries of the Forth and Tay, the splendid railway bridges built last century, and the road bridges built nearer our own time? Before they were built you had to wait for two separate ferries to make the short journey from Edinburgh to Dundee, or else make an enormous detour through Stirling and Perth. Nowadays it is easy by road or rail. Up near Dunkeld, where the Tay has narrowed to a river, is a bridge that looks uninteresting till you learn it was made out of material salvaged from the bottom of the estuary into which part of the old Tay Bridge fell in 1879. In Scotland nothing is ever lost— talent, alas, excepted.

One could write a whole book on the bridges of Scotland. Perhaps someone has. People have written books galore on almost everything else in that astonishing land, so why not? There is at least one book on the Tay Bridge alone. In a land of rivers and other waterways, bridges are a part of the scenery, each adding its own peculiar character to the multiform panorama that is Scotland. Here we can but throw out a hint, a reminder to keep a sharp lookout whenever you see a bridge.

Kirks are also very much part of the Scottish scene. They seem to play the same role in the landscape as do churches in England and France, yet they look strangely different. You expect to see a church in a French or English village; somehow it belongs. You would no more remark at seeing it there, perhaps nestling among the trees, than you would remark at it having an altar. In Scotland the kirks tend to look more cocky, as if they had achieved something rather special being there at all. They stare stonily, as if to remind you that they are not churches but kirks. There is never anything casual about them. They were (and to some limited extent still are) very much part of national life, yet they still do not quite belong to the national scenery.

Some are very old, like the great parish churches and cathedrals of England. The architectural splendors of Scotland do not even begin to compare with those of England or France; nevertheless she does have some gems. A random selection would include the lovely little Norman kirk of Dalmeny, near Edinburgh; the kirk at Leuchars, Fife, with its incomparable Norman apse; and the handsome fifteenth-century Gothic kirk at Linlithgow. Some of the plain little kirks give a better idea, however, of what church-going was like when it was an influential force in Scottish life, which is not very long ago. Unfortunately, partly because of vandalism but even more from the strange incapacity or reluctance of the Scots to think of their kirk as a spiritual home, comparatively few churches of any denomination other than tourist showplaces are open during the week: a pity for those who like to kirk-hop.

Charming nooks nestle in half-forgotten corners of the land. One of the loveliest of them is actually called a nook: the East Neuk of Fife. It includes the fishing villages of Pittenweem, Anstruther, which has an interesting sixteenth-century manse, and St. Monance, where there is a fascinating little kirk on the shore, built by David II in the fourteenth century and still in use. It is small with a squat tower surmounted by an octagonal spire, and is as Scottish as Bannockburn. Pittenweem has seventeenth-century houses of immense charm. The whole of that stretch of Fife on the north shore of the Firth of Forth just before it opens out to the North Sea is as enchanting in its way as is the most romantic *petit coin* in France, but it is also the quintessence of seashore Scotland. Although only across the water from Edinburgh, it is just sufficiently out of the way to qualify as not merely *a* nook but The Neuk. If you like nooks, do not miss this one; all others will pale before your memory of it.

Nearby but unambiguously on the North Sea is St. Andrews, an historic town dominated by the buildings of the University, the oldest in Scotland, described in another chapter. The atmosphere is unique. It is one of the coldest and windiest towns in Scotland, although some diligent researchers claim it also has the highest rating in sunshine hours. It is a gray town whose stones haunt the memory of its sons and daughters with a curiously persistent nostalgia. Green lawns abound to mitigate the icy look of the hard stone, and if you are there on a Sunday you might see the students in their red stuff gowns making their quasi-ceremonial after-chapel walk. St. Andrews is certainly unlike anything else in the world.

So is its history. St. Mary's College, founded in 1538, is straight out of a picture book. The ruins of the twelfth-century cathedral and priory with the pends that are part of the gateway to the latter give an idea of their original scale and the impact they must have made on the medieval pilgrim who penetrated so far north. On the shore are the ruins of the old fortresslike castle, palace of the notorious Cardinal Beaton who was assassinated there. It contains a fiendish dungeon constructed in the shape of a wine bottle. I suspect there is none like it in the world, except perhaps for one at the Castel Sant' Angelo, Rome. When I first saw it as a child, the keeper dropped a kerosene lamp down its neck to reveal the inside; now it is lighted by electricity, which somehow diminishes the horror and one's appreciation of the barbarous cruelty of the punishment. The dungeon is pitch dark. Food was dropped down to the prisoner by a rope, and the sanitary arrangements were zero. After a few months the victim went blind. Before long he became insane. The yells of one were so horrendous they penetrated the cardinal's palace and someone was sent down to beat him senseless. It was used by both Catholics and Protestants, depending on who was in power. At one time the two factions each constructed a tunnel in the grounds, not knowing each other had the same idea. Eventually the one heard the other at work. The diggers missed each other by a few feet. Now you can crawl through one tunnel and up to the other and so enjoy a macabre ecumenism.

St. Andrews has a strangely remote quality. Nothing you have ever learned is of any use to you. It is like joining the Foreign Legion. You are at best a cipher, at worst a nothing, and your knowledge is for naught. It is not an island, yet no island could be more insular. No values are known but St. Andrews values. It would take a lifetime to explain that Salamanca is the St. Andrews of Spain; you could not in a thousand lives get across the notion that St. Andrews is the Scottish Salamanca. It basks in a realm of golf and sand and the deliciously cloistered gardens of an academic Brigadoon. For any Trappist or Carthusian monk who needed to get away from the cares and bustle of the monastery, St. Andrews might be a therapeutic spa. It is almost a polar edition of California's Carmel. To miss it, as so many visitors to Scotland do, is like going to Versailles without seeing the *hameau* of Marie Antoinette. By the way, if you like your ghosts churchy, St. Andrews is doubly for you. I allude to these phenomena in another chapter.

Stirling, at the heart of central Scotland, is the place to honor Wallace and Bruce, the heroes of Scotland's Wars of Independence. But even apart from that it reeks of history. It is dominated by the castle, atop a rock 360 feet high, which is entered by a drawbridge. It embodies, besides the old royal palace, Parliament Hall and a building that once housed the Royal Mint. At the old entrance is an eleventh-century arch. From the esplanade are splendid views of the town and countryside. Stirling is a good center for seeing many neighboring sights, including the field of Bannockburn only three miles away, with its handsome equestrian statue of Bruce. Across the river is the Wallace Monument, standing gauntly on the 340-foot Abbey Craig where Wallace stood before the Battle of Stirling Bridge. His sword is among the relics. Traditionally it is a two-yard sword, but Scots are careful to point out that it is in fact only five and a half feet. The precision helps to call attention to the fact that it is indeed large enough to have needed no exaggeration.

Admirers of that celebrated Scottish outlaw Rob Roy MacGregor, who died in 1734 and has been called the Robin Hood of Scotland, should visit his grave in Balquhidder (pronounced *balwhidder*) kirkyard, Perthshire. His exploits were the talk of his contemporaries and have been immortalized in the novels of Scott. He had the skill and daring of the heroes of the Wild West in its palmiest days, and he exercised his talents while Queen Anne and the first of the Georges reigned in London. According to tradition he had very long arms, so that with the weapon every Highlander carried in his stocking he could be quicker on the draw than any other man alive. As with Charlemagne nine hundred years earlier, fantastic leaps are attributed to him when he was fleeing his enemies, enabling him to escape to safety, since no one else could match them. Well may it be that in Rob Roy's case the truth may have been stranger than Scott's fiction.

Away on the west coast of Argyll, as if in another world, is the popular resort of Oban, which lies in a bay and is well equipped with facilities to please tourists. It is situated in beautiful country and has an air of bustle that is not typical of most Scottish towns. It is an ideal jumping-off place for exploring many of the western islands, which are treated in another chapter.

Loch Lomond is easily accessible by road from Glasgow and is both the largest freshwater loch in Scotland and the most romanticized in song:

> Where me and my true love were ever wont to gae
> On the bonnie, bonnie banks o' Loch Lomond.

It is best to approach it from Balloch and thence to Ardlui by road or by loch steamer. Between Luss and Balloch it is studded with thirty islands, some with ruins of ancient monasteries and castles. A cave named after Rob Roy, but which had been used centuries earlier by Robert the Bruce, lies to the north.

Much history attaches to the region, especially the district called "The Lennox," where Norsemen portaged their galleys across the isthmus to wage war on people in Scottish glens, where, centuries later, fierce clan battles were fought, notably one between the MacGregors and the Colquhouns at Glen Fruin. Loch Lomond is the foyer of the Highlands. On anything like a fair day it is indeed bonnie, a word that says "beautiful" with a very Scottish accent, although no other word can convey the freshness and purity it implies. Like Plato's *to kalon,* it says both "the good" and "the beautiful." In the fall, when the red and gold of the leaves dip into the water's edge and the hills sleep on each other's shoulders as they fade dreamily into the distance, and mile after mile of silvery waters lap your boat, you suddenly know something of the meaning of the peculiarly Scottish yet universal anguish of the song:

> Oh, ye'll tak' the high road and I'll tak' the low road,
> And I'll be in Scotland afore ye,
> But me and my true love will never meet again
> On the bonnie, bonnie banks o' Loch Lomond

No road that you take away from Loch Lomond, high or low, can be trodden without a twinge of what the lovers felt.

From Glasgow in another direction one can sail down the Firth of Clyde. To do justice to its beauties would need yet another book. Dunoon, Rothesay, Largs are all popular resorts, so popular that if you go at the height of the summer season you may think all Scotland has decided to emigrate en masse to escape a national plague. Only those who like crowds should go "doon the water" (as is the Glasgow street idiom) during the peak of the summer season.

In the Trossachs, a pass in Perthshire celebrated in Scott's *The Lady of the Lake,* is an extraordinary mixture of the sublime and the picturesque. Birch and rowan are punctuated by heather and honeysuckle. Ben A'an lies to the north, Ben Venue to the south of the pass between Loch Achray and Loch Katrine. The whole countryside is richly wooded. No wonder everybody goes to the Trossachs.

Everybody also goes to Glencoe, but certainly not for the same reason. True, this awesome pass has a somber grandeur of its own, but no one who knows its history can see it without a gulp of horror at the cruel massacre, the memory of which enshrouds the whole region with a black pall of shame. The clan chiefs had been required to swear allegiance to King William III by January 1, 1692. Not untypically, some Highlanders procrastinated. On

February 12, 1692, troopers in his pay who had received hospitality from the MacDonalds crept up on their sleeping hosts and slaughtered thirty-seven of them. Two hundred escaped into the snow. For a detailed brief account, see *The Massacre of Glencoe,* with facsimile of the order for the extermination of the MacDonalds, a National Library of Scotland publication, Edinburgh 1972.

From Inverness you can explore the wilder parts of the Highlands, including Loch Maree, which is in some ways even lovelier than Loch Lomond, and Glen Affric, perhaps the most beautiful glen in Scotland. The whole region, especially the west coast of Ross and Sutherland, is different from anywhere else, but roads are narrow and driving is slow. It is also a wet region. If you can catch it when it is sunny you will know what the beauty of Scotland really is. Gairloch, Ullapool, Lochinver, and Badcall Bay are each unforgettable. To the east is the so-called "Black Isle," which, as you might guess in paradoxical Scotland, is not an island. It is more accessible and has a distinctive beauty of its own.

My own favorite part of the Highlands is Deeside. Like Perthshire it is less wild than the northwest. From Perth you leave through the Tay Valley and Blairgowrie (see the famous beech hedges near this center of raspberry farming) up into the hills, taking the extremely sharp hairpin bend in the road called the Devil's Elbow, which is the highest point on any road in Britain. You are in Deeside when you have reached Braemar, scene of the Royal Highland gathering in September, which is usually attended by the royal family. This is picture-postcard country if ever there were: pine woods, soft fern, and in late summer the purple of heather, heather, heather. (By the way, white heather is rare and is prized as a good-luck talisman.) From the road you can glimpse the white local granite of Balmoral Castle in romantic Scottish baronial style and perhaps see the royal standard fluttering from a turret. This, of course, is the Scottish home of the royal family, and it is easy to see why they have loved it so.

Queen Victoria in her day drove about the neighborhood in a simple little buggy drawn by a shaggy Highland pony, admiring the scenery and making courtesy calls on the local inhabitants by whom she was truly beloved for her simple graciousness. You may visit Crathie Church, where the royal family worship when at Balmoral. Then on you go through Ballater (games there in August), Aboyne, Banchory, Crathes Castle, and the city of Aberdeen. If you like contrasts, have time to spare, and would like to have your lungs filled as full as your heart, drive north up the coast road to Fraserburgh or (less drastic) south through Stonehaven, lovely Montrose, Arbroath, Carnoustie, and Dundee. Some hardy spirits have found it so health-giving as to make them feel they must have been ill all their life before.

Very different is the border country: gentle, comely, rolling, and dotted with ancient abbeys such as Melrose, Jedburgh, and Dryburgh, and strongholds such as Hermitage Castle. It is the country of Scott and James Hogg "the Ettrick Shepherd": pastoral country through which the rivers Tweed and Teviot gently flow. At the conjunction of these rivers lies the little market town of Kelso, with its large square, oddly French in feeling, and its twelfth-century abbey. Near Melrose is Scott's stately Abbotsford House. Over to the southwest of the Border country is Dumfries, dear to all lovers of Robert Burns for its numerous associations with him. Nationalism is usually most strongly felt near the border of another land, and indeed the Border country is permeated with a more self-conscious Scottishness than you will generally find anywhere else.

Among the most satisfying as well as historically instructive sights in Scotland are the great homes and castles, not least those with lovely gardens such as have been acquired and maintained by the National Trust for Scotland, which is what we might call in America a preservation society. It is one of the best modern institutions in Scotland and has one of the most laudable objectives: conserving in perpetuity many beautiful historic places which, under the crushing British tax laws, would otherwise fall into ruin or be commercialized. Although Scotland cannot at all match Italy or France or England in either the number or the grandeur of its palaces and castles, it does have many that are remarkably distinctive in style and a few that are singularly charming. The work of the Trust is comprehensive. Not only has it already preserved both great ancient castles and historically no less important "little houses" and workers' cottages. It has also safeguarded Bannockburn from becoming a slum and has saved large regions of mountain and forest for the people of Scotland and the world. It has a counterpart in England, by the way, and membership in one gives corresponding privileges in the other. As things are today, there is probably no other organization in Scotland that has a better record or better deserves support. Of course, not all castles and other historic places are National Trust property; but through the generosity of private benefactors it has acquired many, including, for example, places as sacred to Scottish memory as Bannockburn, Culloden, Glencoe, and Glenfinnan. Culross, already mentioned, is a sort of Scottish Williamsburg in miniature.

Before looking at the great houses and castles, first consider some of the humbler homes. Near Glamis Castle, for instance, which is not Trust property, the Trust has preserved a row of handsome little eighteenth-century workers' cottages, furnished as in the period. These show how well life could be lived by some who were not at all grandees. The birthplace of J. M. Barrie in Kirriemuir is also a humble place. The washhouse is preserved where James and a companion performed plays as children, charging for admission a marble or a few pins. The "Arched House" that was Thomas Carlyle's birthplace at Ecclefechan remains very much as it was in his day, including the original kitchen grate.

When it comes to gardens, both those attached to great houses and those that are not, Scotland can hold its own almost anywhere. Inverewe in the northwest has some 2,500 species in twenty-four acres of woodland. Growing in the open air are flowers and plants incredible at that latitude, such as climbing hydrangea from Japan, the scarlet flame flower of Chile, colorful American avalanche lilies, and kaffir lilies from South Africa flowering as late as December. Rhododenrons grow profusely in public parks in Scotland, but here are varieties so delicate that they can be grown nowhere else in the country except under glass. Palm trees grow along the shore of Loch Ewe. If you visit it in spring or summer you might think you were in Burma rather than Scotland, at least till a shiver or two reminded you.

Inverewe was begun in 1862 by Osgood Mackenzie, a Highland laird's son endowed with both intelligence and money, who spent much of his youth in continental Europe. Building could not have been easy: soil had to be carried in creels across the then almost roadless land in that out-of-the-way stretch of the Highlands, where there are gales and up to sixty inches of rain a year. For an obviously necessary outer windbreak, Mackenzie used both Scottish and Corsican pines. By 1880 he was growing eucalyptus and an enormous variety of rhododendrons, some with enormous blooms. Inverewe is an extraordinarily felicitous tour de force, for whose upkeep by the Trust all lovers of Scotland should be grateful.

Also Trust property is the Bachelors' Club at Tarbolton; Robert Burns presided at the first meeting on November 11, 1780. Like other clubs of its day, it excluded only religion from the allowable topics. It had a further provision in its rules: to qualify for membership a man must be a professed lover of one or more members of the female sex, a qualification Burns would have had no difficulty meeting. His exceptional ease in opening up conversation with "the lassies" and winning their love is noted by his contemporaries. He appears to have been admitted a Mason here in the following year. In Alloway near Ayr one may see the very room in the thatched cottage where he was born, as well as the family Bible and other relics. At Kirkoswald, about fourteen miles south of Ayr, is the cottage of "Souter Johnnie," mentioned in *Tam o' Shanter.* (A "souter," by the way, was a shoemaker.)

The scanty ruins of Balmerino Abbey, a few miles to the west of Newport, Fife, provide an example of the many historic treasures of this kind the Trust has preserved. Balmerino was a holy site centuries before it became a Cistercian house in 1226. Perhaps no more typical laird's house of the late sixteenth century could be found anywhere than that of Abertarff, Inverness, with its crow-stepped gables and harled walls. In Musselburgh, near Edinburgh, is Inveresk Lodge, built toward the end of the seventeenth century, an excellent example of the quiet, unpretentious, but in its day very comfortable Scottish villa.

The term "castle" is ambiguous. Edinburgh Castle is obviously a fortress, a military stronghold. Even to this day it is an army headquarters. Stirling likewise is pure army. By contrast, castles such as Crathes and Craigievar were intended primarily as great houses—handsome, civilized dwellings.

Of such castles in Scotland I would choose Crathes (fourteen miles west of Aberdeen) above all others, partly for its own sake, for it is exceptionally charming, but even more for its splendid gardens. Such a choice is obviously a matter of taste. The castle is sixteenth century and has the vertical arrangement that distinguishes Scottish houses of the period from their typical English counterparts. An addition of the nineteenth century was burned down in the mid-1960s; since then the castle looks more as it would have looked four hundred years ago, with its baronial turrets and its odd combination of aloofness and warmth. The warmth comes from its having been designed as a house, not a fortress; the aloofness stems from the fact that the large houses of that period remained the focus of the surrounding lands and echoed the slightly menacing quality of their military ancestors. The result is at any rate captivating. The walled six acres of gardens are divided by huge yew hedges that date from 1702. Each garden has a distinctive quality, some formal, some informal, all not only colorful but eminently satisfying. They are constantly tended. Herbaceous borders add much to the splendor. Within the six hundred acres of land are two nature trails.

Crathes today is a unique jewel in Scotland's crown and one of the most delightful places to spend an afternoon.

Craigievar, only a few miles farther west, was built of Aberdeen granite in the first quarter of the seventeenth century. At the time of its building the skill of masons in dealing with the local material and conditions was at its best, and the result is a perfection of its kind. Craigievar with its high turrets seems to rise out of the ground among the trees as if it belonged so much to its surroundings that it had grown out of them into a living thing. The ceiling in the High Hall is noteworthy. Many, with good reason, would choose this castle above all others. Both Craigievar and Crathes are beautifully maintained by the Trust.

Of a very different genre is the Royal Palace of Falkland. It was a stronghold even before it passed into the Stuart family about 1360. The present building dates from the Renaissance. For centuries a royal palace, it has the appurtenances for hunting and other recreations proper to such an establishment, including the oldest royal tennis court in Britain except for the one at Hampton Court near London. (Royal tennis is an ancient game, more like squash than modern lawn tennis. It has many historic associations.) James V died in this palace. During the 1715 rising, Rob Roy and his men for a time possessed it. The chapel, formerly the banqueting hall, has a lovely old rood screen and a richly tapestried gallery. The King's bedroom is noteworthy. All the restoration work has been most skillfully executed. In summer the large garden is a riot of color with a field of lavender and vistas of flowers too long for the eye to take in at one sweep. Despite an air of maturity it is modern, dating from only after World War II: a tribute to the vitality of the justly celebrated Scottish gardening tradition.

Kellie Castle, in the heart of the East Neuk of Fife, is a more recent acquisition of the Trust than either Crathes or Craigievar. The Oliphant family owned it from 1360 till 1613, when they sold it to Thomas Erskine, who was created the first Earl of Kellie the following year. It is T-shaped, consisting of two towers subse-

Craigievar Castle, Aberdeenshire

quently joined. The Vine Room has an unusual coved ceiling with delicate plasterwork dating from 1676. It was falling into disrepair when Professor James Lorimer, father of the notable Scottish architect Sir Robert Lorimer, bought it about 1875. It has since been rehabilitated. Not on such a grand scale as many other castles one may visit, it does give a good idea of the more average type of home in which nobles of the past lived.

Culzean Castle (pronounced *kilayn*, accented on the second syllable), a magnificent establishment with a suite that was set apart for Eisenhower as a tribute to him during his lifetime and is now reserved for any major dignitary visiting Scotland, lies south of Ayr on a cliff overlooking the sea. From the twelfth to the seventeenth century it was one of a dozen or so small castles belonging to the Kennedy family. Between 1762 and 1792 two bachelor brothers of that family refurbished the entire estate and had Robert Adam crown the terraces with crenellated parapets and pavilions while the new house was being built. Today it is an extremely handsome castle with a formal garden and lovely grounds, including the Swan Pond. Its situation and fine state of preservation make it an exceptionally popular Trust property. Across the water on the Isle of Arran is Brodick Castle, also one of the finest properties belonging to the Trust. It is briefly described in the chapter on islands.

The National Trust maintains many other no less interesting ancient properties. And of course many castles are still privately owned despite the crushing tax laws; some are open to the public at certain times.

Dunnottar Castle, near Stonehaven, about fourteen miles south of Aberdeen, especially merits a pilgrimage. It is not only an exceptionally well-reconstructed fortress situated on a mighty rock that rises high above the North Sea, but is a place of peculiar historic interest. It is there that were hidden, during the Commonwealth period the ancient Scottish Regalia ("the Honours of Scotland") now to be seen in Edinburgh Castle. Fantastic stories are told of how they were later smuggled out. They were taken to the nearby parish kirk of Kinneff, where the minister hid them below the pavement stones that he dug up and then carefully replaced. Private papers of King Charles that the English dearly wanted were also smuggled out of Dunnottar.

For dramatic setting, no film director could concoct anything better by way of an imaginary castle than the actual one that is the ancient stronghold of the Mackenzie clan: Eilean Donan. It is reached by a fine old stone bridge from the shores of Loch Duich in Wester Ross. Eilean Donan Castle, believed to have been built in the thirteenth century, was shattered by English cannon in 1719 after a Jacobite battle at Glenshiel. It has been restored. As Craigievar looks as though it had risen out of the earth, so Eilean Donan looks as though it had sprung out of the water.

By these quick glances at some particularly interesting examples of the scenic glories of the Homeland I hope to have whetted some appetites. If you have even a trickle of Scottish blood in your veins, that appetite should be easy to whet. From the aroma you may find your way to the dish, which is better than any scent of Scotland's glory wafted your way. Innumerable books provide both exhaustive detail and beautiful color photographs of Scotland's scenic wonders and historic treasures. The number of books relating to all aspects of Scotland is incalculable. The danger is that if you stay too long reading them you will never get to Scotland—that would be indeed a pity.

CHAPTER

10

The Islands

From the lone shieling of the misty Island
Mountains divide us and the waste of seas;
Yet still the blood is strong, the heart is Highland,
As we, in dreams, behold the Hebrides.
— David Macbeth Moir, *Canadian Boat-Song,*
which appeared in the September 1829
issue of *Blackwood's Magazine.*

SCOTLAND has 787 islands. Most of them are off the west
coast, in the country's rainiest zone. You could live all your life
in Scotland and never visit any of them—no doubt many Scots
have done so without feeling any great sense of loss. Yet Scotland
without the islands would be as immeasurably impoverished as
would Greece without hers. The Scottish islands are as culturally
remote from Edinburgh and Glasgow as are the Greek islands
from Athens. Steeped in history, legend, and lore, they are extraordinarily varied with their own unique character. Some are
considerable in area with sizable and modestly prosperous popu-
lations, some mere rocks noted only by geographers. Many of the
most romantic are in neither of these categories. The flora on
some islands are entrancing, not least under a shining rainbow,
while other islands are harsh and bleak.

Plainly, no one could hope "to do" all the islands, even the more easily accessible. Not only would it take a year in all kinds of weather to do justice to all reasonable claimants among them; the achievement would be less rewarding (except perhaps to a professional geographer) than a careful exploration of some well-chosen samples. This chapter examines only a few to illustrate the variety available. The omission of others that many would account "musts" is inevitably somewhat arbitrary. Anyone who feels the need of more can go to one of the several very good books available on the subject.

ARRAN: Within the island of Arran is a variety of scenery and atmosphere that reflects in miniature the variety in Scotland itself. Arran, easily accessible from Ardrossan on the west coast not far from Glasgow, is in the wide estuary called the Firth of Clyde. With an area of about 166 square miles and a population of a few thousand inhabitants, it is one of the medium-size islands and certainly a good choice for a tourist who has time to visit only one or two. It is dominated by Goat Fell, from whose summit (2,866 feet) on a clear day can be seen something of both England and Ireland. From Brodick, the principal town, it is not a very difficult climb. Some fourteen villages lie along the coast, and the interior of the island can be explored.

Geologists find a good deal of interest in Arran, whose granite mountains are the eroded remnants of a mass of molten material. Basaltic and other dikes abound, among which is the famous Witch's Step, a great V-shaped chasm. There are several lochs (lakes), mostly on high land, including Loch Tanna, which is about half a square mile in area. In the mild, wet climate grow some rare plants and ferns as well as heather, mosses, and a wide variety of trees, including chestnut, beech, pine, larch, lime, and elm. Many of the cottagers grow apple trees, currant bushes, strawberries, and raspberries. The island has a very special flavor of its own that brings vacationers back year after year.

Brodick Castle, which has been National Trust property since 1958, is one of Scotland's great ancient houses. Like many of them it has splendid gardens, including a formal one dating from 1710. Magnolias, camellias, palm lilies, rhododendrons, and hydrangeas are to be found. The present castle, built on the site of an old Viking fortress, dates partly from the fourteenth century, with seventeenth- and nineteenth-century additions. The National Trust owns over seven thousand acres of land, including all of Goat Fell. Amethyst, agate, cornelian, and smoky quartz are among the local stones. Hand-wrought jewelry containing them may be purchased. The island has long been famed for red deer; there are estimated to be between one and two thousand on the island today. Otters, red squirrels, and seals may be seen. Apart from a large variety of birds, once in a while a golden eagle soars into sight. Fishing is excellent: salmon, haddock, cod, and mackerel. Archaeologists have much to interest them. The Stewart clan has been associated with the island from before the days of Robert the Bruce, who spent some time there while mustering support and preparing to rally his troops before Bannockburn in 1314. Among the famous people who have visited the island are Lewis Carroll (of *Alice in Wonderland* fame) and Robert Browning.

IONA: The island of Iona, less than five square miles in area, contains one of the most venerated of the ancient Christian shrines of Europe. It has been a place of pilgrimage since Columba came to it, bringing Christianity from Ireland in the year 563. The monastery he founded became a great center for scholars in the early Middle Ages, when civilization in continental Europe was at its lowest ebb. The abbey, more than once destroyed by the Norsemen and rebuilt, eventually fell into ruin after the Reformation. In 1938 its restoration was undertaken by George (later Lord) MacLeod, founder of the Iona Community, an ecumenical society of clergy and laity mostly working on the mainland but with a spiritual focus on Iona. The restoration is most impressive, and worship is conducted regularly according to the usage of the Scottish Kirk. It is accessible from Oban. Accommodations are usually limited, however, so arrangements should be made in advance. The sands are very white; the beautiful Iona pebbles, some greenish yellow and some dark green, are found on the shores. Automobiles are forbidden. Iona, now acquired for the National Trust, is unforgettable.

MULL: This third largest of the Hebridean islands is just over 350 square miles, with several thousand inhabitants. It can be approached by air from either Glasgow or Oban, and there is also a car-ferry from Oban. Although less exciting than some of the other western isles, it has fine moorland and mountain scenery. Ben More, the highest peak, is over three thousand feet. One of the ships of the Spanish Armada was sunk in 1588 near Tobermory, a somewhat picturesque little town, the principal settlement of the island. The name means "Mary's Well." Both geologists and archaeologists can find much of interest. Among the buildings is Duart Castle, which dates from the thirteenth century and has been restored in the present century by the Chief of Clan Maclean. The castle walls are fourteen feet thick in some places. Mull has some recreational facilities and fine beaches on the west coast.

STAFFA: From Mull one may make arrangements to visit this small, uninhabited island. In summer steamers from Oban pass nearby. About seventy acres in area, it is not only of unusually great geological interest but of singular beauty. Mendelssohn and Turner are among the musicians and painters who have celebrated its charms. Queen Victoria and Prince Albert visited it in 1847. The name Staffa is Norse and means "Pillar Island": an apposite name, for the island is characterized by the columnar structure of the basaltic rocks, the result of the cooling of lava sheets after irregularly occurring volcanic action. Fingal's Cave, 66 feet high and 227 feet deep, with pillars like organ pipes, is especially impressive. It was the echo of the waves crashing in this cave that fascinated Mendelssohn. Other caves are hardly less alluring. Seabirds abound.

ISLAY: While Iona nourishes religious faith and Staffa attracts geologists, the ancient island of Islay, most southerly of the Hebrides, is devoted to whisky. With an area of just over four hundred square miles and a population of a few thousand, its principal industry is whisky distilling. There are adequate facilities for lodging and recreation, including shooting, fishing, sea angling, bird watching, and a regular golf course. On the western side can be seen red deer, as in Arran. On the southeast tip is Kildalton Chapel, with many plants and shrubs that would be more likely in a subtropical climate than at this northern latitude. In this Islay is, of course, the beneficiary of the Gulf Stream. From the summit of Beinn Bheigeir, about sixteen hundred feet, one may get a good view of less accessible neighboring islands such as Jura, whose three peaks are known as the Paps. Islay can be approached by air from Glasgow.

SKYE: Of all the islands, no doubt the one most celebrated in romantic song and legend is Skye, the most northerly of the Inner Hebrides, accessible by car-ferry from the Kyle of Lochalsh. With an area of 535 square miles and about eight thousand inhabitants, it is one of the largest of all the islands; yet its coast is so indented that no point on the island is more than five miles from the sea. Its sea cliffs are very dramatic. One of the mountains, Quirang, is famed for its spectacular gullies and extraordinarily shaped pillars. Not far from the principal settlement (the little fishing town of Portree) may be seen the Old Man of Storr, a remarkable pinnacle consisting of solidified lava.

Among the five castles on Skye, Dunvegan, some parts of which go back to the tenth century, is the most renowned. It is the seat of the Chief of Clan MacLeod; probably no other family in Scotland has held a castle so long in its hands. Legends about Dunvegan abound. Among the relics it contains are the Fairy Flag, said to have been captured by the Saracens during one of the Crusades, and a lock of Bonnie Prince Charlie's hair. The MacDonalds of Sleat at one time ruled the island along with the MacLeods. Needless to say, feuds between the two families were pursued with full display of the tenacity that Scotland unfailingly musters for such purposes. In the Jacobite rising of 1745, the Chiefs of both clans, although highly sympathetic, kept a low profile. Flora MacDonald, however, played an historic part by rescuing the Bonnie Prince after the disastrous defeat at Culloden. At the time the Prince was fleeing she was living in a cottage on another island (South Uist) and obtained passes to Skye for herself and "a female servant." The servant was in fact the Prince, disguised in a floral dress and going under the name of Betty Burke. Flora is buried at Kilmuir, twenty miles from Portree, and her grave is marked by a twenty-eight-foot cross.

Fishermen delight in the abundance of salmon and trout. Naturalists may observe tawny owls, gray seals, and sometimes red deer. Unlike many of the islands, Skye has a good deal of fertile soil that provides a modest living for the crofters. The island is mountainous. The Cuillins, a range famed in song and story, are a symbol of the mystique of the Hebrides. To the west are the Black Cuillins, composed of gabbro, a very hard rock found elsewhere only in the north of Norway. To the east lie the Red Cuillins, so called because in some lights they glow pink. In Glen Brittle, to the south of the range, is one of the loveliest waterfalls in Britain. Anyone with the slightest Brigadoon tendencies who stays even a night or two on Skye may very well see in the patches of mist mysterious, supernatural sights that tug at the heartstrings of even the sturdiest and may hear heavenly music that can cause the manliest throat to gulp.

LEWIS AND HARRIS: With an area of 770 square miles, this is the largest as well as the most northerly of the Outer Hebrides. Lewis is the part to the north, Harris to the south. Lewis is mainly peat and heather-clad flat moorland, while Harris is mountainous and has a wooded area. In the churchyard of Rodel, a pretty village, is the grave of Donald MacLeod, a doughty Jacobite who is said to have fathered nine children after his third marriage at the age of seventy-five.

Stornoway, the principal town, has regular air service to Glasgow and London. The island may also be approached by boat from the Kyle of Lochalsh. Recreational facilities are plentiful: both sea and fresh-water fishing, water-skiing, golf, and lovely walks. The standing stones and cairns, marking the graves of ancient warriors, are noteworthy, not least those at Callanish.

The island is possibly the best place to see in action what survives of the old Gaelic civilization and culture. The people, for all the rocky stubbornness they share with their compatriots all over Scotland, are courteous and hospitable. Here, too, one may see something of the old Scottish brand of Presbyterianism at work, with unbending tenacity to traditional customs such as Sabbath observance. Above all, the pride and industry of the people is heart-warming. Stornoway has admirable modern facilities felicitously superimposed on the old peasant industry of tweed manufacture. Here the world-renowned Harris tweed is made with pride by a people whose ways echo the old rugged individualism and independent spirit of Scotland. With a population of about thirty thousand, the island has its own technical college, which teaches weaving, engineering, navigation, and other skills.

The people, however, are the greatest attraction. Something of their character may be glimpsed from the fact that, when Lord Leverhulme, the wealthy industrialist who owned the island, offered it in a gift to the people in 1923, they declined because ownership would have entailed taxes. The Leverhulme story, an epic in modern Scottish political and economic history, is told in another chapter.

BARRA: Barra is of special interest to Catholics, for it is one of a few remote places in Scotland that the Reformation scarcely touched. The inhabitants today are nearly all Catholics. Chief among a cluster called the Barra Isles, it is about twenty square miles in area and has a population of between one and two thousand. It is accessible by air from Glasgow or by boat from Oban on certain days. The colors of Barra are memorable: deep green grass, blue hills, and silver sands. The lochs are well filled with trout. The friendliness of the people is striking and of a different sort from that of the people of Lewis and Harris. One recalls the lines of Hilaire Belloc:

Where'er a Catholic sun doth shine
There's love and laughter and good red wine.
At least, I have always found it so:
Benedicamus Domino.

The social life is easygoing and the gatherings merry. There are several Catholic churches and one Presbyterian one.

EIGG: This island (pronounced "egg") has less than half the area of Barra and a tenth of its population. It is a kidney-shaped island that also kept its Catholic tradition through the Reformation and is traditionally MacDonald country. Irish Franciscans visited it in the seventeenth century and helped to maintain the old religion. Protestants eventually came, however, and there is still the site of a building that was at one time divided into three sections: the House of Devotion, the House of the People, and the House of the Sermon. It was an ecumenical venture long before ecumenism became fashionable. Today there are two churches: one Catholic, one Presbyterian.

Eigg is one of a few places in Britain, such as the Northumberland coast and the Channel Islands, that can claim "singing sands." The phenomenon has been scientifically studied. Some romantics have likened the sound to that of the Aeolian harp. To produce it, one presses obliquely with the foot on perfectly dry sand, preferably toward the end of a hot day. You cannot hope to produce much melody, but it is an amusing humming and hissing sound, somewhat like what can be made rubbing one's legs together while wearing heavy corduroy pants.

The island is dominated by Sgurr, just under thirteen hundred feet, and the coast is a little reminiscent of Iceland. Flowers and plants come in enormous variety, providing great interest for botanists.

Many are the gruesome tales of bygone days on this strange island. In a cave near the southeast shore, the MacLeods of Skye are said to have conducted a fierce revenge. Lighting a fire at the entrance of the cave where two hundred MacDonalds were hiding, they massacred them by suffocation. The ruins of Donan's Chapel may be seen, where in the seventh century a priest, while celebrating Mass, was set upon by pirates. He asked them not to kill him till he had finished the Mass. They acceded to his request, then beheaded him and some fifty of his monks. According to legend, these pirates were in the pay of a band of female warriors who wanted the island. In the records, Eigg is sometimes called Nim Ban More, "the isle of the big women." There are waterfalls and caves where rock doves nest, and occasionally one may catch sight of a golden eagle.

ERISKAY: This island, with a population of about three hundred and an area of four and a half square miles, is accessible by ferry from South Uist and occasionally from Barra. It has several claims to fame, and is perhaps most widely known for the beautiful songs that have been collected and preserved, such as the "Eriskay Love Lilt." Even today the women sometimes sing such songs, love songs and rowing songs, as they work on the men's fishing jerseys.

To Eriskay, too, the French frigate *La Doutelle* brought Bonnie Prince Charlie. According to legend, the pink convolvulus to be seen in the bay grew from seeds he scattered there as he landed. (Cynics may murmur that he scattered legends with an even readier hand!) According to the story, the Prince predicted that the flower would never grow anywhere else. Some say they have tried without success and so helped to confirm the prediction. He also brought the recipe for drambuie, the now world-famed whisky liqueur. The secret was passed on to the MacKinnon family and is held by them to this day. Eriskay, like Barra, is Catholic. It is a lovely island with soft colors and white sands. There are virtually no recreational facilities, which helps to preserve a quiet and peace that even the best-behaved of vacationers can destroy. Some of the crofters will accommodate visitors to the island overnight. The chief industry is lobster fishing.

SOUTH UIST: This may be the best of all the Scottish islands in which to see the old Hebridean life continued by the several thousand Gaelic-speaking islanders who inhabit it. They are crofters rather than fishing people, and in accordance with Celtic tradition they spread themselves over the island with no inclination toward developing towns. They are comparatively prosperous and predominantly Catholic. Their faith is expressed in some architecturally fine, simple churches, notably those at Bornish and Eochar, which are among the first Catholic churches built in Scotland after the Roman Catholic Relief Act of 1829, which permitted erection of such buildings. A thirty-foot statue of Our Lady of the Isles, by Hew Lorimer, is a landmark for seamen. The island, twenty-seven miles at its maximum length by about seven miles wide, contains nearly two hundred fresh-water lochs, many of them trout-filled and some providing fishing unexcelled anywhere in the British Isles. As already noted, it was from this island that Flora MacDonald rescued Prince Charlie after his defeat.

ORKNEY: We are now moving from the west coast to a very different region of Scotland far beyond John o'Groats, the most northerly point on the mainland. This is a region that is both historically and ethnically very different: Scandinavian territory till as recently as the fifteenth century. Orkney and Shetland are the two principal islands of groups known as the Orkneys and the Shetlands respectively.

Orkney, with a population of about five thousand, has an area of about 115 square miles. It is accessible by air from Wick, and from Aberdeen and other ports by sea. It is bleaker than most of the western isles. The principal town is Kirkwall, where most of the population live. Kirkwall is an ancient Norse town with an interesting church called St. Magnus's Cathedral, whose tower dates from the fourteenth century. Its fabric is a patchwork of red, yellow, brown, and gray stone. The bones of St. Magnus, who was assassinated in the twelfth century, are believed to have been discovered in recent times. Nearby are the old Bishop's Palace and Earl Patrick Stewart's Palace, built in the sixteenth century in Renaissance style by a hated overlord who, after living in great style with a gorgeously attired bodyguard, was arrested for treason in 1609. The town has its own newspaper, *The Or-cadian,* founded in 1854, which is mailed regularly abroad. Or-cadians have an intensely developed sense of identity as a people. They have also contributed a remarkable share of Scotland's notable sons and daughters.

Stromness, the other main town, is an attractive port and was at one time more populous than Kirkwall. The Kitchener Memorial Tower on Marwick Head was raised by local subscription to commemorate the sinking of the cruiser *Hampshire* with Lord Kitchener, the great hero of World War I, which was one of the greatest tragedies of that global conflict. To the south of the island lies Scapa Flow, the famed British naval base in the two world wars.

The most interesting single sight for the visitor to Orkney is Skara Brae, a few miles from Stromness. Orkney is a paradise for archaeologists. Everyone with even the slightest interest in antiquities will be fascinated by this prehistoric village, excavated in 1868 after its discovery in 1850. Ten unmortared stone huts with their original furnishings—stone beds, stone cupboards, tanks, and fireplaces—may be seen. Archaeologists date the foundations from at least as early as 2000 B.C., probably earlier and therefore at least six hundred years before the time of Moses. The tomb of Maeshowe, excavated in 1861, the central chamber of which is fifteen feet square, is open to the public. It is accounted the finest of its kind in Europe. On the walls are both carefully inscribed runic inscriptions and Viking graffiti somewhat of the sort nowadays found in men's rooms and dating from the time of the twelfth-century crusades. The tomb is far more ancient, however, than the graffiti.

SHETLAND: Shetland, sixty miles north of the Orkneys, has an area of 378 square miles and a population of about thirteen thousand. There is regular air service from Kirkwall as well as from Renfrew on the Scottish mainland. Those with strong stomachs and a love of the sea can go by boat from Aberdeen or Edinburgh. (The North Sea can be very rough indeed.) Fierce winds make the island generally treeless and very bleak, although the west coast with its beautiful voes (inlets) has a beauty of its own. Jarlshof, at the south end of the island, has dwellings from the Stone and Bronze ages, including the "wheel-houses," which date from about the second century A.D. and are so called because of their circular shape with radial walls. Half the people of the island live in Lerwick, the principal town, which has a particularly fine harbor, sheltered by the nearby little island of Bressay. That island, with its small population in an eleven-square-mile area, may be visited by boat from Lerwick.

Every year, on the last Tuesday in January, Lerwick holds the festival of Up-Helly-Aa. This is a reenactment of an old pagan fire festival, marking the end of Yuletide and celebrating the people's longing for the reappearance of the sun. Shetland is only a few hundred miles from the Arctic Circle, so in summer the sun hardly sets, while in winter it hardly rises. Winter, however, is not so bad as one might fear. Thanks again to the Gulf Stream, the winters are rarely very cold, although the summers are by no means warm and there is a good deal of rain and mist throughout the year, and often very severe gales. The darkness of the winters is perhaps the most trying feature; hence the popularity of Up-Helly-Aa, for which a Norse galley is carried in procession to the water and there set ablaze with lighted torches. In Scalloway, the other main town of the island, much older than Lerwick, may be seen the ruins of another castle of the odious Earl Patrick Stewart, dating from 1600. He was given to hanging his victims from an iron ring in one of the chimneys. Nearby is the Tingwall Valley and Loch, in which is a small island where, according to a somewhat doubtful tradition, was held the Althing or open-air Shetland Parliament. This small island can be approached by stepping stones. Shetland ponies, known all over the world, may be seen on the island.

PAPA STOUR: This little island, with a tiny population in an area of about six square miles, is two miles northwest of Shetland. "Papa" is the word used by the Norsemen to designate a Christian priest of the Celtic Church, and the name means "Big Isle of the Priests." The names of several of the Shetland Isles allude to that heritage: Papa Stronsay and Papa Westray, for example. Papa Stour is a comparatively fertile island. What makes it worth visiting are the fantastic caves with exceptionally beautiful coloring. The glistening porphyritic rocks forming their interior are of a multishaded red with some areas green from the seaweed, while the roofs of the caves are adorned with strange purple clumps whose regularity gives the impression of bosses on the vaulting of a medieval Gothic church. Access to the island is by boat from Melby on the main Shetland island.

FAIR ISLE: This interesting island, which lies between the Orkneys and the Shetlands, was acquired by the National Trust in 1954, guaranteeing its conservation. It contains a bird observatory that is perhaps the most notable in Europe, with an incredible variety of birds. The area is about four and a half square miles and the population is small. One of the ships of the Spanish Armada was wrecked on this island; the Spaniards whom the islanders sustained for some time taught them how to make fast dyes from flowers. The islanders have kept the secret, using it to manufacture the world-renowned colorful Fair Isle woven and knitted garments. Apart from that traditional industry, the islanders rear sheep and engage in crofting and fishing. This island is less accessible than many, but it may be reached by air or sea from Aberdeen, Edinburgh, and the main Shetland island.

INCHCOLM: From the wild north we now move southward on the east coast to the region of Edinburgh. Inchcolm is one of several islands in the Firth of Forth, about half a square mile in area and virtually unpopulated. The name means "Columba's island," from the hermit's cell established there by one of St. Columba's monks. Shakespeare refers to it in *Macbeth* (Act I, Scene ii), and the very well-preserved ruins of an abbey built in the twelfth century and reconstructed in the thirteenth may be seen, as well as what purports to be the hermit's original cell. Inchcolm commands good views of both Fife to the north and some parts of Edinburgh to the south. Access is by boat from Aberdour, Fife, or Cramond, Edinburgh. It is popular among knowledgeable Edinburgh residents as a pleasant day's outing from that city.

THE BASS ROCK: This striking landmark three miles off the coast of North Berwick, a seaside resort some twenty-five miles from Edinburgh, stands up stark from the sea. It is to that part of the east coast of Scotland what the Big Sur is to California's Monterey Peninsula. It is, however, as different from the Big Sur as is Edinburgh from San Francisco. Easily accessible by boat from North Berwick, it is about a mile in circumference and rises precipitously to 350 feet, a mass of hard, igneous stone. A natural fissure in the rock runs from east to west, forming a tunnel. It is the home of many seabirds, chiefly gannet. There is only one landing place. Special permission is required to land, but serious ornithologists can usually obtain it. Most visitors simply circle the rock in a boat, with a guide who identifies some of the birds for them.

In the seventh century St. Baldred had a cell on the island, which became a monastic center, then later a fortress. Charles II imprisoned some of the Covenanters there, and in 1691 a group of Jacobites, having captured it, remained there for three years.

As promised, this chapter has surveyed only a selection of some of the more interesting islands, enough to exhibit something of their variety. No description could give a sense of their atmosphere, which is different from everything else on earth. To know Scotland without knowing the islands is to know but half of Scotland. Many of them radiate a holy peace and in all of them mature souls can hear, as in few places on earth, the voice of the Eternal. Nowhere else on earth can be heard the heavenly music in this key. The winds of God blow through the inmost recesses of the soul. The light, at dawn or noon or sunset, seems strangely supernal. The call of the island is a call to new life. Even the island smell is a unique magic. As the song goes:

If it's thinkin' in yer inner he'rt
That braggart's in my step,
Ye've never smelt the tangle o' the isle.

The islands assail every sense we have and can carry us beyond
all of them to an experience such as only mystics know.

11

Ghosts, Monsters, and Other Ferlies

Weel done, Cutty Sark,
And in an instant all was dark.
　　　　　—Robert Burns, *Tam o' Shanter*

"FERLIE" is a good old Scots word for any sort of wonder or mysterious happening, sight, or sound. When I was a little boy, country folk would sometimes ask me playfully: "Did you see any ferlies today?" meaning simply any unusual or noteworthy occurrences or sights. The word carries echoes of the meaning of *theos* as used by Greeks in the time of Socrates. A ferlie is a god, but not anything so solemn or holy as Jews and Christians understand by "God." Anything wonderful or merely notable could be a ferlie, from a football star to an unusual sunset, from a cloudburst to an animal you have never seen before. I remember, indeed, once responding to the question by saying, "Yes, I saw two American sailors." At the time either one of them would have seemed to me sufficiently unusual in my experience to qualify as a ferlie. Ghosts and monsters, however, would always qualify *par excellence* and take precedence over all other members of the ferlie class.

The Loch Ness monster, or "Nessie" as she is affectionately called (since for some reason she is always presumed to be a lady), has been for some years the most fashionable of ferlies, having attained international fame. Nessie, although she has had widespread coverage only in the last fifty years or so, has a much longer history. As early as the sixth century, St. Columba scared off a strange water monster who was frisky even in those far-off days. Columba's performance, indeed, alarmed not only the monster but the Picts who observed him in action. Stories of this ferlie go back to the earliest recorded history.

My maternal grandmother, a highly literate lady who was born in Fort Augustus (which is on the shores of Loch Ness) in 1828, and lived to her nineties, used to tell me about the legend when I was a small child. She did not take Nessie seriously at all, accounting her existence a mere silly superstition propagated by a credulous peasantry, like the popular opinion that the loch was bottomless, reaching down to hell, whence Nessie was presumed by some to come up occasionally for air.

Not all modern scientists, however, would share my grandmother's confident skepticism. A London surgeon happened to be visiting Loch Ness in 1934 when he noticed a definite disturbance in the water about three hundred yards from where he was standing. His claim to have seen a small head with a long neck rising out of the water was attested by a couple of quick photographs of the "beastie," as the local people sometimes call Nessie. In the same year Alex Campbell, water bailiff on Loch Ness for forty years, claimed to see a living object about thirty feet long with a flat, reptilian head. At the base of its long neck was a hump. Campbell was able to take in all these details because it surfaced for several minutes before something disturbed it.

Virginia Woolf tells of a woman who, about the same time, was drowned in Loch Ness. She was alleged to have been wearing a pearl necklace valued at something like $100,000. Divers who were sent down to try to recover the body and the pearls (although the body of no one drowned in Loch Ness has ever been recovered) came back with only a horror story of a sinister underwater cave, black and warm. Although the divers' tale might suggest corroboration of the popular tradition rejected by my grandmother, there are, of course, other less theological possibilities.

No one seemed eager to investigate further what happened to the lady and the pearls. Reports about Nessie continued to come in thick and fast. Soon her characteristics had been established in the minds of many before even her existence had been adequately verified to everyone's satisfaction. Her head, by all accounts, is small and reptilian, her neck about ten feet long, her body about forty feet, give or take a few feet either way. She has also a very long tail and thick skin. Some claim to have seen small horns. She propels herself by means of efficient flippers or the like, hears the slightest noise, and is extremely fast in her movements, which is fortunate for her since she is reputed by almost all observers to be very, very shy. One naturally suspects, at first, some Scottish inventiveness. Legends could be profitable. But many who have claimed to see Nessie would be most unlikely to have any such vested interest in tourism, so the possibility of her existence must be taken seriously enough not to repudiate out of hand.

In Fort Augustus is a long-established and well-respected Benedictine abbey and school. On several occasions monks from this abbey claimed to have seen Nessie. Reports continued to come in. Tourism prospered. Hoaxes were perpetrated: someone made giant footprints on the shore that caused a stir for a while. But such practical jokes were short-lived. During World War II some Royal Air Force photographic experts took pictures, and after the war scientists gradually came to take Nessie more seriously. Some thirty Oxford and Cambridge students spent a few months at the loch in 1960, and two years later another expedition equipped with hydrophones spent a similar period studying underwater noises. No definite results were obtained.

About this time, however, a film showing Nessie disporting herself was shown to four scientists, who were convinced to the extent of affirming that there was indeed a living object in the

loch of such size as warranted careful scientific inquiry. The Loch
Ness Investigation Bureau was set up on a nonprofit basis. In
1968–1969 sonar equipment was brought to the loch and two
submarines were sent down. During their explorations they
located a large moving object that eluded their sonar equipment.
One Nessie enthusiast logged more than twenty thousand hours
watching, day after day for years, and made twenty-three of the
best pictures ever taken. In the course of an expedition made in
1970 by the Academy of Applied Science, large moving objects
were detected in the loch. During a further expedition two years
later, pictures were taken of two large moving objects, one of
which clearly showed a flipper whose length was estimated between four and six feet. Further scientific expeditions followed.
They have at least established that the loch has a series of very
deep channels that could easily house the now almost less-than-
hypothetical "beastie."

The loch is deeper than the Atlantic and other waters that
surround Britain. At one point at least it is deeper than the North
Sea at its mean depth. So the old superstitions about the stupendous depth of Loch Ness had not been entirely without foundation. Moreover, Loch Ness, now an inland loch, was connected,
millions of years ago, to the ocean. It is the largest loch in Scotland, Loch Lomond excepted. My grandmother told me that
when she was a little girl of six (about 1834), she and her mother
fell in Loch Ness while boarding a small boat, and that the crinolines they were wearing buoyed them up till help came. At the
time I did not appreciate the full gravity of their situation. The
local superstition that the loch "never gives up its dead" is sub-
stantiated by the fact that there is no record to show that the body
of anyone who has actually fallen into the loch and apparently
drowned has ever surfaced or been recovered. What grisly fate
might they have met in that watery deep? I suspect that my
grandmother, despite her official skepticism, was more than ordi-
narily grateful for those crinolines.

What scientists know about the loch, together with the pictures that have been taken, make plausible the theory that some sort of animal believed to have been extinct millions of years ago may have survived. Such creatures have turned up in other waters. Nessie might be, for instance, a plesiosaur, a species of dinosaur. A small family of plesiosaurs could conceivably have survived the supposed extinction of the species and continued a somewhat incestuous line. This, however, is but one theory among many, although it does seem more plausible than some. Nessie may be a gigantic eel or a huge amphibian or an enormous sea worm. Adherents of rival views have not been slow in airing them.

Who can tell what is the truth about Nessie? At the time of this writing, however, Nessie's existence does seem at least more plausible than her nonexistence. Moreover, if a small tribe of plesiosaurs has so successfully maintained itself in such seclusion for millions of years, the task of capturing any one of them would seem to be as unpromising as that of extracting a bag of gold from a Scotsman's sporran. After a few million years in seclusion, even the most gregarious plesiosaur could hardly be expected to be notably sociable today. Thus the persistent opinion that Nessie suffers from shyness toward strangers would be (if the theory is correct) something of an understatement.

Monsters are one kind of ferlie; ghosts are another. The British Isles have long been noted for their large ghostly population, but not even Cornwall or Ireland can outdo Scotland in the number of ghosts to the acre. In addition to ghosts there are other species of semivisible gentry too numerous for even a Linnaeus to collate. Elves, fairies, pixies, and other "wee folk" abound, and here and there a kelpie, which is a sort of ghostly water horse and by no means to be lightly regarded. Nor may you with impunity suppose that just because you do not know the proper name for a Scottish leprechaun you may conclude disbelief in its existence.

I once asked an old Highland shepherd whether he had ever encountered any uncanny creatures of that kind. He was as hardnosed a son of the soil as ever you met. He could read a sheep's mark at the other end of a valley, and he spoke habitually in a sharp, clear, matter-of-fact tone. I knew I would get an answer. I did, but the voice curiously changed to honey dew, as if to warn me that we were now moving on to a different language level. " 'Tis not a thing that I would be speaking about to everybody. But oh, yes. Yess indeed indeed. Sometimes maybe when the moon is full and you are walking alongside yon river and thinking of nothing but the day's work and the fine warm fire that is awaiting you . . . well, you will maybe see . . . well, ferry, ferry strange things." He spoke eerily, with seriousness, and almost as though he were translating from another and unspoken tongue.

"Ghosts?" He raised his eyebrows, then lowered them as he relit his pipe. I thought he had relapsed into silence and I was about to press him harder, for I was in no mood to let it go at that. But at last he spoke, this time more mysteriously than ever. "Aye," he said. Then he added in an even more mysterious tone and in a sort of choking gasp: "And maybe . . . maybe worse."

"What could be worse?"

But this time he was not to be drawn further into such uncharted waters. Pursing his lips just a little and turning his head away casually, he left me in no doubt that the conversation was ended.

"It iss a bit chilly tonight, iss it not?" he remarked in his ordinary voice. Then with a Highlander's instinctive politeness and hospitality: "What would you be saying to a wee dram?" In the Highlands an allusion to a dram of whisky has perhaps concluded more interesting conversations than it has begun.

Scottish ghosts are not necessarily human. Should you happen to be taking a walk near Castle Douglas, Kirkcudbrightshire (pronounced *kirkoobrihshih*), a black dog may play up to you. He is so friendly that you will soon be patting him on the head. Since you are unlikely to have a mirror handy, you may not notice that your own face, perhaps even your own hair, has turned instantly as white as the dog is black when you find that your hand has gone right through him.

Most Scottish ghosts, however, are green. Green Jean is a lady ghost who may be seen in Ashintully Castle, whither she regularly returns. She does so to make sure you do not forget that her uncle murdered her for her money. She may also be seen any Halloween at Newton Castle. In Crathes Castle, which was singled out in a previous chapter for its loveliness, you may also occasionally see a green lady ghost picking up a baby from the hearth. The baby is also a ghost.

Some ghosts, however, are pink. There is a pink one at Stirling Castle: a ghostly lady who stalks across the courtyard, headed for a place nearby where the ladies used to watch the men jousting.

Mary, Queen of Scots, who after husband Darnley's murder came to Borthwick Castle as Bothwell's bride, left it disguised as a pageboy. As you would expect, she haunts it as a pageboy. Bonnie Prince Charlie haunts Culloden House, near Culloden Moor, scene of his final defeat. Ghosts galore haunt Dunvegan, ancestral seat of the MacLeods, where you may be shown the Fairy Flag. Culzean (pronounced *kuhlayn* with the second syllable accented), is haunted by a ghostly piper. At Balcomie Castle, Fife, you may hear a ghost whistling. That is fitting, for he was hanged as a boy for the offense of whistling after having been clearly instructed not to do so. When the death of a chief of Clan Campbell is impending, a ghostly galley may be seen sailing down the loch at Inveraray. Clan Campbell has a very liberal supply of ghosts.

Ghosts tend to come of aristocratic families, which seems odd in a country with such a reputation for democratic ideals. There are plebeian ghosts, but they do not often make a name for themselves. Perhaps, as I have suggested elsewhere, Scotland is less egalitarian in practice than in theory and reputation.

The last witch burning in Scotland occurred in 1727 at Dornoch, Moray. According to Graham's *Social Life in Scotland in the Eighteenth Century,* she was taken from a cold cell and, feeling the air warmed by the fire that had been laid, remarked: "The air o' the fire is kindly." Presumably the poor woman did not know she was to be presently burned in a tar barrel in the fire she felt so comforting after the cold of her cell. A very elderly friend of mine tells me that when his mother came into the warm house on a cold day she would sometimes quote the gruesome words, which even by her time had lost their fearsome connotation. At any rate, Scotland had in the past such a large indigenous population of witches that if you do not encounter the ghost of one of them, it must be that you just do not know where or how to look. Moreover, I cannot help very much here, since witches, by their very nature, are capricious, so their ghosts are unlikely to follow determinable patterns.

Why warlocks, their male counterparts, are so much less common no one knows. Perhaps at some time the witches waged a successful witches' liberation movement that emasculated them. The only warlock ghost that comes immediately to my mind is a hateful paedophiliac pervert who perpetrated horrible crimes on children, capturing them and using them in diabolical experiments. The local people captured him and threw him into a barrel of molted lead, naïvely supposing to make an end of him forever. Little did they know that he would return regularly to Hermitage Castle, Roxburghshire, to haunt the scene of his foul crimes.

The sites of battles are sometimes visited by the participants. Killiecrankie and Glenshiel are good bets if your time is limited. If, in that overwhelmingly gloomy and eerie pass of Glencoe, scene of the unspeakably cruel massacre, you are unable to see even a single ghost, then I fear you must face the fact that you simply do not have the gift.

The gift of "second sight" as it is called in Celtic circles enables you to do more useful, though perhaps no less fearsome, things than ghost watching. By means of it you can also peer into the future. Among those who possess the gift, elderly women predominate. Now that witch burning has become unfashionable, they may be more willing than in the past to disclose their powers. I would advise no one to treat lightly of such powers, or of the psychic phenomena you may hear about. Of course many are phony concoctions that the Scottish Tourist Board is unlikely to be very active in discouraging; but from that premiss the deduction that all are phony is illogical. If only you stay long enough, you will know what every Highlander knows about them and you will never be the same again. For that, however, your passport may need repeated renewal.

Glamis Castle, birthplace of Elizabeth Bowes-Lyon, who married the future King George VI, and also of their daughter Princess Margaret, is so full of ghosts that even in so spacious a home one suspects they must suffer from cabin fever. It was in this great house, some of which goes back to the eleventh century, that Macbeth murdered Duncan. Janet Douglas, who was burned at the stake in the sixteenth century for practicing witchcraft and plotting to kill the bride of James VI as she was disembarking from the ship that had carried her from Denmark, is a frequent visitor to the Clock Tower. Glamis Castle is the ancestral seat of the Strathmore family, one of whose less worthy representatives long ago was excessively addicted to drink and to card playing. When urged to mend his ways, he replied with Scottish dourness that he would go on playing till Doomsday. If you did not know how aristocratic is the lineage of the Strathmores, you might not guess with whom he continues to play. It is His Satanic Majesty himself: the Devil.

When work was done on Glamis some time ago, the workmen found a door that had been long bricked up. Such was the terrible secret they discovered that it was thought better to persuade them to leave the country. Who can tell what it was? Suspicion, however, rests on a vampire who is periodically born into the Strathmore family and who lives for several hundred years at each incarnation. No doubt in face of such a tradition the proper devotion is a prayer for the monster's longevity, since it is presumably better to live with an old vampire than to have a brand new one in your own lifetime. The less credulous may prefer the theory that the secrets of the room relate to Masonic furnishings or ritual.

The venerable antiquity of the Strathmore family is reflected in the pleasantly apocryphal story that went the rounds at the time of the betrothal of Elizabeth Bowes-Lyon with the Duke of York, the future George VI. Legend had it that when the Earl was consulted for his approval of the proposed marriage, he replied that it would be all right, although the family into which his daughter was marrying was rather a new one. Although a mere after-dinner story, it does exhibit the peculiarly strong family pride that is so very Scottish. In such a family-minded atmosphere, ghosts are bound to prosper.

I have mentioned the lady ghosts that wander around so gracefully in their green and sometimes pink gowns. Not all lady ghosts, however, walk with such courtly poise. Lady Anne Douglas, for instance, would find that difficult. She may be seen at Drumlanrig, Wigtownshire, cuddling her head, which she carries in her hand. The reason is straightforward: before she became a ghost she had the misfortune to have literally lost her head. At Rait Castle, Nairn, is a perhaps even more dispiriting sight: a ghostly young lady with no hands. She was the daughter of the Chief of the Comyns and fell in love with a young man of the enemy Clan Mackintosh. Plainly the family had to do something about that. They took the obvious course of inviting the Mackintoshes to dinner so as to provide themselves with a convenient opportunity for murdering them. (One must have thought twice in those days before accepting dinner invitations even from those with the best cuisine in the land.) Imagine the consternation of the hosts when the guests arrived armed. The girl's father was so enraged that he blamed his daughter for tipping them off, betraying her own family. He thereupon cut off her hands. In her distress she leapt from the tower to her death. One may be grateful that she did not also lose her head, as did Lady Anne, for without arms how could even a resourceful ghost tote around her head?

St. Andrews, not unexpectedly, is marvelously well stocked with ghosts. It has the advantage of proximity to the sea, whence comes the "haar" that helps ghosts manifest themselves even to the ungifted, tactually as well as visually. If you happen to see a phantom coach, watch carefully for the driver. He is not there. The horses, however, are audible as well as visible: you can hear a strange ticking sound on the road. Among the rest of the ghostly population are a smothered piper, a screaming skull, and the beautiful white lady who seems indigenous to almost all parts of the Spooklands of Scotland. One would think it unlikely, moreover, that either Patrick Hamilton or the despicable prelate who watched with satisfaction his superlatively cruel burning at the stake in 1528 would neglect to make at least occasional courtesy calls, unless it be (as many believe) that the wicked cardinal has been permanently detained in a much warmer clime.

If pressed for time, do not go to remote castles to look for ghosts. Robert Louis Stevenson tells of a lady in white "with the most beautiful clear shoes upon her feet" who was known to frequent a district near his native Swanston, which is only a pleasantly long walk from Edinburgh. The Hunters' Tryst, once a woodside inn nearby, was haunted by none less than the Devil himself. He "shook the corners of the building with lamentable outcries, beat at the doors and windows, overthrew crockery in the dead hours of the morning, and danced unholy dances on the roof." He defied all the ministrations of the local clergy and all the prayers and psalm singing of the good neighbors, who sometimes sat up all night trying to help exorcise the infernal guest. After years of such alarming disturbances, he suddenly left the place, no doubt with other business on his mind. So if you do go ghost hunting, watch the company you keep. By no means are all ghosts friendly.

Yet what is the use of going to Scotland if you are squeamish about getting close to ghosts? Anyone who wants to avoid them would have to stay exclusively at modern hotels and motels that no self-respecting ghost would be seen dead in. I wonder, however, whether even with such contemptible subterfuges it would be possible to see Scotland without at least a few whiffs of the supernatural. The two dimensions so interpenetrate that unless you are the merest oaf from across the border (in which case you would not be reading this book), you will find it impossible to go anywhere in Scotland without seeing more ghosts of the past than present people. That is only fair, for were you to see merely the people, you would be getting only a very one-sided picture of this enchanted land.

A final word of warning: never ask a Lowlander about ghosts. He is unlikely to know unless he has Highland blood in him. Better still, ask no one. Just listen and look. Ghosts do not like to work through diplomatic channels.

12

The Varieties of Local Speech

Poo pa poo. If ye dinna wanna poo pa let ma poo pa.
—Excerpt from a Glasgow conversation

THE number of persons in the Scottish Homeland speaking Gaelic today is estimated at under 100,000. It is a difficult language, as are Irish, its close cousin, and Welsh, its distant ancestor. In Gaelic the predicate comes before the subject and the adjective comes after the noun. The indefinite article does not exist. Tense, gender, and number are indicated by changes in the initial consonant. Pronunciation is also difficult: the value of consonants changes with the adjacent vowels. Moreover, even if you were to learn to speak it impeccably, you would probably have difficulty finding anybody with whom to converse, despite strenuous and admirable efforts to keep the language alive. Like three-dimensional chess, it is not something that is going to be much of a social asset to you as a visitor. In Nova Scotia there is a college that actually uses Gaelic as its regular medium of instruction and conversation. In the Scottish Homeland, however, the vast majority of people are as unable to speak it as are most Americans. So unless you are a philologist or the like, stick to English.

The everyday language of the Scots is English. It is their

mother tongue, but they speak it with a remarkable variety of regional peculiarities. Moreover, even in the best society they may now and then use words that have gone out of vogue in standard English or that came to Scotland in the first place as imports. In general use today are words such as "ashet" for platter and "cundy" or "gundy" for street drain. Yet many Scots would not know what a "cundy" is, for while "ashet" is still used in the best households, "cundy" has become somewhat less acceptable, although there is nothing wrong with it. As in England, speech usage varies from class to class, although (except in Edinburgh and a few other places), the Scots on the whole are a bit less self-conscious about such differences. Lowland shepherds will still call their sheep "yowes" or "wethers" or "tipps." Most Scots, if not hopelessly urbanized, will understand such talk but would not readily adopt it for regular use. Almost all Homeland Scots, however, both understand and use "rone" for roof gutter, although educated Scots would tend to follow standard English usage even here, especially when talking to non-Scots. Americans, being accustomed to a heterogeneous environment, are generally much better at grasping unfamiliar patterns of English than are the inhabitants of England, who, except in cosmopolitan London, usually make not even the slightest attempt to follow the slightest deviancy.

In Scotland today, as in England, the difference between the speech of the educated upper classes and that of the crowd is striking. A few centuries ago the situation was somewhat different. Some judges and other dignitaries still spoke in words and accents not noticeably different from those of the common folk, although their grammar and logical construction would be much better. As we shall see in a later chapter, the fashion began to prevail, after the Union of the Parliaments in 1707, of trying to anglicize both speech and literary style. The Scots never took well to that. Even the educated classes were not very good at it; the common folk hated it and to a very large extent still do. With the improvement of transportation in the nineteenth century, and the tendency of the upper classes to send their sons to English schools such as Winchester and Eton, well-bred Scots today have few of the peculiarities traditionally associated with Scottish speech. Today, if you visited a law court, the difference you would hear between the judge and a policeman making his report would be striking.

If you want to hear and try to follow the dialects of Scotland, you must talk to common folk. You must also distinguish between the speech of common folk in the rural areas and those in the cities. The former often include in their speech archaisms, picturesque words, and quaint locutions that are very interesting to anybody with a flair and an ear for language. The latter, the urban dwellers, speak a sort of Scotch Brooklynese. The difference in regional accents is as great as any to be found in the United States. The difference between the intonations of a farmer from Ayrshire and one from Caithness or even Aberdeenshire is certainly at least as striking as between a farmer from Georgia and one from New England. Both climate and history affect language, and the Scottish climate varies enormously within short distances.

Let us begin with the largest city, Glasgow. This is the accent most widely heard abroad, since by the laws of probability more Scots abroad will have a Glasgow origin than any other. The intonation is very distinctive and to some ears monotonous. It conspicuously lacks the modulation to which educated speakers of English, French, German, and other languages are accustomed. The Glasgow sentence proceeds with a slight inflection upward followed by a tremendous and sudden fall in pitch at the end. The speech is, however, pleasantly soft, lacking the harshness of the east coast. The softness may be partly due to the softer, rainier climate of Glasgow; but the gradual absorption of Highland elements into the Glasgow scene in bygone times is likely to have done something to determine long ago this aspect of the notorious Glasgow accent. Hostile critics liken a Glasgow discourse to gobs of treacle dropped on a rainy sidewalk, followed by the thud of a pile of books on top of the mess. But in small doses it is not by any means a charmless kind of diction. Like all urban speech, it tends to accelerate just at the point where you have rashly concluded that you are going to understand it, so that you end up wishing it were only a foreign language, which you would either learn or not attempt to follow at all. Its worst feature, perhaps, is the tendency to slur consonants and in some cases to substitute for them a sort of glottal stop, usually represented by nonspecialists in phonetics by an apostrophe: "wa'er" for "water" and "bu'er for "butter." It is very unpleasant to most educated ears.

The Glasgow influence extends far beyond the official boundaries of the city, of course, and while a Professor Higgins could distinguish many dialects within the general sphere of Glasgow's influence, the casual listener would not. In common with the inhabitants of other large cities, the Glaswegian tends to incorporate much local slang and to interlard his sentences with current wit and humor that become very tedious clichés long before they go out of style. All this, on top of a vocabulary that is fairly general in Scotland (including such words as "ken" for "know," "blether" for "gossip," and even "clipe" for "telltale" or "stoolpigeon") provides a quite sound assurance of unintelligibility. You will probably end up congratulating yourself on having understood a few words here and there. The visitor to Glasgow has nevertheless one great advantage: the friendliness of the people is such that they will often go far out of their way to promote not only communication but genuine understanding.

The example cited in the exergue is an extreme case: "Poo pa poo. If ye dinna wanna poo pa let ma poo pa." It is a boy's protest when in a boat with his parents on the Clyde, his father being at the oars. "Row, father," he is urging. "If you don't want to row, father, let mother do it, father." When expectorated by childish lips, with the distinctive Glasgow inflection, and at breakneck speed, it is about as intelligible as Cantonese. It is almost as unintelligible to many Scots not born near the banks of the river Clyde.

Dundonese is in almost every way a different approach to the problem of human communication. Where the Glaswegian relaxes his whole vocal apparatus before beginning the process, the Dundonian gives the impression that he is ready to bite you. There is indeed a doggy sort of quality in Dundee speech. It barks at you, as though the speaker were trying to talk above the noise of the North Sea wind and waves. The Dundonian, even when he is slovenly in his speech, rasps it out with the peremptoriness of a drill sergeant. From a tenement window in Dundee you might hear a mother call to her little boy in the street below: "Mupp furz and wull gupta yer granniz angowertyer antiz on the wye." Translation: "Come up for me and we'll go up to your grandmother's house and go over to your aunt's on the way there."

"Stoap skytin yergirdin the plenniz," would be no less puzzling: "Stop striking your hoop on the sidewalk." In Dundonese, "plennies" means sidewalk, while "pletties" means "tenement balcony." Such, at any rate, is classical Dundonese. One does not hear it today so often in such purity as a generation or two ago. The BBC has gradually made inroads into the local usages, but you will still frequently hear fairly close approximations. "Oh meh, whit a peh!" (oh my, what a pie!) is as current as ever, and you might well hear an old woman say of another: "Aye, she's fleh," meaning that she is cunning or shrewd. Flies, which in Dundonese are pronounced "flehz," are notoriously skillful at avoiding human entrapment. Dundonians account themselves very "fleh."

Aberdeen, seventy miles north of Dundee, is strikingly different in speech. One basic characteristic is the substitution of "f" for "wh," as in "faurs the fisky?" (where's the whisky?). But it is not as simple as it sounds, since the vowels also change, as in "foo dye no ken fae wiz at the feel fistlin?" which would be translated as "why don't you know who was whistling at the wheel?" Like Dundonese, the dialect of Aberdeen is sharp and staccato. It has more music in it, however, for it echoes the lilt of Scandinavian speech. In the north of Aberdeenshire, the region called Buchan, which includes Fraserburgh and the neighboring flatlands near the Moray Firth and the North Sea, the characteristics are much more pronounced and the use of Scandinavian words more frequent. In all of Aberdeenshire, however, you will hear variations of a dialect peculiar to that general region and with roots in a long past. It may claim, for this reason alone, to be a peculiarly authentic kind of Scottish speech.

Aberdonese is a speech that few natives entirely discard, even after a lifetime in England or America. You will also hear its curiously rapid Scandinavian ring among all classes. This is exemplified in the story of the Londoner who visited Aberdeen to try to clear up an insurance claim. Being unable to make head or tail of a question put to him, he concluded that it was because the questioner was not a very well-educated man. He asked an Aberdeen lawyer to interpret. The question had been "Fa dee dee dee oh?" (What did he die of?), which the lawyer explained was due to the first questioner's lack of education. What the man meant, explained the attorney, was: "O fa dee dee dee?"

All the pronouns in Aberdonese tend to be pronounced alike, a peculiarity that does nothing to facilitate easy communication. I knew, as a boy, an old tenant farmer who voiced his complaint about landlords in this way: "Ee ken, ee ken, ee dinna ken, ee ken, it's ee lahnlords, ee ken, ee think ee'z ahbody, ee ken, an ee'z naebody." The first nine words constitute merely a general introduction to any statement purporting to contain a considered reflection. They might be rendered: "You know, you know, I don't know, you know." Then follows the substantive assertion: "It's these landlords, you know. They think they're everybody, you know, and you are nobody." Robert Burns, from the other end of Scotland, would have had much difficulty understanding that man, although he would certainly have felt instant sympathy with the sentiment if he could have understood that expression of it.

Edinburgh, the capital, fosters the belief that no particular accent or peculiarity of speech is discoverable in its inhabitants. That, of course, is a legend less credible than the existence of the

Loch Ness monster. What gives it slight plausibility is that Edinburgh, as an administrative rather than an industrial city, and one to which a good many expatriate Scots like to retire, tends to house a fairly large proportion of speakers whose speech has been modified either through long residence abroad or from much contact with England. The local speech of working folk is as broad and as distinctive as that of Dundee or Glasgow, although it has a little more affinity with the speech of the border country than with either of these cities. Where Glasgow's intonation comes down with a sudden thud, Edinburgh's goes up gradually with a slightly querulous pop. Class distinction, however, operates more strongly in Edinburgh. As in London, where phoneticians have discovered at least ten different socially acceptable upper-class modes of speech, Edinburgh has a fairly large and probably growing crop of these, mainly but not exclusively modifications of good standard English. Its special riches lie in the remarkable variety of its middle-class accents, of which one of the best known is attributed to Morningside, an area on the south side of the city. It is an ultra-selfconsciously genteel speech entailing much pursing of the lips. Women tend to achieve greater perfection in it than men. The letter "a" is flattened as in standard American but without the American robustness, while as far as anatomically possible the entire vocal production occurs between the teeth, with occasional timid excursions as far as the front of the palate.

A typical example would be: "Eh don't lehk to be kehtty, but Eh wish Mehggie would beh herself a new heht. The one she's wearing looks as if she had ehksidentally seht down on it and behsht it." Translation: "I don't want to be catty, but I wish Maggie would buy herself a new hat. The one she is wearing looks as if she had accidentally sat down on it and crumpled it."

As in Sweden, every important profession sooner or later acquires or affects a special mode of its own. So there is a clerical speech that few clerics who live long enough in Edinburgh succeed in avoiding, another mode characteristic of the medical profession, and two distinctive ones pertaining to the lower and higher branches of the legal profession. Edinburgh businessmen tend to cultivate a peculiar brand of speech unlike anything else in the English-speaking world. It is fortunate, indeed, that Shaw did not send his Professor Higgins to Edinburgh, where there is already a whole colony of Eliza Doolittles making more or less unsuccessful attempts at refining their speech without benefit of the Professor's instruction. Except for Sweden, there is perhaps no society on the entire planet so extraordinarily class conscious as Edinburgh—and none can be more inexpert at translating its class consciousness into the kind of speech it is trying to affect.

Edinburgh can claim, however, the inimitable Harry Lauder, whose speech became known to millions throughout the world as that of a typical Lowland Scotsman, for he was born in Portobello, Edinburgh, in 1870. The much-beloved comedian who began life as a millboy, worked as a coal miner, and was eventually knighted for his stage performances, made popular the sentence "It's a braw, bricht, moonlicht nicht the nicht," as the epitome of Scottish homespun. In the back streets of Edinburgh you will still hear people talking much as did Sir Harry in his palmy days on the stage, from which he charmed generations of admirers, including the royal family. Harry's fabulous success was partly due, by the way, to two factors: (1) he never embarrassed his audiences with bawdy jokes, and (2) he strove to be at least moderately intelligible to London audiences.

The homespun speech of Robert Burns, widely acclaimed as Scotland's national poet, was the basis of what he wrote in his native Ayrshire dialect. Burns was very much a son of the soil, and much of his greatness lay in his ability to express his finest thoughts in the rustic speech of his particular corner of Scotland. Two hundred years after his death, the country folk still speak much as he wrote. Yet, although his dialect is generally intelligible to Lowland Scots anywhere in the country, it is by no means the natural speech of all, and it is not too much to say that it represents Scottish speech only as Kentucky's represents that of the United States. No doubt every American knows the songs of Dixie and appreciates their charm, but that does not mean their idiom would come naturally to a native of Minnesota or of Vermont. To recognize the variety of the dialects of Scotland is to go far toward appreciating the complexity of the history and character of the Scottish people. After all, there is no more reason to expect all Scots to talk like Harry Lauder than there is to expect William Buckley to talk like Mark Twain.

Travel south almost anywhere in the border country and you will find the main characteristics of all Lowland speech uttered with defiant exaggeration. There, as in border country all over the world, nationalist feeling is heightened. "They" (the English) are just over the Border, so "we" feel a duty to utter our Scottishness with muscular emphasis. If you want the full flavor of Lowland speech in all its pungent earthiness, you can hardly do better than listen closely in the Border country. If you have a good ear you will soon detect the basic principles. Among the most conspicuous of these is the use of pure vowels, vowels not diphthongized as in most other parts of the English-speaking world, and of course the celebrated trilled "r"; but there are many other general characteristics that are best learned just by listening.

In literary circles we have heard much in the last fifty years or so about Lallans, which is an attempt to revive the old Lowland Scots tongue purified of the peculiarities of local dialect and various extraneous influences supposed in one way or another to have debased it. More will be said about it in the next chapter.

Highland speech is radically different from any form of speech you will normally hear in the Lowlands. It may be heard best in the remoter areas of the Highlands and in the Islands. It is an English spoken as a foreign language; hence the oft-repeated claim that the best English in all Britain is spoken in Inverness. It is best in the sense in which a well-trained German sometimes speaks English more correctly, according to "the book," than any English you will ever hear from the lips of a native speaker. A Highlander's English is delightful, however, being soft yet precise, luscious yet crisp, and above all nothing if not lyrical. The sentences flow like poetry. Once you have found your way to a Gaelic-speaking island or to a remote Highland glen and have heard the lilt of English as spoken there (which, by the way, is generally far more intelligible to American ears than any form of "street" Lowland Scots), you will feel that you have reached Scotland for the first time. It is like first tasting honey after having had syrup palmed off on you for years. All English spoken north of the Border, however, is remarkably different from anything you will ever hear in any part of England, from Cumberland to Kent, except of course in the case of a few speakers whose speech has been thoroughly anglicized.

Diction, accent, and pitch are not the only distinguishing features of the forms of English to be encountered in Scotland. Apart from special dialect words such as the Aberdonian "speir" for "ask" (a few others are listed in an Appendix), Scottish usage conserves some antique words that are sometimes incomprehensible south of the Border. "Ashet" for "platter" has been already cited. Some Scots still speak of "the forenoon" for "the morning" and especially for "the late morning." Lawyers, always a conservative breed, cling to words and phrases such as "anent" for "concerning" and "furth of Scotland" for "beyond Scotland." The influence of the BBC has modified such picturesque peculiarities. But many persist, strange and puzzling to both English and American ears.

Sometimes such archaic usages are worse than puzzling. A very general usage at one time was "intercourse" for "conversation." Its occasional use even today among old-fashioned people can give rise to embarrassing situations, as in the perhaps not entirely apocryphal story of the old Scottish Moderator of the Kirk who, during his year of office, was talking to the Queen, who had to leave him for a few minutes. On her return she politely expressed the hope that he had not been bored, to which he courteously rejoined: "Not at all, Ma'am. I have just been enjoying intercourse with your lady-in-waiting."

So much for some of the language difficulties one may encounter. What will be expected of *you?* Even today most untraveled Scots in the Homeland think of American speech as monolithic, the monolith consisting of a cross between Brooklyn and Chicago with a slender topping of Tennessee. Their expectation is derived chiefly from an impression first made on their parents in the early days of the "talkies," in which speech, most of it American, was distorted and exaggerated. On the whole your speech will not offend anyone so long as it is not tainted with any form of English spoken south of the Border, which is the only kind of English that causes intemperately murderous thoughts in the mind of the average Scot.

The educated Scot has been for centuries notoriously pedantic and still is. That is why, unless he happens to have both an exceptionally good ear for languages and a thorough training in phonetics from an early age, he is so funny when he tries to speak a foreign language. An educated Englishman or American will usually blunder away in French or Italian with expected slipshod grammar to match the impossibility of his diction. Even the French will accept him as a foreigner, since he cannot be expected to do much better. The average educated Scot, however, will insist on an elegant flapping of subjunctives such as *"Auriez-vous voulu, Madame, que je passasse?"* and will say it in an accent to which no self-respecting Spanish cow would descend. So beware of a Scot who *does* speak French like a Parisian; he may be a member of an international spy ring. The Italians have a saying, "An Englishman italianate is a devil incarnate." They have not yet found out how diabolical is a Scot with comparable linguistic talent.

For a recent technical study of Gaelic and Scots and of the accents of Standard English in Scotland today by phoneticians and others, see A. J. Aitken and Tom McArthur (eds.), *Languages of Scotland* (The Association for Scottish Literary Studies: Occasional Paper number 4). Edinburgh: W. & R. Chambers, 1979.

13

Literature and Song

Be it granted me to behold you again in dying,
Hills of home! and to hear again the call;
Hear about the graves of the martyrs the peewees crying,
And hear no more at all.
                        —Robert Louis Stevenson, *To S. R. Crockett*

MOST people throughout the world, when they think of Scottish literature, think first of Robert Burns, unless they happen to be academic specialists. They will think also of Scott and Stevenson, of course, and probably of some others such as Barrie and some other writers of the "Kailyard School" such as Ian Maclaren or S. R. Crockett. Burns, however, will spring first to mind, as would Shakespeare in English literature.

What is so special about Burns that, rightly or wrongly, he has won such a place, even apart from his having captured the imaginations of all who have the slightest drop of Scottish blood in their veins? It cannot be merely that he wrote some lovely, tender, earthy poems, along with some others that even his admirers would call pedestrian. At the time of his death in 1796, not even the most perfervid of these could have foreseen the kind of recognition he was to be eventually accorded. Indeed, many English critics for long habitually classed him as a minor poet, setting

189

down his esteem in Scottish circles to peasant taste and maudlin, not to say drunken, sentimentality. Meanwhile, he has been translated into a wide variety of languages, including Russian, French, Italian, and Hungarian. His plebeian origin, style, and outlook cannot in themselves account for the estimate of him by these critics, for the same critics denigrated his patrician counterpart, Sir Walter Scott (1771–1832), whose novels not only were unparalleled best sellers in the capitals of Europe but influenced English literature far beyond the context of the romantic revival in which, like Victor Hugo, he wrote.

To understand the unique place of Burns that has resulted in the founding of innumerable Burns clubs throughout the world —many of them very lively indeed and often with some members displaying impressive, serious scholarship—one must first know something of the history of Scottish literature and also of what was happening to it during his lifetime. The tradition of the "makar," that is, the maker of verses, goes back into the Middle Ages, long antedating William Dunbar's *Lament for the Makaris.* Dunbar (*c.* 1460–*c.* 1520) is by some standards Scotland's greatest poet; but he wrote in a medieval context that would be strange to many today. Till the Reformation, Scotland was politically and culturally tied, through France, to continental Europe. The work of the Scottish writers of that age must be judged accordingly. Robert Henrysoun (*c.* 1420–*c.* 1490), for example, was as different in temperament and outlook from Dunbar as any two contemporaries could be. Yet both wrote with that same European background, both as part of the great medieval Catholic tradition. Dunbar's celebration of Christmas is beautifully medieval:

> Celestial fowlis in the air,
> Sing with your notis upon hicht;
> In firthis and in forestis fair
> Be mirthful now, at all your micht,
> For passit is your dully nicht;
> Aurora has the cludis pierc'd.

The sun has risen with glaidsome licht,
Et nobis puer natus est.

Yet like all great medieval writers, Dunbar was nothing if not a humanist speaking the language of universal humanity:

What is this life bot ane straucht way to dede,
Whilk has a time to pass, and nane to dwell?

Such writers were continuing and developing a Scottish literary tradition that went back to at least the beginning of the fourteenth century, when John Barbour (*c.* 1320–1395) had been writing of freedom and of Robert the Bruce:

Freedom all solace to man givis:
He livis at ease that freely livis!

"Blind Harry the Minstrel," who flourished in the following century, wrote of love and war and William Wallace, much in the same tradition.

Gawin Douglas (*c.* 1475–1522), through a literary learning notably expressed in his translation of Virgil's *Aeneid* into Scots, immensely enriched the vocabulary of the language and its potentialities within that same medieval tradition. Sir David Lyndsay (*c.* 1490–1555) is no less within it, for although his task as a satirist on the politico-ecclesiastical corruptions of his day was a very different one, it reflected the mood of continental Europe on the eve of the Reformation, when people were longing for a way of cleansing the Church without the drastic measures that eventually became inevitable. The Reformation movement in Scotland was itself, as is well known, on very European lines.

Up to about this time, Scotland had been culturally as well as politically quasi-European, while England had been pursuing a more insular way. Scotland, although distant from the mainstream of European culture, had been part of it, looking to it for inspiration and feeling with it through her own historical roots.

Now that she was beginning to cast her lot with England, her cultural roots were cut and a certain literary confusion followed. An old oral tradition prospered, however: the ballad and the folk song. This was not a professional tradition of the kind we have so far been considering. Ballads were composed by local lairds and the like on amateur lines. That is not to denigrate them; no one who knows anything about the ballads would seek to do that, for they have a unique vitality and their images are vivid:

> The king sits in Dumferling toune,
>   Drinking the blude-reid wine:
> "O whar will I get a guid sailor,
>   To sail this schip o' mine?"

They are also a part of Scotland's heritage. Their development calls our attention, however, to a collapse of the old tradition in Scottish literature that comes with the Union of the Crowns. Literature certainly declined, so that in the seventeenth century the very spirit of poetry seems to have departed from the land. In its place were tedious disquisitions of the pulpit and the dreary debates of ecclesiastical assemblies at the very time that Shakespeare was flourishing in England. What authentic Scottish literature there was in that period was, on the whole, amateurish. Still, it kept the stream trickling, and with Allan Ramsay (1685–1758) it began to pick up force. Ramsay could not be called a great poet, but he did save the day and pave the way for Burns.

With the Union of the Parliaments in 1707 came a new attitude among the upper classes who were to set the fashion in the eighteenth century and thereafter. The Scottish gentry did not disparage much less wish to suppress the old vernacular tradition, but they saw it as pertaining to "the lower orders" of society. One does not disparage a kitchen mop, although one does not like to see it in the living room. At heart the gentry very much relished that vernacular tradition. It was in their blood. As we have seen, the various orders of society had lived close together in Scotland. As a consequence, they understood one another well. The upper classes enjoyed the earthy simplicity of the old Scottish songs in no spirit of condescension but because their spirits had been saturated with them from time immemorial. They could no more shed them than they could shed their hearts. They not only sang them but often composed them. Soon, however, they were to be loving them only as we love Westerns, which appeal to us because there is a little of the frontiersman in every American even if he or she be sipping chartreuse in a Park Avenue apartment.

Gradually these Scots were adopting an attitude somewhat like that of the "brahmins" of Boston society a hundred and fifty years ago, who well understood but tried to look away from the folk songs of the hinterland. Even today New Englanders who all warm to the refreshing sound of Vermont folk speech may, if gifted with a talent for mimicry, reproduce it for amusement or to win casual applause, although it would never occur to them to use it as a normal means of communication at their club in Boston or New York. Other parallels include the attitude of the ruling class in Russia who, before Pushkin, generally overlooked or even despised their native language as a literary medium and affected French. The fact that French is such an exceptionally beautiful and ductile medium for the communication of human thought and human feelings does not make it the best medium for the expression of specifically Russian sentiments and moods. Similarly the Flemings, before the revival of Flemish in the early twentieth century, having learned to account their language a peasant tongue and French the only one fit for use on any cultural or literary level, trained themselves to adopt it, often with pedestrian results.

In the case of Scotland, the eighteenth-century attitude was particularly regrettable. Not only had all Scottish literature been written in the Scots vernacular, but a Scottish literature patterned on the literary fashions of London simply did not exist. Such patterning no doubt looked at first deceptively easy to educated people. It was not. When people felt such a literature had to be created, they had to start from scratch, and their attempts sometimes bordered on the ridiculous. True, some writers, such as John Knox, had anglicized their spelling two centuries earlier, but that was a trivial matter. After the Union, all Scots who sought acceptance in the highest society—and especially any who hoped for recognition in the literary world—felt they must purge their writing and their speech of Scotticisms. This they tried hard to do, as they tried to conform in every way to the manners of polite London society. I suspect that a sense of inferiority was usually remote from their minds. On the contrary, they are much more likely to have felt, at least in the first flush of their enthusiasm, more than equal to the task. The Homeland Scot is seldom troubled by suspicions that he might not be superior to the rest of humankind.

Unfortunately, this particular enterprise was much less easy for the Scots than they probably expected. Profoundly conscious though they were of the radical differences of outlook, thought, and temper between them and their southern neighbors, which are almost as great as between the Germans and the French, they seem to have underestimated the difficulties. Political realities were forcing them into molds few Scots could ever hope to fit. It was not that they lacked a literary tradition. Although they had spawned no Shakespeare, they had, as we have already seen, a literary tradition any small country might envy. It is remarkable enough that they had any at all in view of the limits set on it by their country's extraordinarily unfortunate experiences with Church domination both before and after the Reformation. Their family-mindedness, their love of the soil, their fierce independence, and their geographical isolation made such a cultural and linguistic transference intrinsically difficult for them. The difficulty was compounded by the fact that English looked so similar to their ordinary speech, especially in the written form. The womenfolk had identified easily with the Lass of Lochryon as she cried:

> O wha will shoe my bonnie foot?
> And wha will glove my hand?
> And wha will lace my middle jimp
> Wi' a lang, lang linen band?

Now they were being told to admire Addison. Even village children were encouraged to improve their speech by anglicizing it, at least in school and, in view of the infinite faith that prevailed in the efficacy of the tawse, the children were no doubt treated to copious wallops for lapses into their native tongue. In good society the old robust speech of the Scots was beginning to be looked down on as coarse. It was less offensive, presumably, than swearing, but felt to be moving in that general direction.

Men of the upper classes, ambitious for their sons' future careers, sent them to Eton and other English schools, not so much for any particular educational advantage but that they might learn English ways and speak the English of London society. The result is readily imaginable. But we need not rely on our imagination only, for there is abundant contemporary evidence to show it was as we could not but expect. J. W. Oliver quotes a letter that had appeared in *Ruddiman's Magazine* for September 17, 1772, complaining that "an itch of Englifying prevails among us, which, being for the most part an uncouth mixture of bad English with Scots, has the stiffest and most absurd appearance." The fashionable English the Scots tried to emulate at that time was not the best model. It inclined to favor latinity in a way that has now gone completely out of style, and the Scots, with their natural deliberateness of speech, exaggerated the worst qualities in that then current fashion. What began by seeming ponderous soon sounded pompous.

The result of all this feverish anglicization was to lose the best Scots speech, the language of the gentry, who had moved so easily with the common folk. Nothing much was left in its place but street language and rustic talk. A century or so after the

Union, Scott refers to the "slow, pedantic mode of expression" used by Scots and their distinctive "intonation."

In short, the difficulty the Scots experienced was almost as great as if they had been asked to make Italian or Spanish their customary mode of communication. Indeed, as we have seen in another chapter, Gaelic speakers have done better just because they have been forced to recognize English as to them a very foreign language. Among the circumstances aggravating the difficulties these Scots faced was one akin to a special problem that Britishers have in coming to America such as Germans and others escape. The language seems so similar that they naturally but mistakenly tend to assume the whole national outlook is approximately the same. So they measure everything by their British outlook. It is a mistake that Germans and Italians could never possibly make, if only because they are confronted with a radically different language.

Nevertheless, a new literary culture did develop, with Edinburgh as its center. A very remarkable culture it was: so remarkable that one tends to forget that it had really no antecedents at all. David Hume and Adam Smith emerged in a milieu that had seen absolutely nothing like them before. It is not merely that their thought attracted worldwide attention; they were pioneers in a new medium of communication. A generation or so later, Edinburgh certainly accounted itself a literary center that could match many in Europe. The claim was not without foundation. Literary and debating societies abounded, such as the Easy Club, the Select Society, and the Speculative. The latter, founded in 1764, is still very much alive and continues to hold its meetings by candlelight in its main hall, much as it did in the eighteenth century. Many clubs, like the "Spec" and the Dialectic (founded in 1787), were for the most part societies of young men who debated questions of the day with earnestness and conviviality and sometimes reached conclusions that older generations must have frowned upon. This was an age of great new vitality. Cockburn, Brougham, Jeffrey, and many others were a breed that could not possibly have emerged a century earlier. The tradition grew and prospered. Scott was secretary of the "Spec" in his youth, and Robert Louis Stevenson (1850–1894) was its president two generations later. Yet Edinburgh's position in the world of letters was special, standing apart from all else and expressing a new mood that had captured and intoxicated ambitious Scotsmen. A native growth, it was at the same time a sort of transplant.

What was left of the native Scottish tradition survived precariously in a sort of backdoor, kitchen-entrance existence, and even that thanks only to Allan Ramsay and a few other poets who tried as best they could to keep it from extinction in face of the tremendous pressure of fashion in the other direction. Their efforts were so much against the fashion that Scottish poetry might well have seemed to have no future, but for one important fact. Fashion or no, the hearts of the fashion-makers were by no means unsympathetic to the tune they could hear from the kitchen even as they talked and wrote in parlor or salon.

Alexander Geddes (1737–1802) was voicing the sentiments of many when he pilloried the pretentiousness and folly, not to say vulgarity, of the movement that seemed so bent on anglicization that it was constrained to treat with contempt the native literature that deserved so much better of Scottish society:

> For tho' 'tis true that Mither-tongue
> Has had the melancholy fate
> To be neglekit by the great,
> She still has fun an open door
> Amang the uncorruptit poor,
> Wha be na weent to treat wi' scorn
> A gentlewoman bred and born,
> But bid her, thoch in tatters drest,
> A hearty welcome to their best.

Geddes goes on to allude to England's disparagement of every language but her own, which, he adds, is like herself,

> A vile promiscuous mungrel seed
> Of Danish, Dutch an' Norman breed,

decked out in finery and all painted and powdered,

> While ours, a blate and bashfu' maid,
> Conceals her blushes wi' her plaid.

He invites his readers then to strip them both and see which has the finer shape, which less that of a monkey,

> An' whilk, in short, is the mair fit
> To gender genuine manly wit?
> I'll pledge my pen, you'll judgment pass
> In favor of the Scottis lass.

One can almost hear Burns say the *Amen* to that!

One of the most remarkable poets of this period who wrote in the Scottish tradition was Robert Fergusson (1750–1774), a contemporary of Burns for whom Burns had great admiration. He wrote more than a hundred poems, mostly in his early twenties. Utterly spurned by Edinburgh society (he contracted syphilis and died in misery at a very early age), he showed every sign of genius. Well educated, he was able to satirize the English, whom he disliked and distrusted, being a foe of the Union and all it stood for. He does so, for instance, in his address to Dr. Samuel Johnson, by the use of grandiloquent adjectives mockingly alluding to his "dictionarian skill" far beyond the ken of

> mortalic shapes,
> As we, who never can peroculate
> The miracles by thee miraculiz'd,
> The Muse, silential long, with mouth apert
> Would give vibration to stagnatic tongue
> And loud encomiate thy puissant name,
> Elogiated from the green decline

Of Thames's bank to Scoticanian shores,
Where Loch Lomondian liquids undulize.

His counsel to the gifted is, rather:

> Ye wha are fain to hae your name
> Wrote in the bonny book of fame,
> Let merit nae pretension claim
>   To laurel'd wreath,
> But hap ye weel, baith back and wame,
>   In gude Braid Claith.

Burns needed no such encouragement to write in the language of his own Ayrshire folk. He almost always wrote badly when he departed from it or "improved" his own work with anglicization, as he was almost always at his best when he most faithfully adhered to it. He was fifteen when Fergusson, at twenty-four, died prematurely in a cell in a lunatic asylum. Burns's own life was short: he died at the age of thirty-seven, all his life lived completely cut off from both the English and the European Renaissance, cut off indeed from almost every cultural influence but his own genius. His father had seen to it that poverty would not deprive him of the ability to read and write. With typical Scottish thrift and love of education, he had joined with other parents to pay a teacher to help him. But for the rest Robert had to shift for himself. No poet could ever have written out of a more parochial environment, and few out of much greater poverty. Although his work varies much in quality, it is at its best as perfect a lyrical expression of an extraordinarily sensitive soul in a red-blooded sensuous body as is to be found anywhere in the literature of the world. The universal popularity he has attained is indeed well deserved.

The fact remains that the old tradition of the "makars" had been lost. Burns was writing in a local dialect, as other writers since him have done in theirs, not in the language of a whole people, as Barbour and Dunbar had written in their day. That is the situation modern Scottish poets such as Hugh MacDiarmid (C. M. Grieve) have tried to rectify by the invention of Lallans, mentioned in the previous chapter. On the whole, their work, for all its merits, shows no sign of coming near the genius of Burns at his best. It may be that Lallans is an artificial language, a Scottish Esperanto; or it may be that we do not have today such poetic genius. But in one way or another we certainly do not have a Burns.

Not only did Burns write his feelings with disarming simplicity and translucent sincerity; his feelings were a unique combination of the tender and the earthy, the fine and the robust, gentleness and strength. Therein, no doubt, lay much of his appeal to women and the unusually easy rapport he was able to make so quickly with every girl he met, according to the testimony of his contemporaries. His understanding of women made it easy for him to express not only the love of a man for a maid, but the love of the maid for her man. He could poke fun without rancor and could weep without mush. Such literary tradition as was available to him in Scotland was in too much of a shambles to constrain him. He took from it what he needed and learned a few tricks, but at his best his genius surmounted all his models. The century in which he lived is known to historians of thought and culture as one that theorized much about man and nature. Burns seems too much in tune with both to need to think much about either. He is everyman, smiling at the paraphernalia of those who bury their humanity under the trappings of rank or wealth:

> The rank is but the guinea's stamp,
> The man's the gowd for a' that.

Yet he can feel as much tenderness toward a little mouse that he had turned up in her nest with his plow one cold November day as if it had been a human child, so close is he to all that lives and breathes. He offers his apology:

> I'm truly sorry man's dominion
> Has broken Nature's social union,
> An' justifies that ill opinion
>   Which makes thee startle
> At me, thy poor, earth-born companion
>   An' fellow mortal!

In his reverence for all life, he is not content to talk down to the trembling creature he has disturbed. He raises her up to his own stature:

> But, Mousie, thou art no thy lane,
> In proving foresight may be vain;
> The best-laid schemes o' Mice an' Men
>   Gang aft agley,
> An' lea'e us nocht but grief and pain,
>   For promis'd joy.

His gentle mockery of those who put on airs and graces is the occasion of one of his most celebrated utterances. Seeing a young lady in the village church dressed in her finery on which a louse has chanced to stray in full view of his observant eye, he concludes a spree of merry lilting with a noble wish:

> O wad some Pow'r the giftie gie us
> To see oursels as others see us!

His contempt for religious hypocrisy is less gentle. Nevertheless, even in the satire in which he pillories the self-righteousness of an elder of the Kirk (and at the same time the predestinarian theology of the Establishment of the day), he is able to make the laughter comparatively venomless. In this poem he effectively combines two styles: the grandiloquence of the pulpit alternating with the speech of the bothy. "Holy Willie," at prayer, expresses his amazement at the predestinating grace of God that has selected him to be:

a chosen sample,
To show Thy grace is great and ample:
I'm here a pillar o' Thy temple,
          Strong as a rock,
A guide, a buckler, and example
          To a' Thy flock!

The elder, in his prayer, recalls his various fornications. But such
is his sense of ownership of a pew in heaven that all sins can be
set aside as trifles:

Maybe Thou lets this fleshly thorn
Buffet Thy servant e'en and morn,
Lest he owre-proud and high should turn
          That he's sae gifted:
If sae, Thy han' maun e'en be borne
          Until Thou lift it.

It is in his love songs that Burns has won millions of hearts:

O wert thou in the cauld blast
          On yonder lea, on yonder lea,
My plaidie to the angry airt,
          I'd shelter thee, I'd shelter thee.

He celebrates love in all its aspects. Now the very young:

My love, she's but a lassie yet,
My love, she's but a lassie yet!
We'll let her stand a year or twa,
          She'll no be half sae saucy yet!

Then the old:

John Anderson, my jo, John,
          We clamb the hill thegither,
And monie a cantie day, John,
          We've had wi' ane anither;

> Now we maun totter down, John,
>   And hand in hand we'll go,
>   And sleep thegither at the foot,
>   John Anderson, my jo!

And of course the sorrow at faithless love:

> Ye banks and braes o' bonnie Doon,
>   How can ye bloom sae fresh and fair?
>   How can ye chant, ye little birds,
>   And I sae weary, fu' o' care?

Lyric poetry is notoriously difficult to translate. Although some admirable translators have used great skill with Burns, the results are often ridiculous. The famous lines in *Tam o' Shanter,*

> Weel done, Cutty Sark,
> And in an instant all was dark,

were rendered by Ulisse Ortensi into Italian:

> "Benissimo la Camicia-corta!"
> Allora in un istante tutto si fece oscuro.

One cannot fault the translator. French is equally daunting, as translators are the first to recognize. The opening lines of *Of a' the Airts* become:

> Entre tous les points d'où le vent souffle,
>   Je préfère beaucoup l'ouest;
> Car là demeure la jolie fille,
>   La fille que j'aime le mieux.

German is a more promising language for Burns. But when L. B. Silbergeit, one of Burns's innumerable German translators, renders the opening lines of *To a Mouse,*

> Du kleine Maus, du graue Maus du,
> Was eilest so aus deinem Haus du,

the result is absurd. As a rule, however, German translations do better, as, for example, K. Bartsch's *Auld Lang Syne:*

> Sollt' alte Freundschaft untergehn
> Ganz in Vergessenheit?
> Sollt' alte Freundschaft untergehn
> Und gute alte Zeit?

Latin, in the hands of Alexander Whamond, comes out surprisingly well in the first stanza of *Scots, Wha Hae:*

> Cum Valla, Scoti, qui vicistis,
> Et sub Brussio pugnavistis,
> Macti, ad mortem venistis
> Aut victoriam.

Burns has not lacked translators in Russian, Dutch, Hungarian, Welsh, Swedish, Czech, Danish, and both Scottish and Irish Gaelic. So much has an impossible task challenged so many!

Burns has had many imitators, among whom Robert Tannahill (1774–1810) is probably best known. Not very much can be said in praise of his work, and indeed for long the most gifted poets after Burns gave up the whole idea of writing in any distinctively Scottish medium, contenting themselves instead with following the essayists and others who were trying to write fashionable English. T. S. Eliot has mentioned Lord Byron (1788–1824), who had a Scots mother and received his basic education in Scotland, as an example of a Scottish genius doing his best with the medium of English. That may be indeed part of the reason why Byron has been so much more highly esteemed in France than in England: his work often has the flavor of one who is writing European sentiment yet in English such as a European might well covet. James Thomson (1700–1748) is another example of a

Scottish poet who did well in English. Meanwhile, a few such as James Hogg (1770–1835), writing in his own Border dialect, at least kept Burns alive in the minds of his compatriots, though he had little of Burns's genius.

The novel is, of course, a comparative newcomer to the literary scene. When it emerged, Scotland was already well committed to the use of English for narrative prose. Writing prose in a foreign language is always easier than writing lyrics, since the latter involve an intensity of feeling that could not be sustained in an essay or a novel, and feeling is what is most difficult to express well in a language other than one's own. So Scott could not have done otherwise than write his novels in English, using Scots only where the dialogue demands it. Still, Scott had other reasons for his use of English. His manner of writing and his interminable descriptive passages are ill adapted to modern tastes. At some stages in his career he churned out novels that were far below the standard of some of his earlier ones. yet his place is assured, all criticism notwithstanding, if only for what he did to exhibit, through his historical fiction, some of the richness and moral grandeur of Scotland's heritage.

Alexander Carlyle, once the idol of literate Scots, is no longer very popular with his compatriots. He chose to leave Scotland for London, and although he was as thoroughly Scottish, both in his shortcomings and in his abundant virtues, as any man could be, he is nowadays disliked by many in the Homeland, perhaps because he reminds them too much of the rugged individualism and independence in Scotland's past. His style, striking in his day, is belittled by many modern critics, and his wisdom is far too little appreciated. Perhaps, like George MacDonald, he will be "found" again.

Much has been written, mostly disparaging, on what is called the "Kailyard School" of writers. Examples are: J. M. Barrie, S. R. Crockett, and Ian Maclaren. These all had in their day an enormous vogue. They treated of simple life in cottages in old-fashioned rural areas and of social customs that were passing or had passed away. They conjured up scenes that evoked intense nostalgia among those who had left such scenes or who had only heard of them at their mother's knee. In a way they were a sort of prose counterpart to the poetry that was being turned out in imitation of Burns; but on the whole they were much better than the latter. They have been denigrated mainly, I think, because of the part they have played in stereotyping Scottish life in the eyes of Londoners too insular to inspect the real thing. Yet Scottish literature cannot surely be so derelict as to be unable to afford a decent place to the "Kailyard School." Lewis Grassic Gibbon, whose *Scots Quair* (a trilogy) is certainly among the best fiction modern Scotland can offer, echoes in many ways that nostalgic intensity that the Homeland Scots tend to dislike or to be afraid of. The Scottish terror of sentiment is itself very Scottish.

Among twentieth-century poets, Violet Jacob (1863–1946) has a sure sense of Scottish feeling and of the rhythm of the Scottish life of her youth, not least in her *Tam in the Kirk:*

> O Jean, my Jean, when the bell ca's the congregation
> Ower valley and hill wi' the ding o' its iron mou',
> When a' body's thochts are set on their ain salvation,
> Mine's set on you.

Charles Murray (1864–1941) wrote in his own Buchan dialect, with all the Scandinavian elements of the speech of that part of Aberdeenshire. Like so many other Scottish writers, he emigrated, in his case to the Transvaal. Of all Scots who have written poetry in their native dialect, he is probably the most genuine poet other than Burns, who would have had difficulty understanding him, such are (as we have seen earlier) the disparities of regional speech. Murray's dialect is much more difficult for most Americans than that of Burns, and for that reason he is too little known, which is a great pity. Many of his best poems are collected under the title *Hamewith* (including *The Whistle* but not another of his best, *It Wasna His Wyte*) and should not be neglected by a lover of Scotland. Their tempo is quicker than that of Burns, and they certainly cannot be charged with the mawkish sentimentality that so many find in the "Kailyard School." The people in Murray's region are as hard as flint, at any rate to all outward appearance.

With Hugh MacDiarmid (C. M. Grieve) we enter a new stage and a very controversial one. To many he is the saviour of the old tradition of the "makars." "Not Burns but Dunbar" was the spirit in which he entered the fray. A Borderer by birth and a perfervid nationalist with Marxist sympathies, he deplored the fact that Scottish poetry had been able to survive only in dialect forms such as those of Burns and Charles Murray. He was certainly a catalyst, an influence on almost everybody who came near him. Edwin Muir (1887–1959) was one of those who did, and MacDiarmid expected much of him as a companion in the struggle for the renaissance of Scottish literature as he understood it. Muir turned out differently—and in MacDiarmid's eyes a traitor to the cause—largely because of Muir's acquiescence in the realities of the Union. The result was inevitable: a bitter feud. Put two Scots in an empty room and they fight over the furniture. Yet when all that is said, MacDiarmid has been a turning point in Scottish literature. Scores of poets in Scotland today are writing differently because of him. No less a figure than Denis Saurat has expressed admiration for him, recognizing that he is European in a way that Burns never could have been. Burns has become a European celebrity, indeed a celebrity all over the world (excepting England!) precisely because his appeal is to the universal feelings of humankind. But such were his circumstances that he could not conceivably have been in his own time the European that Saurat sees in MacDiarmid. Personally, I am inclined to think that Saurat reads too much of the "good European" into MacDiarmid; but he is right in seeing in him a landmark in Scottish literature.

One of MacDiarmid's best-known poems is *A Drunk Man Looks at the Thistle,* published in 1936 when the author was thirty-four.

It is not an easy poem. Passionate Scottish nationalist that he is, he berates his country as Burns could never have thought of doing or seen any point in doing. That is because Burns was simply writing. MacDiarmid is always writing for a cause: the nationalist one, support for which, as we shall see, is paradoxically easier to get almost anywhere in the world other than Scotland.

The drunk man sees "wee Scotland" in relation to the spinning wheel of the infinite universe:

> He canna Scotland see wha yet
> Canna see the Infinite,
> And Scotland in true scale to it.

After contemplating the historical procession of his countrymen "baith big and sma'," he launches his attack:

> They canna learn, sae canna move,
> But stick for aye to their auld groove
>> The only race in history who've
>
> Bidden in the same category
> Frae start to present o' their story,
> And deem their ignorance their glory.
>
> The mair they differ, mair the same,
> The wheel can whummle a' but them,
>> They ca' their obstinacy "Hame",
>
> And "Puir auld Scotland" bleat wi' pride,
> And wi' their minds made up to bide
> A thorn in a' the wide world's side.

This is a mood Burns could not have conceived. But as we shall see in our last chapters, it springs from a clear perception of the Homeland today. It is not a mood the Scot abroad can readily understand, and it is one the Homeland Scot too often does not wish to understand. For all that, it may be that MacDiarmid will one day be to the Homeland Scot what Burns will always be to the Scot abroad. He is certainly a strange figure. Moray McLaren, a not unsympathetic literary compatriot, describes his appearance as the unlikely combination of Shelley and a thistle.

Among writers in the MacDiarmid tradition, as we may now call it, are Maurice Lindsay, Thurso Berwick, William Tait, William Soutar, Robert Garioch, Douglas Young, Tom Scot, William Scott, George Mackay Brown, Hamish Henderson, and, above all, Sydney Goodsir Smith. Opinions differ about the respective merits of such contemporary poets, but most critics would rate Sydney Goodsir Smith high, if not preeminent, after MacDiarmid. Other poets, such as Kathleen Raine, have chosen to walk in the steps of Edwin Muir rather than in MacDiarmid's. Of those poets writing predominantly in Gaelic, who for that reason are likely to be inaccessible to most readers, the names that stand out are those of Sorley MacLean and George Campbell Hay. A convenient collection of Scottish Gaelic poetry in English is provided by G. R. D. McLean, *Poems of the Western Highlanders.* London: S.P.C.K., 1961.

Scottish prose writers today, having no MacDiarmid for a focus, are not at all easy to categorize. Robert Cunninghame Graham (1852–1936) towers high among twentieth-century Scottish writers. He was a patrician Scottish laird, a most unusual man, immensely impressive in appearance and in manner. He had some Spanish blood in him, although just enough to accent his Scottishness. He was a supporter of the downtrodden classes; for his part in a demonstration in London he was sent to prison in 1887. The nobility of his own character and outlook is expressed in what he wrote in 1902: "Success, which touches nothing that it does not vulgarize, should be its own reward. In fact, rewards of any kind are but vulgarities." For the rest of the panorama of modern Scottish prose writers, choice is very difficult. Certainly no list could omit Moray McLaren, James Bridie (O. H. Mavor), or John Buchan (Lord Tweedsmuir), Neil Munro,

Eric Linklater, or Compton Mackenzie, who have devoted their gifts mainly to Scottish themes.

One naturally cannot help wondering whether any modern Scottish writer, poet or novelist will wear as well as Burns or Scott or Stevenson. No one can tell. Those writers who, like MacDiarmid, write so specifically for the Homeland, trying to get their compatriots to see more clearly the ills to which they point with such poignant anguish, can hardly expect to capture the imagination of the Other Scotland, the Scottish Diaspora. They write, indeed, as though it did not exist, or at any rate as if its existence could have no bearing on the future of the Homeland. The paradoxical fact remains: those Scots who, like Burns and Charles Murray and Violet Jacob, have written in their own regional dialects without caring to be good Europeans, with no conscious didactic purpose, and certainly with no special eye on Dunbar, are the ones who have spoken loud and clear to humankind. May not it be that in doing so with a Scottish accent they have best served that Scotland that is so much more than the Homeland peninsula, being spread over all the earth?

14

Scottish Nationalism

NATIONALISM is a fact of life. Most Americans tend to see it as a regrettable if not a retrograde step. That is natural, since American history has been largely the history of an extraordinarily successful enterprise in assimilating people of varied languages, cultures, and national heritages. If peoples can be welded together in America, why not in Europe and Asia? Indeed, in view of the smallness of many of the sovereign states of Europe, both in area and in population, why not perhaps even more easily there than here?

Very different indeed is the European viewpoint, which has been reached after long, painful, and even demoralizing experience of failure to overcome nationalist feeling. Europe has seen too many unions of nations that have turned out to be so unsuccessful that they have led in the long run to a proliferation rather than a decrease in sovereign states. The Scandinavian peninsula was at one time united, but in 1905 Norway formally declared her independence. The Netherlands were also united. Not only have they been long ago carved up, but Belgium, one of the smallest countries in Europe, has been for most of the present century sorely divided into two factions bitterly hostile to each other, each pointing to its very distinctive language and cultural heritage. The great Hapsburg Empires of central Europe have been carved up every which way. Ireland provides perhaps the best-known example. For centuries part of the British Isles, Ireland became in 1921 officially (except for a few counties in the north that were later still to become the focus of fierce conflict) the independent Republic of Eire.

Whenever the question of Scottish nationalism is raised, the case of Ireland naturally comes to mind. Both Ireland's area and her population are similar to those of Scotland, and they are both obviously part of the unity we still call the British Isles. If Ireland can do it, why not Scotland? The fact is, however, that the histories of Ireland and Scotland are very different and today the two peoples are poles apart in much of what is relevant to nationalistic enterprise. Americans who have learned the fact that the Scots who joined with the Picts to make up much of Scotland came directly from Ireland are inclined to deduce that a strong connection must exist today. That invasion, however, took place more than a thousand years ago. One might as well expect, on learning that in India the Aryans in the north descended upon the Dravidians in the south, that the north of India today would be a developed area and the south a primitive one, when in fact the case is now rather the other way around. Much water runs under any mill in the course of a thousand years. Today the Irish and the Scots have little in common save a deep social and political unhappiness, and even their respective unhappinesses are singularly different. After all, a Baptist and a Jew might both be unhappy with the Pope, but that would not bring them an inch nearer one another.

We have seen that the Union between Scotland and England that was formalized in 1707 was unpopular at the time in Scotland and that the unpopularity was never wholly extinguished. So great, however, were the economic advantages it brought to Scotland from the first, and especially in the early Victorian period, that no intelligent Scot, however deep his nationalist sentiment, could have argued very seriously for separation, particularly in view of the notable cultural, religious, social, and educational independence his country enjoyed. Scotland seemed to many to be having the best of two worlds, and the fact could not escape the notice of the proverbially shrewd Scots. In the later Victorian period, that surge of economic prosperity waned, but not badly enough to make any radical difference. Although romantic and sentimentalist expressions of nationalism flourished, the Union still seemed secure. This sense of indissolubility was strengthened by the promise of the gradual devolution of government from Whitehall to Edinburgh, a token of which was seen in the establishment in 1885 of a separate Secretaryship of State for Scotland. Political conservatives in Scotland called themselves Unionists. The Scottish Liberals favored more devolution. But nobody with any sense of political responsibility stood for separation, for that was too far removed from practical politics to be considered by any perceptive Scot.

By the beginning of the present century, however, vague rumblings were heard. Demand for a Scottish nationalist party was voiced in one of the short-lived papers of the time, *The Scottish Nationalist,* which appeared in 1903 under the editorship of Charles Waddie. Nothing happened. Then John Wilson, whose *Scottish Patriot* had carried a leading article under the heading "Wanted! A Scottish National Party," decided to form one on his own. It was founded in May 1904 with the name Scottish National League. Still nothing much happened. Others tried with similar lack of success. Those who felt strongly about nationalism had to be content with trying to get candidates in the major parties to promise to do more to get Home Rule for Scotland, which no thoroughgoing nationalist can really accept as a final goal. Trying to rouse even hotheads in Scotland to any kind of political action was in those days apparently futile, despite the strong undercurrent of innate nationalist feeling.

Not till after World War I did a serious Scottish nationalism emerge, and then very slowly indeed. Many reasons contributed to the reluctance of most Scots to entertain the notion seriously. In the first place, the rank and file of the Scottish people were not as politically minded as most Europeans, and in this respect very unlike Americans. Secondly, there was no easily identifiable common front. Some proponents of the political doctrine wanted total independence like Ireland; others wanted Home Rule; others were asking for only a little more devolution than was currently forthcoming. Some were far to the left, even with an admiring eye toward Russia; others seemed to be sentimentally hankering after Jacobite and other long-lost causes. In one way or another, the nationalist platform seemed to the majority of the people either fanatical or utopian or both, not at all fit for a people who like to think of themselves as having heads as level as they are hard. The Scots are notoriously dour. In the depression of the early Thirties many became also sour. At first it was a natural reaction to their feeling of helplessness; then it became a habit of mind.

The Scots are also and less explicably very bad at cooperation with one another. Infighting is certainly one of the major characteristics of Scottish society and has been ever since the Middle Ages, when the nobles spent much of their time in internecine war. This propensity has hindered Scottish enterprise, for without cooperation no enterprise can ever conceivably succeed. Many of the pioneers of Scottish nationalism, moreover, were Marxists of one sort or another. The literary efforts of some Scots early in the century did stir some nationalist concern. Among them were the Hon. Ruraidh Stuart Erskine of Marr, who had tried to obtain a separate Scottish representation at the Paris Peace Conference at the end of World War I, and John Maclean. Two journals, the *Scottish Review* in English and the *Guth na Bliadhna* in Gaelic, survived throughout the war and carried articles by Erskine and other pioneers in Scottish nationalism. The poetry of Hugh MacDiarmid eventually aroused some dormant nationalist feeling.

A burst of such feeling had already flared up in the late Twenties. On June 21, 1930, at a great demonstration at Stirling, a "covenant" was launched, carefully worded not to offend extremists. It called for self-government for Scotland. The policy of the National Party of Scotland at that time was to call for the restoration "to the ancient Scots Nation and People" their "former Freedom to govern themselves." Despite attempts to please all shades of opinion, the internecine warfare that plagues Scottish discussions ruined all prospects of genuine agreement even among the leaders.

Then in 1934 a new organization emerged under the name of the Scottish National Party. It seemed to have a well-established platform and a policy of self-government. The original program called for this to be based on the notion of "Scotland as a partner in the British Empire with the same status as England." The Scottish Parliament would be the final authority on all Scottish affairs, including taxation. Hopes ran high of getting representatives of the new party elected to the British Parliament. But in this respect the new party did even worse for the movement than had the old. Recriminations poured forth, and no substantial progress ensued. Purges were duly made. War with Hitler looked more and more probable; the time was again inauspicious for the movement. From the end of the war till the mid-Sixties, the greatest achievement the Scottish National Party could claim was bare survival. Grand statements of aims were promulgated, notably one adopted in 1946; but the effect on the majority of the Scottish people was negligible. Men and women who were as Scottish as heather and oatcakes, and loved their native land deeply, would shrug off the name of any nationalist leader with a smile or a sigh.

What no political analysis could do, the Leverhulme saga may. So I tell the story. Lord Leverhulme was a very rich and successful English business magnate, founder of a company (Unilever) that was one of the twenty largest in the world; he was also an unusually farsighted and benevolent employer whose name was a by-word in working-class households as the exception to their customary ugly picture of the capitalist ogre of selfishness, cruelty, and greed. Leverhulme was a kind and intelligent man who saw that good relations between capital and labor were in the interests of both. When he and his wife happened to visit the island of Lewis in 1880, they both fell in love with it. His wife died just before World War I. At the end of that war Leverhulme, then sixty-six, bought the island as a peaceful haven on which to live in his approaching old age. The previous owner (Sir James Mathieson) had bought Lewis for £200,000 and had invested £500,-000 (then an enormous sum of money) in developing it: introducing various schemes for improving the crofters' output and providing better roads, schools, and other amenities. Not only had his return on this enterprising and seemingly farsighted investment been negligible; the market value of his holding had actually diminished: Leverhulme bought it for £143,000, much less than Sir James had paid.

Leverhulme characteristically set about becoming the perfect landlord. He was thoroughly sympathetic to the islanders' dislike of tourism, for he despised the practice of the rich English visitors who came for a few weeks of fishing and then left with not the slightest interest in the land or its people. He would help the people and improve the region. The backward conditions of the crofters pained him. He found three thousand crofters each paying a rent of only two pounds a year for six acres and earning a miserable eight shillings a week that entailed the carrying of eighty-pound loads of peat by their womenfolk: almost twice the load permitted by law at that time for African women in the Congo. Moreover, in the fishing season the men could and often did earn six pounds a week. Why not develop the fishing industry? Seeing a vision of well-paid men with well-fed families supported by a modernized fishing industry, Leverhulme urged the people to let him help them achieve this goal. No, they would not give up the crofts. He saw how a little technology could turn the old weaving of Harris tweed into a mighty modern industry, without any displacement of the people from their ancient land. The people did want industrial advancement. He would provide the capital to help them. No, they would not change their ways. What frightened the people was not a vision of big factories on the island or grand new roads. Rather, they feared possible desecration of the Sabbath and other such changes in their customary habits.

Still, the Lewis folk liked and respected him. They saw he meant well, and they probably murmured now and then the old saying that the path to hell is paved with good intentions. He went ahead with his plans anyhow, but at every turn he encountered obstacles. Not hostility, just obstacles. He got radio-equipped planes to spot the herring shoals and to signal to Stornoway where to go for the fish. He introduced an air service to supplement the old shipping line. He built fine, solid, modern houses for the people. They preferred their old crofts. The Secretary of State for Scotland at the time happened to be the son of a minister of the Free Kirk, which is strong in Lewis. He sided with the people against Lord Leverhulme. Returning ex-servicemen came to squat on private property he owned, claiming it was theirs, having been taken from them centuries earlier. Leverhulme prosecuted them, but then withdrew or suspended proceedings, partly because he loathed being put into the position of the wicked landlord (which he certainly was not) and partly because he was beginning to see there was in any case no way of attaining his sensible and benevolent ideals. Altogether he had spent an estimated million pounds, with little return, on the island he loved, whose people he wanted so much to help. At length he made a final gesture of goodwill. In 1923, having paid off his personal staff, he offered the entire land to the people as a gift. The crofters declined, for if they were to become owners of the land rather than tenants they would have to pay taxes! In uttering the customary *nyet*, they probably thought themselves very shrewd businessmen. If ever the Scots did get an independent seat in the United Nations, perhaps they might make the

Russians seem to be going out of their way to be cooperative!

Therein lies the essence of the problem. The crofters wanted the factories as they wanted other improvements and modernizations, but they did not want the conditions they entailed. They wanted modern methods of fishing but did not want to fish that way. They would not pay the price. Above all, these people, for long rooted to land they did not own, must surely have wanted to own the land they so deeply loved; but they would not pay the price of the taxes. To the average American it may seem like refusing to accept a large gold nugget because it would entail renting a safe-deposit box at the bank.

The tragedy, however, does not lie only in the stubborn narrow-mindedness of the crofters but in its conjunction with the age of socialism, into which, with the rest of Britain, they were moving. The crofters were doing in their little way what all Scotland, as we shall see, was eventually to do: they were dramatically showing the truth of Oscar Wilde's saying that "All men kill the thing they love."

The death of Scottish nationalism, however, was by no means at hand. On the contrary, by 1950 hopes were running so high that a party leader, J. M. MacCormick, was put up for election to the office of Lord Rector of the University of Glasgow, an honorific sinecure whose nature was indicated in the chapter on education. With the aid of a few of the customary shenanigans—such as raiding the offices of the Conservative magazine, stealing the entire stock, and reissuing all copies the following day with the headline "Churchill says vote for Fyfe" overprinted in vivid red so as to read "Churchill says vote for MacCormick"—MacCormick was actually elected. That was a big shot in the arm for the campaign on which the nationalists were embarking: the collection of signatures to a Scottish nationalist document entitled "Covenant," a name no doubt intended to evoke secular counterparts to the religious emotions generated three centuries earlier by the Solemn League and Covenant. Soon the nationalists were claiming two million signatures.

More, however, was felt to be needed to dramatize what they represented as the will of the Scottish people. The dramatization took the form of a remarkable escapade, the success of which astonished even the adventurers themselves: the theft of the Stone of Destiny (Stone of Scone) from Westminster Abbey and its removal to a hiding place in Scotland. The Stone is a block of red sandstone twenty-six by sixteen by ten inches, which had been used in the coronation of Scottish kings from very early times. Captured by the English under Edward I in 1296, it had been taken as a prize of war. Although most Scots had welcomed its use in the coronation ceremonies of monarchs after the Union of the Crowns in 1603, many had come to resent the fact that it is housed nowadays in Westminster Abbey rather than in some suitable place in the land of its origin, such as St. Giles', Edinburgh. According to a theory dear to some Scots, the original Stone of Destiny had been actually kept in Scotland and hidden, causing Edward I in 1296 to carry off instead a substitute. That is extremely unlikely, if only because the hypothetical original would surely have been produced for Bruce to sit upon after his victory at Bannockburn in 1314. In fact, thirty years after Edward's removal of the Stone to England, attempts were made to recover it for Scotland, which is a very improbable move to have made if the Stone was spurious. Be all that as it may, the proposal to carry off the Stone of Destiny from Westminster Abbey was certainly as dramatic as anyone could have wished.

The maneuver was successfully completed on Christmas morning, 1950. Apparently the thieves (or removal squad, as their supporters might have called them) entered the Abbey before closing time and then, next morning, while the custodians were on their rounds, slipped out, presumably with a rubber-wheeled contraption softly carrying off the precious slab. No Sherlock Holmes was needed to guess the intended destination. All the national papers were full of the story, of course, and the police were watching all roads to Scotland. Snow lay deep everywhere. The docks were also watched, in case the Stone might be shipped by steamer. By a remarkable combination of youthful ingenuity and fantastic good luck, the perpetrators managed to get the Stone across the border and to a hiding place.

In London Scotland Yard's sleuths worked diligently. A net was spread all over the land. Questions were raised in Parliament. While many fumed anxiously over the safety of the incomparable treasure, few who had any sense of humor at all could fail to chuckle at the daring, the drama, and the miraculous success of the audacious enterprise. Meanwhile, nationalists proposed that if the Government gave assurances that the Stone would be kept forever safely in some suitable place in Scotland and the perpetrators promised indemnity from prosecution, the Stone would most surely be restored. The British authorities would make no such undertaking. By this time Scotland Yard had narrowed the list of suspects to four who were now in fact more than suspects. A war of nerves ensued. Eventually, persuaded that the game was up, the adventurers resolved to make the Stone available. As mysteriously as it had disappeared from Westminister Abbey, it appeared, draped in the flag of Scotland, on the high altar of Arbroath Abbey. Within fifteen minutes a police check on all roads leading from Arbroath was instituted. No arrests were made, but the stone was duly returned by the authorities to the place where Edward I had taken it seven hundred years before. The Scottish nationalists felt they had made their point. The story was told later in a book by Ian Hamilton, who had played a leading role in the escapade: *No Stone Unturned.* Despite all the furor and the widespread sympathy expressed by many Scots for the cause, no decisive political success ensued.

The Marxist tendencies that had been in the movement from the beginning had not entirely disappeared in the Fifties, but the party had become much more comprehensive. Some leaders were now appealing to the traditional old Scottish independence and enterprise. Among these none was more respected than Robert McIntyre, who brought to the movement an almost Calvinistic fervor that contrasted with the more academic style of Douglas

Young and others who gave the popular impression to some of being not up to practical politics. Yet no matter who led the field, nothing much ever happened. In 1967 the party polled only 2.4 percent of the national vote. None of its fifteen candidates had been returned to Westminster. At last, at a by-election that year, a young woman, a Glasgow lawyer, was voted in. That achievement, however, was a danger signal to those in control of British affairs, so elaborate provisions were made by Westminster to increase the devolutionary sops.

At the General Election in 1974, a new effort was made. The party's seventy-one candidates opposed every Conservative and Labour seat. This time they gained eleven seats and claimed over 30 percent of the national vote. Poll after poll, however, was showing that while more than two-thirds of the voters indicated some desire for more political control over Scottish affairs, fewer than a quarter of them seemed to be prepared for national independence.

At a by-election in 1978, the combined votes of the Conservative and Labour parties, both talking of devolution without breaking ties with London, came to over 64 percent, seemingly a clear announcement that the Homeland Scots, for all their devotion to the ideal of national independence, were unwilling to pay the price, especially with Conservative and Labour parties in turn openly wooing them with little dollops of devolution. Nor were all Scots unaware that since the Thirties much of Scotland had benefitted from financial assistance from the British Government to attract new employment. Between 1960 and 1971 such assistance to Scotland had been over a third of the total for all Britain, although Scotland's population was a tenth. Many could feel cozier than ever. Enterprise had been not merely forgotten, it had become a disvalue. A new generation had seen the thrift of their elders rewarded by the penury inflation brings.

Nevertheless, nationalist demands continued. On March 1, 1979, a referendum was before the Scottish people: did they want a new assembly with limited Home Rule? The proposed measure needed 40 percent of those eligible to vote. Among those who voted, the proposed measure was approved by a majority. But they numbered only 33 percent of the electorate, so it failed— because a third of the electorate did not show up at the polls. Eloquent was the lethargy. It could hardly any longer be blamed on fear of adverse economic circumstances. Scotland was now the third largest center in electronics for the assembly of integrated circuits, after California and Massachusetts. Everybody seemed to believe, rightly or wrongly, that North Sea oil, now flowing, would make Scotland capable as never before of economic independence. More industry was being attracted to Scotland. Why did the referendum get too little support to pass?

Whatever the reason, hot on the heels of its failure came loud and clear confirmation that no mere accident or indifference had brought it about. Two months later, at the next general election (at which the Conservatives, with Margaret Thatcher as the first woman Prime Minister in British history, ousted the Labour Government), the Scottish Nationalist Party had to try to keep its eleven seats, if not gain more. It gained none and lost nine of the eleven. Furthermore, the new Prime Minister and her party were openly against even moderate proposals for a measure of Home Rule. Bruce Millan, Secretary of State for Scotland under the ousted Labour Government, who won reelection for a Glasgow constituency with a ten-thousand–vote margin, declared: "The Nationalists are a spent force. Their bubble has finally burst." With no friends in either of the major parties and only two seats in Parliament, the movement seemed to be back to square one. Indeed, some may have thought it was, rather, the square of minus one: nowhere.

Theoretically it would seem that the passionately strong nationalist sentiment that is supposed to lurk in every Scottish heart would have had to show itself at the polls in one way or another, especially with signals set as they had been. On the contrary, it had been the Scottish voters themselves who had precipitated the election in May out of pique at the Labour Government, causing it to fall on a no-confidence vote. They exchanged a party that had tried to curry nationalist favor for a party openly committed against even the more moderate aspirations of the nationalists.

Will Scottish nationalism rise again? With the astounding propensity for infighting that runs through the Homeland society from top to bottom, it does not seem likely: certainly not, at any rate, at first sight. In patrician circles that infighting is all the more vitriolic because it is veiled from public view. Internecine warfare conducted in an aura of Byzantine secrecy is even more self-destructive than exuberant public brawls. Informed political analysts have proposed federalism of the Swiss type as a solution to Britain's nationalist problems. Theoretically it is the obvious remedy. But how could it work in a country so habitually divided over emotional issues that could not possibly count for much if nationalism were really a ruling sentiment in all Homeland hearts?

That the most northerly nation in the British Isles, whose people can be the kindliest on earth when so disposed, can have so ready a supply of spleen for unprofitable causes and such energy for self-destruction is not easy to understand. Some dare to suggest that the explanation lies in a strange form of self-hate in the Homeland Scot today. But every such suggestion evokes only new howls from nationalist hotheads and dour sullenness from others. Yet all know well that the Scots have for long distrusted themselves, to say nothing of their sons and daughters abroad. Scotland is nowadays a more complex country than many appreciate.

Perhaps many years ahead, perhaps literally tomorrow, a vigorous nationalist movement might conceivably bring about civil war. It might no less conceivably bring about the destruction of Scotland's identity as a nation. The hope is that both Scotland and England will have more sense than to bring about either catastrophe. Yet the difficulties and dangers are not to be underestimated. As was written as long ago as 1549, in the *Complaynt of Scotland:* "There are not two nations under the firmament that are more contrary and different than are the English and the Scots, though they are within the same island and neighbors and of the same language." That is still substantially true and does not augur well for mutual understanding. Such understanding, however, is not all that is needed; it might even be dispensed with. What is indispensable for a functioning Scottish national independence is a radical renaissance of political sanity and savoir faire among all who espouse that cause. That is precisely what shows no sign of coming about.

15

The Homeland and the Diaspora

Breathes there the man with soul so dead,
Who never to himself hath said,
  "This is my own, my native land!"
    Whose heart hath ne'er within him burn'd,
    As home his footsteps he hath turn'd
  From wandering on a foreign strand?
      —Sir Walter Scott, *Lay of the Last Minstrel*

BY the Scottish Diaspora I mean those persons of Scottish birth or descent who are living permanently anywhere other than the Homeland. Although no one can tell how many there are as accurately as one might know, through the latest census, how many people are living in Scotland at the present time, the number in the United States alone is estimated to be at least five times that of the present population of Scotland.

By any reckoning the Scottish Diaspora is vast compared with the Homeland population. Moreover, the latter is by no means any more "purely Scottish" (whatever that might mean) than is the Scottish Diaspora, since modern Scotland has a large number of Irish immigrants and a considerable number of other residents who could not claim as clearly Scottish a lineage as can many Americans and others in the Diaspora.

The difference between Homeland and Diaspora attitudes is profound. Diaspora Scots have been, in the vast majority of cases, thoroughly naturalized and attached to the country of their adoption. While they look with affection (especially perhaps after the second generation) on the Homeland, sometimes even with passionate devotion, their whole life is geared to their adopted land, to its laws, customs, and ways of thought. There is certainly nothing remotely like a Scottish Zionism. They look to Scotland more as an American Catholic looks to Rome: a place of pilgrimage, not a home. No matter how many planeloads of Diaspora Scots descend upon Prestwick Airport every summer, these Scots have almost all returned to America or elsewhere before the first nip of frost. Even those who go over for three months at a time cannot be said to live in the Homeland. And it is where you live that counts; that is what determines your basic outlook on life.

The consequence is obvious. No matter how deep your devotion to the Homeland, you will always be a foreigner to those who inhabit it. Nor will you stay long without having to recognize, however reluctantly, that the Homeland Scot is a foreigner to you. Nevertheless, if you love the Homeland Scots, as do most Americans of Scottish descent, you must be prepared to find the love a bit one-sided. That is by no means to say you will not be warmly welcomed. Most Scots have a kindly disposition toward all their guests. However, the fact that you or your ancestors have left Scotland, and that the exodus has been for Scotland the most unprofitable export she has ever made, will be always before the minds of your hosts, consciously if they know their own history well, unconsciously even if they do not. Most Scots in the Homeland know very little about the history or the character of the Diaspora. They do sense, however, that the Diaspora is a credit to Scotland. They do not blame us. If they did, the relationship might be easier. What makes it awkward is that they blame themselves: not consciously, of course, but, which is psychologically far more potent, unconsciously. So even as the Homeland Scot and his Diaspora guest clink glasses and join in the toast,

Here's tae us. Wha's like us?
Damn few, and they're a' deid,

the Homeland Scot is troubled by the thought that his country is poorer because you or your ancestor left it and gave your Scottishness to an alien land.

Scotland's case is strikingly different from Ireland's. Generally speaking, the Irish were forced by intolerable and enslaving circumstances to emigrate. Of some Scots this was also true, but many could well have stayed. What made them leave was lack of opportunity for the full exercise of their native Scottish enterprise, and with every shipload was exported some more of that most precious quality. With every shipload, therefore, the situation worsened. So your very love for the Homeland is a reproach. Worse still, it is the ultimate reproach. A mother guilty of child abuse can receive no greater punishment than the child's forgiveness and abiding love. The Homeland Scot could take any insult or rebuke you offered him, accepting it with stolid calm or lordly disdain as the case might be; but he cannot take forgiveness and love. He retaliates by calling you sentimental. He chides you for not knowing some trivial detail about his home town when he himself has never even been to Inverness. In short, there is nothing you can do to please him. The love traffic, all protestations to the contrary notwithstanding, tends to be one way.

I happened to be talking recently with a Justice of the Supreme Court of Iowa who confessed that his love of Scotland, where one of his grandparents was born, had become for him an absorbing passion. He had a large collection of books on the country. He could hardly be a mere sentimentalist, this jurist whose daily work consisted of reviewing cases that had come up for an appellate judgment and writing his judicial opinions on them for submission to his colleagues on the Supreme Court bench. He was certainly in no danger of confusing Scotland with Brigadoon. Yet he had never been to the Homeland in his life. Naturally I asked why. He remained silent for a considerable time as if mulling over a difficult case. Then he murmured in a serious and thoughtful whisper: "Perhaps I'm afraid I might be disillusioned."

This reply was so apt that it almost took my breath away. What more eloquent expression could there be of the gulf between the Homeland and the Diaspora? He could not possibly have been disillusioned by the scenery. The pageantry could not have disappointed him. Even if this or that might be less than he had hoped, the total could not but have made the trip worthwhile for one with such a strong sense of his ancestral heritage. Only one thing could have disillusioned a man so deeply in love with Scotland: a negativity in the Homeland Scot. I felt at once that in his discernment of such a possibility he showed a keen judicial mind.

What has brought about that negativity, that dog-in-the-manger attitude that disappoints so many of the Diaspora? Is the British Welfare State to blame? Surely not. An excess of welfare and governmental interference may have aggravated the situation. But the situation is the inevitable result of the letting go, decade after decade, century after century, of the cream of the nation.

It *was* the cream that was lost, constituting the richest export Scotland has ever made, the one for which she has received absolutely nothing in return and can never reap any reward, since no monetary or other such reparation could ever compensate for the loss of generation after generation of a country's most enterprising citizens. This fact is attested in many ways, notably by the singularly successful record of the Scottish Diaspora in the countries in which it has been naturalized. This success is not merely economic but is a moral achievement that has won extraordinary respect. Sir Charles Dilke, an impartial witness indeed, explicitly recognized this a century ago, affirming also that for every Englishman abroad who has prospered "you find ten Scotchmen." Beneath the façade of unconcern that the Homeland Scot affects lies the painful knowledge of all this and of the irreparable loss to the Homeland you or your ancestors have helped to bring about. The Scots do well with their exports of Scotch and tweeds and woolens, and they feel they may do even better with the larger measure of prosperity they expect to ensue upon the North Sea oil now flowing fast. But you: you are the one export that has brought them not merely no profit but inner shame, even a sense of disgrace. By draining the Homeland of its moral vitality you have committed matricide! In their eyes you have killed the Homeland you profess to love as your mother. The mother may go on living out her days in quiet dignity (even modest prosperity, if her hopes are fulfilled) but deserted by the best of her children: a cheerless old age indeed for any mother.

Is it really true that Scotland, notorious for her canniness, has exported such moral and mental riches as if they were of less value than heather or peat? It has been shown over and over again that in salesmanship, in business organization, in industrial research, Scotland has fallen behind England, despite a better record in some areas. Some of these have been already noted in the last chapter. Most educated Scots perceive that in modern Scotland it is not merely that, as everywhere, a prophet is not without honor save in his own land. Among the rank and file of Scots in the Homeland today, a Leonardo would be belittled as a generalist and Schweitzer mocked as a visionary. But was it ever any better? No, the attitude seems to have been much the same in the past. At any rate, we read plenty of complaint along the same lines two hundred years ago. Yet the record of accomplishment in creative science and technology before the effect of the exodus had become visible is astonishing, and no less amazing is the decline in the last fifty years or so. Nor can anyone pretend that conditions for creativity were better than they are now. On the contrary, they were worse: most unpromising, if one thinks in terms of favorable conditions for work. Today the conditions are of course far better.

Consider only a few of the scientific discoveries and technological inventions of Scotsmen between, say, 1750 and 1900. We certainly cannot mention even all the important ones but must be content with random examples. Joseph Black, who discovered carbon dioxide in 1754 and specific heat in 1760, founded the first chemical society in the world. (This was at a time when Scotland had barely recovered from the Jacobite rising. Edinburgh's old city moat was drained only in 1760, and not till 1772 was a wooden bridge erected to do the work of the present North Bridge. Edinburgh was still a cramped medieval town.) Thomas Melvil discovered the basis of spectrum analysis in 1752, and in the same year John Pringle demonstrated a relation between putrefaction and the spread of disease. In 1769 John Robinson proved the inverse square law in mechanics. (John Napier had discovered logarithms in 1614.) In 1776 James Lind showed lemon juice to be the best available cure for scurvy. Robert Whytt discovered the sympathetic nervous system in 1764. About 1775 William Meikle developed the first successful threshing machine, and the following year Patrick Ferguson invented the breech-loading rifle. Daniel Rutherford discovered nitrogen in 1772. In 1780 John Brown discredited the time-honored practice of bloodletting. In 1785 James Hutton expounded the uniformitarian theory of the formation of the earth. Thomas Charles Hope discovered strontium in 1792, and five years later William Cruickshank discovered the ovum in mammals. To John Loudon McAdam (1756–1836) we owe the macadamized roads that bear his name.

To James Watt (1736–1819) must be attributed the invention of the steam engine that made possible the railroad systems that transformed the world. He came of humble parentage. According to a persistent legend, he was watching, as a little boy, a kettle coming to the boil on the kitchen fire. If so small a quantity of water could raise the heavy iron lid of that kettle, why should not a correspondingly large quantity move a truck? As he was pondering this, the kettle boiled over, making a mess, whereupon his overwrought mother came by and "wahrmed his ear-rs," calling him an "idle, lazy loon." The story may well be a later fabrication, but by whom? No doubt by someone who in later times perceived how plentiful had been creative genius in the Scotland of those days and how cheaply rated.

The concept of motion pictures was foreshadowed in 1816 when David Brewster, who two years earlier had discovered the polarization of light, invented the kaleidoscope. In 1831 Robert Brown, a botanist, discovered the cell nucleus. Alexander Forsyth invented the percussion lock in 1800. In 1812 Henry Bell built the first steamship in Europe, the "Comet." James Jardine was the first to determine the mean level of the sea, and Thomas Henderson was first to measure the distance to a star, Alpha Centauri. Charles Mackintosh, when he developed the process of rubberizing fabrics in 1823, gave us the raincoat that still bears his name: a mackintosh. In 1827 Robert Wilson invented the screw propeller. In 1834 James Chalmers printed samples of perforated adhesive postage stamps. In 1828 James Beaumont Neilson invented the hot blast furnace and William Nicol the polarizing prism that is named for him. The following year James Esdaile used mesmerism in surgery. A decade later Kilpatrick Macmillan made the first bicycle. William Fairbairn built the first iron ship in 1830, and in 1850 the first crane. John Goodsir discovered the nature and function of cells. The seismometer was invented by James Forbes in 1842.

To James Young Simpson we owe the use of chloroform, which in 1847 initiated the revolution in medicine that anesthesia was to bring about. Lord Lister initiated another revolution in medicine: the principle of asepsis in surgical and hospital practice. (The well-known mouthwash is named for him.) Lord Kelvin not only discovered the laws of thermodynamics but also invented the tidal gauge and improved the compass. James Nasmyth invented the steam hammer in 1839 and John Stenhouse the gas mask in 1860. James Bruce Thomson pioneered criminal psychology. Peter Guthrie Tait laid the foundation of the kinetic theory of gasses. James Young founded the petroleum industry. After John Dunlop had used rubber hose on bicycle wheels, William Thomson invented the rubber tire in 1845, the pneumatic tire in 1867, and the fountain pen in 1849. Alexander Graham Bell invented the telephone in 1876. Edward Forbes made oceanography feasible.

That is certainly no more than a random list of a few inventions and discoveries by Scotsmen of that period. Of course scores of others have been omitted, some of them equally important. The list could fill a book and would be tedious.

What of our own twentieth century? In 1924 John Logie Baird invented television; in 1923 John Macleod, with another scientist, discovered insulin; in 1928 Alexander Fleming discovered what was to make penicillin possible. But by that time the flow had already shown signs of drying up. Soon it had all but evaporated. At least it has ceased to be remarkable compared with that of other nations.

All the names I have mentioned are of native Scots. Except for Patrick Ferguson (who was killed in North Carolina), Bell (who died in Nova Scotia), and one or two others who may have died south of the Scottish border, all also died in the Homeland.

We cannot escape the fact that the cream of Scotland's greatest resource has been exported, although Diaspora Scots obviously cannot say that in the Homeland, at any rate not in a loud voice. Why did Scotland let that happen? The answer is not easy, for the blame cannot be placed squarely on one group, nor can the tragedy be explained by the presence of a single circumstance. Nevertheless, there is one fact that should be carefully examined by anyone who seeks a full explanation. We have seen that the Scots have conspicuously cherished the family, which is indeed a stabilizing institution. That is the fair side of the coin. The dark side is that as a result they have attached too much weight to hereditary stock. The Scots, despite the democratic tradition they helped to foster, developed an elitism of their own: a family elitism, which may be the most pernicious of all. Over and over again, especially in patrician circles but even among people of very humble circumstances, one still hears: "He comes of a good *stock;* he's a Sinclair" (or, of course, a MacLeod or whatever) as though one were talking of an Angus bull prized for its breeding prowess. Heredity, like any other aspect of our environment (for, of course, heredity is part of that), plays an important role in determining our looks. Cattle farmers rightly watch it closely in trying to produce the best beef. It is very far indeed from determining creative genius. The Scots, lip service to the contrary, have seldom fully recognized this. They have seen that talent may come out of a cottage, but on the whole they have so highly valued the family as to look to heredity for the great qualities of leadership and creativity.

The Diaspora Scot should also remember that the Homeland Scots have been for the better part of three centuries so closely tied to England that they could not conceivably have escaped developing some English prejudices as well as their own. The English have a most fertile supply of these. By the time you have both sorts of prejudice working together, prejudice hangs over all things like a funeral pall. The Scots have acquired some of the English aggressiveness in business without always matching it with the qualities needed to make it work. They have acquired much of the notorious English insularity without the very peculiar qualities that made English insularity work long before the British Empire emerged. So we must not expect to find the Scots of today with either their own warts or their own beauties in a state of pristine purity.

One of the great virtues of the Scots of the Diaspora has been their adaptability. This does not mean that they have been eminently assimilable, as have been the Irish and the Italians, for instance. But their adaptability has made them look assimilated. A young Scots couple who came last year straight out of Muthil or Tobermory to take up life in Nebraska or Tennessee will be as likely as not to be seen sauntering down Fifth Avenue next year with the nonchalance of Americans who came over on the *Mayflower*. Their relaxed adaptability captures all hearts before they have had an opportunity to exhibit their even greater qualities. Their adaptability may spring from the fact that to them London and Los Angeles, Bombay and Paris, are all the same because they are not Scotland. No matter. It endears them nevertheless to their hosts from the first day. The Diaspora Scot who has seen this in recent immigrants may expect to find it in the Homeland. If so, he is likely to be much disappointed. *He* has changed; they have not. Most Homeland Scots today are not only unadaptable, they do not want to be otherwise.

All this may sound a little depressing, but it need not be if one is prepared for it and ignores the negativity somewhat as one learns to ignore billboards and television commercials. The more enlightened Homeland Scots are well aware of the disease and live with it rather comfortably. Why not you? It should not be difficult for you, who know and love your great heritage.

Also bear in mind that till recently the Homeland Scot could plead one genuine extenuating circumstance for some of his outlook. As recently as the Fifties there were at least as many automobiles in Southern California as in all of Britain. The average Scot had little opportunity for travel within his own country. In many cases he, and oftener still she, hardly ever went more than twenty or thirty miles from home. Cicely Hamilton, an English observer writing in the Thirties, noted that Dundonians grumbled if they were asked to live beyond walking distance of their work, even to get better housing a short bus ride away. Although all that has changed, attitudes die hard, and for a Glaswegian never to have seen Aberdeen or Inverness is usually accounted hardly more remarkable than that a San Franciscan should never have been to Hawaii or Japan. The upshot is that the Homeland Scots, for all they may talk of Scotland, often know less of it than many a Diaspora Scot gets to know of it in a month. Yet almost all Homeland Scots, of whatever station in life, will chide (not to say rant at) their Diaspora counterparts for not seeing Scotland the way they do. How could they? Not even the resident physician, let alone visiting friends, knows the hospital the way the patient knows it.

If the Diaspora Scot can get over such hurdles, the rest is easy. Beneath the curt and laconic speech of many Scots lies a unique kindliness that the Scots of the Homeland are half afraid to show only because they are afraid their own warmth will carry them

away. Once you see that and set it in the context of your own
devotion to your ancestral land, you will fall in love with the
Homeland Scot almost as much as you have already fallen in love
with the Homeland itself.

Once that happens, Scotland your mother will never let you go.
You will have been captured forever in the arms of her encompassing love. The irritants will chafe no more than your mother's
Harris tweed coat. Her love will haunt you wherever you go. Even
in moments of exasperation, you will know that you have found
your way home at last and that your heart will be forever there,
although your body and your brain be firmly established in Chicago or Berne.

Robert Louis Stevenson, a literary genius as thoroughly Scottish as Scott or Burns, whose travels took him to Monterey and
to the island of Samoa that he came to love so much and where
he died, wrote for himself an epitaph beloved by all who have
found freedom:

> Under the wide and starry sky,
> Dig the grave and let me lie.
> Glad did I live and gladly die,
> And I laid me down with a will.
>
> This be the verse you grave for me:
> *Here he lies where he longed to be;*
> *Home is the sailor, home from the sea,*
> *And the hunter home from the hill.*

Yet even as you may wish to make the epitaph your own, for use
wherever you die, in Antarctica or Athens, Siberia or the Sahara,
Park Avenue or Bel Air, your heart, on its last beat, will go home
to Scotland.

APPENDIX
A

Some Gaelic and Norse Elements
in Scottish Place-Names

Note: Gaelic is found in a great many Scottish place-names, whose meanings are therefore much more easily understood if one has even a slight acquaintance with the Gaelic words they contain. For instance, Tighnabruaich (a small town in the Kyles of Bute): *tigh* (house), *na* (of the), *bruaich* (bank or slope); Drumnadrochit (a village in Glen Urquhart near Loch Ness): *druim* (back), *na* (of the), *drochaid* (bridge); Inverness (capital of the Highlands): *inbhir* (mouth of [the River Ness]). Terms may be slightly anglicized, as in *inver* for *inbhir*, *drum* for *druim*, and *ben* for *beinn* (mountain). Other place-names, however, are of Norse origin, and some Norse roots (e.g., *voe*) are included in the list. For a much more comprehensive list, see *Place Names on Maps of Scotland and Wales*, published by the Ordnance Survey, Southampton, 1973.

aber, mouth of a river
ald, stream
ard, aird, height, promontory
bagh, bhaig, bay
baile, bhaile, village
ban, bhain, fair, white
bard, bhaird, meadow
beag, bheag, small
bealach, mountain pass
beinn, ben, mountain
beith, birch
beull, mouth
binnean, peaked hill
blar, bhlair, plain
bo, cow

brae, bread, height
bruach, bruaich, bank, height, slope
buidhe, yellow
cairn, heap of stones
caol, strait
cas, steep
clach, cloiche, stone
clachan, stone-built hamlet
cladach, shore
cleuch, ravine
clunie, meadow
coill, coille, choille, wood
coir, hollow
creag, craig, rock

cruach, heap
dearg, red
drochaid, bridge
druim, drum, back
dubh, dhubh, black
dun, duin, fort, castle
eilean, island
esk, uisge, water (same root as "whisky")
fad, fhad, long
gair, gearr, short
glas, green
gorm, ghorm, green-blue
inch, innis, island
inbhir, inver, mouth of
ken, kin, head
knock, little hill
kyle, strait
lag, hollow
lairig, pass
lax, salmon (Norse)
liath, grey
linn, port
lios, garden
lomond, beacon
lyng, heather (Norse)
machar, machair, sandy plain
mam, round hill
marn, meall, round hill

monadh, hill
mor, mhor, big
na, of the
ob, oban, bay
oe, island (Norse)
raineach, rannoch, fern
ramh, raimh, oar
riabhach, riach, greyish
rudha, promontory
sean, old
sgor, sgur, scuir, rocky peak (Norse)
sron, stron, point, nose
stac, cone-shaped hill
steinn, stone (Norse)
stob, point
strath, valley
tairbeart, narrow isthmus
thing, ting, ding, assembly (Norse)
tigh, tay, house
tir, land
tober, well
tom, hill
uamh, weem, cave
uig, bay
uisge, water (see "esk")
vik, wik, creek (Norse)
voe, narrow bay (Norse)
yel, sandy slope (Norse)

B

Sovereigns of England from William I and of Scotland from Malcolm III to the Union of the Crowns, and Some Other Historical Notes

England		Scotland	
William I	1066–1087	Malcolm III	
		(Canmore)	1057–1093
William II	1087–1100	Donald Bàn	1093
Henry I	1100–1135	Duncan II	1094
Stephen	1135–1154	Donald Bàn	
		(restored)	1094–1097
Henry II	1154–1189	Edgar	1097–1107
Richard I	1189–1199	Alexander I	1107–1124
John	1199–1216	David I	1124–1153
Henry III	1216–1272	Malcolm IV	
		(the Maiden)	1153–1165
Edward I	1272–1307	William I	
		(the Lion)	1165–1214
Edward II	1307–1327	Alexander II	1214–1249
Edward III	1327–1377	Alexander III	1249–1286
Richard II	1377–1399	Margaret	
		(Maid of Norway)	1286–1290
Henry IV	1399–1413	John Baliol	1292–1296*
Henry V	1413–1422	Robert I	
		(the Bruce)	1306–1329*
Henry VI	1422–1461	David II	1329–1371

*Intervals between reigns attributable to political disputes or unrest.

England		Scotland	
Edward IV	1461–1483	Robert II (Stewart)	1371–1390
Edward V	1483	Robert III	1390–1406
Richard III	1483–1485	James I	1406–1437
Henry VII	1485–1509	James II	1437–1460
Henry VIII	1509–1547	James III	1460–1488
Edward VI	1547–1553	James IV	1488–1513
Jane	1553	James V	1513–1542
Mary I	1553–1558	Mary ("Queen of Scots")	1542–1567
Elizabeth I	1558–1603	James VI	1567–1603

At the Union of the Crowns in 1603, James VI of Scotland acceded
as King of Great Britain and Ireland.

MNEMONIC

For enabling us to get the events and developments of a nation's history
into perspective, nothing is more useful than a knowledge of the chrono-
logical order of the reigns of those who have ruled it. In my schooldays,
on the eve of examinations in English history, we resorted to the following doggerel lines as an effective mnemonic:

> Willie, Willie, Harry, Ste,
> Harry, Dick, John, Harry 3.
>
> One two three Neds,
> Richard 2.
>
> Harry 4, 5, 6, then who?
> Edward 4, 5, Dick the Bad,
> Harries twain, then Ned the Lad.
>
> Mary, Bessie, James the Vain,
> Charlie, Charlie, James again.
>
> William, Mary, Ann Gloria,
> Four Georges, William and Victoria.

I have never heard of one for Scotland but would suggest the following:

Canmore, Don, Dunc, Don restore,
Edgar, Lex, Dave, Malc once more.

Bill the Lion, Lex no worse,
Alex 3 and Marge the Norse.

Baliol, Bob, Dave, Bob (again!)
Five Jims, Mary, James the Vain.

C

Important Dates in Scottish History

The following key dates should help get Scotland's story in perspective:

80–500	Roman invasions to the north of Hadrian's Wall between the Solway and the Tyne. They left little mark. By about the end of this period Picts, Scots, Britons, and Angles had all settled in Scotland.
563	Saint Columba's landing on Iona began Scotland's conversion to Christianity.
844	The kingdoms of the Picts and the Scots united under Kenneth MacAlpin. By this time had come a Norse conquest of Orkney and Shetland and Norse settlements in the Western Isles.
1018	Malcolm defeated a Northumbrian army and became the first King of Scots, ruling a territory roughly coextensive with the modern Scottish mainland.
1068	Malcolm III (Canmore) married Margaret, a Saxon princess, who introduced Roman innovations into the Celtic Church, English speech and customs, and elements of the feudal system.
1263	Under Alexander III, the Scots won a victory over the Norse at Largs, leading to a return of the Western Isles to Scotland.
1291–1328	Wars of Independence over the English King's claim to feudal overlordship over the King of Scots, leading to the Scots' entry into what is now called "the Auld Alliance" with France, England's traditional foe, with which, along with other European countries, Scotland had already established extensive trade and other associations. Bruce, crowned King of Scots in 1306, defeated the English at Bannockburn in 1314, leading to the Treaty of Northamp-

242

ton in 1328, formally establishing Scotland's independence.

1470	Orkney and Shetland annexed to Scotland.
1503–1513	James IV of Scotland married Margaret Tudor of England in 1503. In 1513 he attacked England (to support France), resulting in the disastrous defeat of the Scots at Flodden in 1513.
1542	Accession of the infant Mary, Queen of Scots, daughter of James V. She was executed in England by Queen Elizabeth in 1587.
1560	Scottish Reformation under John Knox.
1603	Union of the Crowns of Scotland and England under James VI of Scotland and I of Great Britain. The two countries continued, however, with separate parliaments and as separate states.
1638–1690	Scotland's struggles between Presbyterianism and Episcopacy. In 1638 nobles and common people alike joined in signing the National Covenant against episcopal government in the Church. During the Civil War in England (1649–1660), the Scots supported Parliament against the King at first but then turned to the royalist cause. In 1651 Charles II was crowned at Scone. Cromwell's soldiers invaded Scotland and subjugated the country for nine years. At the restoration, Charles II restored episcopacy. Many Covenanters were martyred. At last, under William and Mary, Presbyterianism was reestablished by law as the national religion of Scotland.
1707	The Union of Parliaments.
1715	First Jacobite rising.
1745	Second Jacobite rising.
1746	Defeat of the Jacobites at Culloden. Kilt banned.
1782	Right to wear the kilt restored.

APPENDIX

D

Some Annual Events

Note: The months listed are in some cases approximate and of course many more sporting, musical and other important events take place whose dates vary. The Scottish Tourist Board, 23 Ravelston Terrace, Edinburgh, publishes an annual brochure, *Events in Scotland*, providing exact dates for a large number of events in the year covered.

JANUARY

Curling	Nationwide
Burning of the Clavie	Burghead (Doune Hill)
Soccer	Nationwide
Robert Burns's Birthday (25th)	Nationwide
Up Helly Aa	Lerwick, Shetland

FEBRUARY

Scottish Dairy Show	Glasgow
Curling	Nationwide
Soccer	Nationwide
Callants' Ball Game	Jedburgh

MARCH

Spring Flower Show	Edinburgh
Soccer	Nationwide
Lacrosse	Nationwide
Hockey	Nationwide
Whuppity Scoorie	Lanark

APRIL

Drama Festival opens (continues into October)	Pitlochry, Perthshire
Rugby Sevens	The Borders
Royal Scottish Academy opens	Edinburgh

Kate Kennedy Pageant	St. Andrews
Carnegie Festival	Dunfermline
Links Market	Kirkcaldy

MAY

May Day celebration (traditionally, girls wash faces in early morning dew)	Arthur's Seat, Edinburgh
Skye Week	Portree, Skye
Festival	Stirling
Golf Week	Nairn
Anglers' Fortnight	Pitlochry
Music Festival	Aberdeen
Agricultural Show	Cupar Fife
Royal and Ancient meeting	St. Andrews
General Assembly of the Kirk	Edinburgh
Golf	Nationwide
Fishing	Nationwide
Beltane Festival with Crowning of the Queen	Peebles

JUNE

Riding of the Marches	Selkirk; Linlithgow
Common Riding	Hawick; Selkirk
Beltane Festival (with horse racing and other sports afterward)	Peebles
Guid Neighbours' Day	Dumfries
Lanimer Day	Lanark
Piping Society Competitions	Drumnadrochit, Inverness
Festival	Melrose
Braw Lads' Gathering	Galashiels
Gaelic Mod	Oban
Festival of Music, Art and Drama	Montrose
Agricultural Show	Skye
Welcome Week	Arran
Pageant Week	Kirkcaldy
Sea Angling Festival	Eyemouth
Bannockburn Day	Bannockburn
Highland and other games	Perth; Alloa; Markinch; Ceres; Cupar Fife; Crook of Devon; Aberdeen; Forfar; Kirkconnel

JULY

Riding of the Marches	Annan
Summer Festival	Duns, Berwickshire
Common Riding	Langholm
Masque	St. Andrews
Braw Lads Gathering	Galashiels
Horse Fair	St. Boswell's
Scottish sheep-dog trials	Various places
Golf	Nationwide
Fishing	Nationwide
Civic Week	Castle Douglas
Crowning of Carberry Queen	Leven, Fife
Highland and other games	Lochearnhead; Kelso; Dingwall; Strathmiglo; Oxton; Alva; Airth; Fort William; Dunbeath; Jedburgh; Luss; Balloch; Stonehaven
Gala Week	Wick

AUGUST

International Festival (music, drama, film, etc.)	Edinburgh
Military Tattoo	Edinburgh
Riding of the Marches	Sanquhar (pronounced *sangker*)
Common Riding	Lauder
Cleikum Ceremony	Innerleithen
Festival	Invercauld
Gala Week	Bonar Bridge
Cowal Highland Gathering	Dunoon
Scottish Tennis Championship	St. Andrews
Highland and other games	Dornoch; Ballater; Aberlour; Drumnadrochit; Bridge of Earn; Inverkeithing; Taynuilt; Strathpeffer; Morebattle; Nairn; Strathdon; Crieff; Murrayfield, Edinburgh; Kinlochrannoch; Nethy Bridge, Milngavie (pronounced *milgye*, accented on second syllable); Ballater; Whittinghame;

Glenfinnan; Strathallan;
Mallaig; Invergordon

Bon Accord Festival	Aberdeen
Horse Show	Edinburgh
Arts Festival	Dunbar

SEPTEMBER

Royal Highland Gathering	Braemar
Flower Show	Edinburgh
Sheep-dog Trials	The Borders
Royal and Ancient meeting	St. Andrews
Highland and other games	Aboyne; Dunblane; Pitlochry; Oban; Birnam; Shotts

OCTOBER

National Gaelic Mod (An Comunn Gaidhealach)	Edinburgh
Border Shepherds' Show	Yethold
Dog Show (championship)	Various places
Halloween: the "Guisers"	Nationwide

NOVEMBER

Motor Show	Glasgow
Freemasons' Torchlight Procession	Melrose
St. Andrew's Day (30th)	Nationwide

DECEMBER

Hogmanay (New Year's Eve) with "first-footing" and other specifically Scottish customs	Nationwide

E

Heraldic and Miscellaneous Notes

THE national flag of Scotland is the Saltire: a white St. Andrew's cross (**X**) on a blue background. In Scottish hearts it creates feelings of pride, warmth, and general satisfaction.

The red lion rampant on a field of gold is the flag that pertains to the Sovereign and is flown from royal residences and elsewhere to symbolize royalty. It is *not* for general use.

Such matters and all that pertains to the use of heraldic emblems (coats of arms and other insignia) are controlled by the Lord Lyon King of Arms (the Scottish counterpart of the Earl Marshall in England) and lie within the jurisdiction of his court, which has authority to prosecute for misuse. The authority has actually been exercised within recent times in some flagrant cases. It does not extend abroad, however, and the display of erroneous or phony arms in places such as Wisconsin and Tennessee is unlikely to result in your extradition for punishment by Lyon, as he is called for short. Lyon is also the authority to whom application is made for grants of personal arms.

The patron saint of Scotland is St. Andrew.

The national emblem of Scotland is the thistle (corresponding to the English rose, the Irish harp, and the Welsh leek), which is fitting for so prickly a people as the Scots. According to legend, a Danish invader stepped on a bed of thistles and cried out in pain, to the delight of the Scots whom his cries had alerted.

The national motto is *Nemo me impune lacessit:* "No one provokes me with impunity" or, more colloquially, "Wha daur meddle wi' me?" ("Who dare interfere with me?") or again "Touch me gin ye daur!" ("Touch me if you dare!"). It is also the motto of the Most Ancient and Most Noble Order of the Thistle, Scotland's counterpart of the English Order of the Garter.

The Scottish Regalia, anciently called "The Honours of Scotland," consist of the Crown, the Sceptre, and the Sword of State. The Crown was remodeled by James V in 1540 but is of greater antiquity, although its exact date is unknown. The gold in it came partly or wholly from Scottish mines. It is adorned with numerous stones. The Sceptre was presented to James IV in 1494 by Pope Alexander VI along with a gold rose. It consists of a rod of gilded silver, hexagonal in form, with a head flanked by dolphins between which are three small figures (Mary with the Infant Jesus, St. James, and St. Andrew), surmounted by a globe of rock crystal that is in turn surmounted by a small oval globe on top of which is a Scottish pearl. The Sword of State was presented to James IV by Pope Julius II in 1507. Both handle and scabbard are richly ornamented. For a succinct but detailed account of the remarkable history of the Scottish Regalia, including the episode alluded to in Chapter 9, see W. D. Collier, *The Scottish Regalia* (second edition). Edinburgh: Her Majesty's Stationery Office, 1970.

Scotland has no official national anthem, but traditionally "Scots Wha Hae" has been used. Since the tune is somewhat lugubrious, the stirring alternative, "Scotland the Brave," has attained immense and much deserved popularity. As a finale for reunions and other festive occasions, notably Hogmanay (New Year's Eve) gatherings, "Auld Lang Syne" is traditional. All verses should be sung and with gusto, and at the words "weary fut" the foot should be stamped vehemently on the floor. The "s" in "syne" is hard as in "hiss," never soft as in in "rosy" unless you want to be put down as English and therefore presumptively effete, which is always a pity in Scotland since it excludes so many nice people from the popularity that they would otherwise be likely to attain. Nor should one sing "For the sake of auld lang syne," but simply "For auld lang syne."

If one might speak of a national grace before meals, it would be the one attributed to Burns and called "The Selkirk Grace," which is:

> Some hae meat and canna eat,
> And some wad eat that want it,
> But we hae meat and we can eat,
> And sae the Lord be thankit.

A popular good-luck symbol is the Luckenbooth brooch, which before the 1745 rising was sold beside St. Giles' Cathedral, Edinburgh. Exchanged between lovers on bethrothal, it was also pinned on the shawl of the first baby, so that mischievous fairies would not steal the child. Over the brooch is a crown, which is held to be a symbol of Mary, Queen of Scots.

If you should wish to send Christmas greetings in Gaelic, you would write: "Nollaig chrideil agus bliadhnu mhath ur," meaning "A merry Christmas and a good New Year." More people would understand you, however, were you to write or say, as a New Year's greeting: "Lang may yer lum reek, and may ne'er a wee moosie leave yer meal-poke wi' a tear in his e'e," which means "Long may your chimney smoke, and may never a little mouse leave your larder with a tear in his eye." Philistines who ask silly questions such as "Why should the mouse be there in the first place?" simply do not understand the magnanimity of the Scottish heart.

Those who wish to pursue in greater depth studies on any Scottish topic may be directed to bibliographical sources such as:

A. Mitchell and C. G. Cash, *A Contribution to the Bibliography of Scottish Topography.* Edinburgh: T. & A. Constable, for the Scottish History Society, 1917.
P. D. Hancock, *A Bibliography of Works Relating to Scotland, 1916–1950.* Edinburgh: Edinburgh University Press, 1959–60.

Many of the great American university and other libraries have large holdings of books on Scottish topics.

APPENDIX
F

Cuisine

CONTRARY to a prevalent opinion, Scottish cuisine can be excellent. The best place to find it is in well-to-do private homes and good social clubs. Only a few decades ago, finding a restaurant open when you wanted one was like finding a parking place in Manhattan. But that has changed a good deal, although even now you should not expect to find a meal in the smaller towns any time you happen to want one. In recent years international restaurants have sprouted in Edinburgh and Glasgow. By far the best counsel is to eat Scottish fare, which at its best is delectable.

As to be expected in this land of paradox, you will be told that haggis is the national dish, yet you will very rarely find it on a menu unless you are at some festive affair such as a Burns supper, at which it is as *de rigueur* as the flag on a State Capitol. It is ceremoniously addressed in Burns's own words:

> Fair fa' yer honest sonsie face,
> Great chieftain o' the puddin' race.

It is made of ground ox liver, heart, and kidney mixed with oatmeal, suet, onions, and other ingredients stuffed in a bag. Most people find it edible; nobody finds it by any means indispensable. You need never meet it. It is really more of a civil sacrament than a national food.

For breakfast you are likely to be offered porridge made from fresh oatmeal and served with salt, never sugar (unless they take you for English). You might also have bacon and eggs or a kipper or finnan haddie and perhaps oatcakes. Coffee is used more than most Americans tend to expect, but tea is still the national nonalcoholic beverage.

Tea is almost always served with cream or milk. You first pour boiling water into a teapot, which should be made of pottery, not silver, although transgressors abound. You then empty out the water and immediately put in one teaspoonful of tea for every cup you will need, plus one "for the pot." Thereupon you no less immediately pour boiling (not almost boiling) water and let the brew stand under a tea cosy for four minutes. It may then be poured into cups into which milk has been poured already. Before pouring the tea, the cup should be covered with a strainer—sterling silver if you want to be elegant. If you think this makes the Japanese tea ceremony kindergarten stuff, you may be almost right. At any rate the results are admirable, which is fortunate, since tea is drunk at any hour of the day and in any circumstances. Tea pouring is the only act you can always perform in Scotland in certainty that you cannot be acting improperly.

Fish are plentiful in Scotland and usually very good. Finnan haddies are so called from the town of Findon, Aberdeenshire. They are haddocks hung up a chimney over a peat fire and are to be distinguished from smokies, which are haddocks prepared by smoking in the Arbroath manner over birch or oak chips. Two hundred years ago salmon were so plentiful that servants' contracts sometimes contained a clause providing that the servants would not be expected to eat them oftener than so many times a week. Fresh salmon is by no means so common today, but it is certainly the fish to order when it is offered. If you want the Scottish counterpart of a hot-dog joint, your best bet is a fish-and-chip shop. You might prefer to omit the chips, which are sometimes fried in fat that looks as though it had been in continuous use from the time it was freshly poured in Malcolm Canmore's kitchen.

Meat is not often cooked to suit the American palate, but it is usually excellent if you can accustom yourself to the way of cooking it. The Scots like meat very well done. Steak and kidney pie is deservedly a favorite. In upper-class houses you may be served wild fowl, especially grouse and pheasant. Vegetarian food can be obtained by those who prefer it. Scots of all classes tend to eat less salad than Americans and far more desserts, which they used before England did, having borrowed the idea from the French. The Scottish passion for sweets and candies in every form is insatiable. All the best pastries, including shortbread and black currant bun, are very delicious and outrageously fattening, so if you are overconcerned about your waistline you had better cancel your plane reservation to Scotland. Resistance to such goodies is too much to expect of mortal flesh.

Homemade griddle scones (usually called girdle scones in Scotland, to the puzzlement of many an American lady) are also delicious. They are served with butter and jam and are highly recommended by tailors and dressmakers since after a few weeks of such food you will have to give them an order. Strawberries and raspberries are plentiful in season and are also irresistible, being served with fresh cream. The cream is no less a dressmaker's delight.

You may have heard of pease brose. You are unlikely to be offered it, for which you need feel by no means aggrieved. It is made of crushed yellow peas mixed with boiling water and is splendid if you plan on plowing a few fields before lunch.

Whisky is a matter too sacred to be treated in a general appendix. A special one will be devoted to it later. Although it is of course the traditional drink of the Scots, it has become too expensive for the average person nowadays and has been supplanted to a great extent by tea and beer. Beer should be approached with respect: most of it is much more potent than the brands generally favored in the United States. Remember, too, that the imperial pint used in Scotland contains twenty ounces, not sixteen as in the American pint. Two pints of Edinburgh beer can be a heady brew. Wines are all imported and are either poor in quality or very expensive. There exists a tendency in Scotland to treat them as though they cannot be served otherwise than in fine crystal, and one is made to feel one should don a coronet before drinking them. If you are accustomed to very good inexpensive wines for everyday meals, you might as well steer clear of the whole business so as not to feel as though you were eating hamburger off a gold plate. If you simply must have Château Margaux or something of that order, you might as well emplane for France rather than order it in Scotland.

APPENDIX
G
Whisky

"SCOTCH" is the international name for what is sold from Greenland's icy mountains to India's coral strand. If you ask for it under that name in Scotland you will be understood, but you will get along better there if you simply ask for whisky or, in pub or bar, "a half." Your host may invite you to have "a dram" or "a wee dram." In the latter case you should not take the adjective too literally. It is a mere linguistic convention. Whisky is sometimes poetically called "usquebaugh."

The word "whisky" or "usquebaugh" comes from the Gaelic *uisge beatha,* meaning literally "water of life" *(aqua vitae).* No one knows exactly how long it has been used in the Homeland, whence it is nowadays so widely shipped. It is mentioned in the Scottish Exchequer Rolls in 1494 but is of much greater antiquity than that, having been very possibly brought with Christianity from Ireland by St. Columba. It may well date earlier still. Some Scots might go so far as to decry as pedantic all attempts to trace its origin, on the ground that exercises of this kind diminish the opportunities for practicing the art of drinking it, an art they reverence more than mere scholarly research.

Most whiskies consumed throughout the world are blended from two kinds of whisky: malt and grain. Malt whisky is made from malted barley, by the pot still process; grain whisky is made from a combination of malted barley with unmalted barley and maize, by the patent still process. In the process of making pure malt whisky, four distinct stages are recognized. First, the barley is soaked and spread out to germinate. Then it is dried in a kiln. Second, the dried malt is ground and mixed with hot water, so as to form a sweet liquid. This is the mashing stage. Third, yeast is added to convert the sugar into alcohol. Fourth, the liquid is heated to a vapor that rises up the still and, having passed into the cooling plant, condenses. Two distillations are needed.

Now that the whisky has been produced it must be matured. For this, oak casks are used. The best malt whiskies are allowed to mature for fifteen years or more. Malt whisky has a very different taste from the blended whiskies commonly drunk all over the world. A few distilleries, such as Glenlivet, export some bottles of malt whisky, and it may sometimes be bought at duty-free export shops at the airports. Most of it, however, is used for blending, an art that entails knowledge of how best to mix whiskies produced at the various distilleries, each of whose products is affected by water, soil, and other local conditions. Generally speaking, water in most parts of the Homeland is exceptionally good—and water is a very important part of the total process.

Some decades ago, at one of the distilleries in the Glenlivet area (one of the very best for the finest whiskies), a memorable error occurred. Someone inadvertently turned a tap the wrong way, sending two weeks' produce of the sacred liquid into a neighboring stream. According to reports at the time, which in the nature of the case are likely to have been subjected to imaginative ornamentation, the cattle, once they had staggered ashore, danced an elegant shantruse. The demand for milk rose rapidly.

If you are drinking cheap whisky you may put ice in it if you feel you must, with soda or what you will. Good whisky, however, ought to be consumed straight. After all, the water is such an important element that to pollute it with the admixture of anything is accounted sacrilegious, or at the very least like flavoring fresh salmon with canned salmon paste.

Where whisky is used for purely medicinal purposes, additives are permitted. Whisky diluted with hot water and flavored with lemon juice and sugar is called a "hot toddy" and is an effective and widely used remedy for colds and the like. Athol brose is made with whisky to which heather honey, cream, and some oatmeal have been added, making a pleasant drink. Such concoctions, however, do not constitute whisky drinking. They are merely medicinal aids or culinary adjuncts, not sacramental. By the way, whisky is the proper accompaniment for the haggis.

Drambuie, a whisky liqueur, is used as an after-dinner drink. Whisky is used anytime. Were it not so heavily taxed it would be used much oftener.

The simplest and most general Highland toast is: "Slainte mhah" (pronounced approximately *slantchi va*), meaning "Good health!" A more elaborate one is: "Slainte na Ban-righ agus na cuideachd gu leir" (even more approximately pronounced *slantchi na bannree agus na kootchach gu lehr*), which means "A health to the Queen and all the company!" I would strongly recommend, however, that ambition be curbed. Many educated Scots will understand the first of these toasts even if your pronunciation is poor; but the second, even if your diction were to be impeccable, might well lead the average Homeland Scot to the unjust conclusion that you were showing off your skill in Hawaiian or Iroquois. The literature on whisky is considerable. For an extensive treatment, see Brian Murphy, *The World Book of Whiskey*. New York: Rand McNally, 1979. It is informative, but it should not be carried about obtrusively in Scotland, since it spells "Whiskey" the Irish way. You would not wish to be guilty of indecency. You need have no such misgivings in using a more modest little pamphlet by Iain Cameron Taylor, *Highland Whisky*. Inverness: An Comunn Gaidhealach, 1968.

APPENDIX

H

Scots Law

EVEN by the time of Wallace and Bruce, Scots law was recognizably different from English law. After then its development proceeded on nationalist lines. Feudal law persisted with elements of Roman and medieval canon law, but the Scots consciously ignored English law and looked instead to the continental European centers of legal learning for their inspiration: Bologna, Pisa, Paris, Orleans, Leyden, and Utrecht. In such ways the Scots lawyers came more and more under the influence of Roman law, which appealed to them and has left its mark ever since.

The publication of Viscount Stair's *Institutions* in 1681 provided the Scots lawyers with a systematized presentation of their legal learning. It is still a basic work, supplemented by Erskine's *Institute* in 1773, though not much used. Although with the Union of 1707 came inevitably some English influences, the continental European traditions that had already deeply affected the development of the legal system of Scotland remained.

Scots law today is in important ways fundamentally different from English law; nevertheless they have come closer. Traditionally, the Scots have preferred principle to precedent, but under English influence have come to follow English practice here and have also rejected to a great extent the large-scale codifications characteristic of continental systems. In such matters as modern business law, Scots lawyers must rely, of course, on the same "black letter law" as the English. American lawyers see similarities in practice between Scots and English law where both systems differ from their own, such as the distinction between two branches of the profession: solicitors and members of the Bar. The latter, who have the sole right of audience in the higher courts, are called barristers in England and advocates in Scotland. Solicitors, who are also called law agents, may be members of a professional society, the most distinguished of which is that of Writers to the Signet. A client must go to a solicitor in the first instance. He deals with all the more straightfor-

257

ward legal problems, writes wills, and attends to most ordinary legal needs. If the services of a member of the Bar are needed, the solicitor approaches one that he thinks best in the circumstances. Barristers' and advocates' clients are the solicitors. Hence the most unsuitable gift you can make to a member of either the English or the Scottish Bar is one of those house signs reading: NO SOLICITORS.

Still, the differences between English and Scots law are profound. For instance, the English and American distinction between law and equity does not exist in Scotland. Scotland also subordinates the remedy to the right. No importance is attached to forms of action as such. Laws relating to marriage and divorce have for long differed, and there are differences even today. For example, a Scottish divorce decree is always final: there is no decree *nisi* as in England. Scotland also gives minors more rights and responsibilities. Following the Roman law distinction between pupil (under puberty) and minor (after puberty), boys of fourteen up and girls of twelve up can make a valid will and can enter into contracts. In contract law promises can be enforced without the English insistence on consideration.

Torts in English and American law are called, in Scotland, "delicts." In this realm the principle has been that fault or breach of duty is required to create a liability to make reparation. English law has no such requirement. Scotland allows not only the wills of minors but also holograph wills, which, being in the testator's handwriting, need no witnesses. A distinctive feature of Scots law forbids the disinheritance of one's spouse or one's children, who are entitled to fixed portions of the estate. Land law differs notably, being perhaps the most feudal of any systems in use elsewhere in the civilized world, though surviving remnants of feudalism are being phased out.

The highest civil court in Scotland is the Court of Session, founded in 1532. Its decisions are subject to appeal only in the House of Lords. It consists of an Inner House and an Outer House. The former hears appeals from the latter and also exercises an original jurisdiction in certain kinds of cases. Much civil litigation is conducted in the Sheriff Courts, of which there are more than sixty throughout Scotland. The Sheriff is an important judicial officer of the Crown, dating back to the twelfth century. Another distinctive feature of Scots law is the practice of requiring written pleas, which ensure that the parties state their respective cases very precisely at the outset, for though adjustments may be made the end product is a "closed record" and the factual contentions of the opposing sides are set out in numbered paragraphs.

The highest criminal court in Scotland is the High Court of Justiciary.

It was founded in 1672. From its decisions there is no appeal to the House of Lords or elsewhere. The well-known "not-proven" verdict, peculiar to Scotland, is intended to provide for cases in which everyone believes that the accused is probably guilty but insufficient evidence is available for a conviction. The accused goes free, not declared guilty but nevertheless not specifically awarded a "not-guilty" verdict. The merits of this peculiarity are debatable, but without it juries tend to vote "guilty" on the ground that the doubts are insubstantial. Thus the "not-proven" alternative, if it errs, does so on the side of the accused. The High Court travels on circuit and the judges sit with a jury of fifteen. Unanimity is not required, only a simple majority. When sitting in Edinburgh this court receives and disposes of appeals in criminal cases. Murder and other major crimes must be tried in the High Court, but the Sheriffs deal with the vast majority of criminal cases.

In the handling of the earlier stages in criminal proceedings there are several important peculiarities. The police report to a local official called the Procurator Fiscal, who corresponds in some ways to the District Attorney in the United States. He has authority to decide whether or not to prosecute, and if so what is to be the charge. The police do not prosecute. He also investigates sudden deaths, since there is no coroner's inquest as in England and no public proceedings of any kind at this stage. The confidentiality is intended to avoid publicity prejudicial to the fair-minded conduct of the case. At the trial, if there is to be one, no formal opening speeches are made, so that the jury knows virtually nothing about the case till they hear the witnesses' testimony at the trial. The Procurator Fiscal works under the direction of the Lord Advocate, to whom he reports serious crimes, and who alone makes the decision whether to have the case tried in the High Court before judge and jury or dealt with in the Sheriff Court with Sheriff and jury or even more informally with the Sheriff sitting alone. The Procurator Fiscal and especially the Lord Advocate have therefore enormous discretionary powers.

Scottish judges did not always work within a system so favorable to the accused. In the eighteenth century, a judge such as Lord Braxfield, notorious both for his use in court of the old Scots tongue and for his readiness to impose the death sentence, would be heard to mutter, as he surveyed an accused: "Aye, he would be nane the waur o' a hangin'." When an advocate made an impassioned plea for mercy for his client, reminding the judge that Jesus Christ commended that disposition in all men, Braxfield is reported to have remarked sardonically, "Muckle He made o' that—He was hangit!" before imposing sentence of death. After pronouncing it on another man who happened to have been for long his companion at chess, he is reported to have added jocosely as the man destined for the scaffold was taken from the court: "Checkmate, Willie!" Today, in extreme contrast to such horrific methods, criminal evidence and procedure in Scotland are designed to lean backwards in favor of the accused, preferring to let the guilty go free rather than risk the unjust punishment of the innocent.

The dignity of the law is upheld in externals. Advocates and judges wear gowns and wigs, as in England. Solicitors usually wear gowns when pleading in Sheriff courts. In the higher courts the judges' robes lend colorful grandeur as well as solemnity to the proceedings: in civil cases, blue with plum facings and crimson crosses, in criminal cases, scarlet with silk facings and crimson crosses.

A more detailed account in small compass can be found in a pamphlet by Lord Cooper, *The Scottish Legal Tradition,* published by the Saltire Society, 13 Atholl Crescent, Edinburgh, Scotland.

I

Glossary of Mainly
Lowland Scots Words

The principal function of this brief glossary is to help understand Scots words used in this book. With few exceptions, therefore, only these are included in the list.

a'	all	dede	death
ae	one	deid	dead
airt	quarter, direction	dinna	don't
		dool	mourning, sorrow
ashet	platter		
auld	old	doon	down
baith	both	e'en	even; evening
blate	shy, bashful	fae	from (Aberdeenshire usage)
blude, bluid	blood		
bogle	hide-and-seek		
bonnie, bonny	pretty and lovely	fain	eager
		faither	father
braggart	boastful, boasting	ferlie	strange or wonderful being or occurrence
braid	broad		
brig	bridge		
cam'	came	fly	cunning
cantie, canty	cheery, lively	fowlis	birds, fowls (old Scots)
claith	cloth		
clamb	climbed	frae	from
cludis	clouds (old Scots)	fu'	full; drunk
		fun	found
cundie, cundy	street drain	gae	go
cutty sark	short shirt	gait	walk, road

gang	go		Throne after
ghillie	attendant,		the Union,
	hunting		Prince
	guide		Charles
gie	give		Edward
giftie	giver, gift		Stewart
glaidsome	joyful	jimp	slender,
gloaming	twilight		scanty, neat
gowd	gold	jo	sweetheart,
gowff	golf		dear
guid	good	jougs, juggws	neck irons
haar	hoarfrost;		formerly
	frozen dew		used for
hae	have		punishment
haffets	temples (sides		of public
	of the		offenders
	heads)	kail	cabbage or any
hame	home		green
hap	wrap up		vegetable
	(especially a	kailyard	cabbage patch,
	person, for		kitchen
	warmth)		garden
he'rt	heart	lane, len	alone (e.g., by
hicht	height		his len, by
howff	inn, pub		himself)
ilk, ilka	each, every	lang	long
	(*note:* of that	lea	tract of open
	ilk, of the		ground,
	same; e.g.,		especially
	grant of that		grassland
	ilk or grant	licht	light
	of grant)	loup	jump
ingle	hearth	lyart	gray-haired
jabot	ornamental	mair	more
	frill on shirt	makar	poet, maker of
	or dress		verses
Jacobite	follower or	maun	must
	supporter of	micht	might
	the	michty	mighty (used
	Pretender to		as mild oath:
	the British		mercy me!)

monie	many		in front of
mou'	mouth		kilt
nane	none	stane	stone
ower	over; too	straucht	straight
peewee	lapwing	swankie	lusty lad
plaidie	plaid: a tartan	syne	ago
	overgarment	tae	to
poo	pull	tawse	strap for
puir	poor		punishing
quhilk	which (old		children
	Scots)	toune	town
reid	red	wad	would
sae	so	wae	woe, woeful
sair	sore, difficult	wame	belly, womb
sark	shirt	waur	worse
shieling	shepherd's	wha	who
	hut; grazing	wham	whom
	ground for	whar	where
	cattle (shiel	whilk	which
	means hut)	whummle	whirl
sma'	small	wifie	wife, woman
sonsie	jolly looking	wight	luckless person
sporran	leather or fur		or thing
	pouch worn	wyte	fault, blame

Index